POWER
AND
METHOD

Critical Social Thought

Series editor: Michael W. Apple
John Bascom Professor of Curriculum and Instruction and
    Educational Policy Studies, University of Wisconsin-Madison

Already published

POWER
AND
METHOD

POLITICAL ACTIVISM AND
EDUCATIONAL RESEARCH

EDITED BY
ANDREW GITLIN

ROUTLEDGE
New York • London

Published in 1994 by

Routledge
29 West 35 Street
New York, NY 10001

Published in Great Britain by

Routledge
11 New Fetter Lane
London EC4P 4EE

Library of Congress Cataloging-in-Publication Data

Power and method : political activism and educational research /
    Andrew Gitlin, editor.
        p.   cm. — (Critical social thought)
    Includes bibliographical references and index.
    ISBN 0-415-90689-X(hb) — ISBN 0-415-90690-3(pb)
        1. Education—Research—Methodology.   2. Education—Research—
    Political aspects.   3. Critical pedagogy—Research.   4. Feminism
    and education—Research.   I. Gitlin, Andrew David.   II. Series.
    LB1028.P585   1994
    370'.78—dc20   93-15749
                                                                            CIP

British Library Cataloguing-in-Publication Data also available.

CONTENTS

SECTION TWO: POWER AND METHOD IN CONTEXT

Relationships Within Qualitative Research

SECTION THREE: POWER AND METHOD REVISITED

ACKNOWLEDGEMENTS

Volumes such as this often reflect ongoing discussions and relationships that have taken place over a long period of time. Several people at the University of Utah have taken part in these discussions and, through their ideas, criticisms, and support, have shaped the nature of this project. I would especially like to thank Donna Deyhle, Harvey Kantor, Frank Margonis, and Audrey Thompson.

Perhaps our greatest thanks needs to go to the progressive students, educators, and political activists who have suggested that academics need not only to produce new knowledge but also to make a difference in the world. In particular, feminist scholars have created a space for books like *Power and Method* by focusing our attention on the researcher/"subject" relationship and by raising questions about the link between understanding and change. These scholars and many others working outside the educational arena have provided a forum to discuss further ideas on educational research.

We want also to give special thanks to Michael Apple, the series editor, and Jayne Fargnoli of Routledge, who have given us critical feedback, editorial suggestions, and encouragement. Robyn Turner's endless patience and insight also was essential to the completion of this project.

An earlier version of Patti Lather's chapter, "Fertile Obsession: Validity After Poststructuralism" was published in the *Sociological Quarterly* (1993) 34 (4): 673–93.

SERIES EDITOR'S INTRODUCTION

Power and Method is an unsettling book. Usually this word—unsettling—has negative connotations. It speaks of nervousness, the loss of certainty, feelings of discomfort. Yet, while each of these descriptions is accurate as far as it goes, I use the word, and these descriptions, in a much more positive way. Certain things *need* to be unsettled, need to be shaken. For those of us in education, among the most important assumptions that deserve to be "unsettled" is the belief that research—as it is currently done in both its quantitative and qualitative forms—is a "good thing." If done well, with particular attention to the existing canons of research protocol, it is a significant tool in understanding and ultimately improving educational policy and practice.

But what if this assumption is naive? What if it is based on an unexamined foundation that begins to crumble when looked at closely? What if research is a political act? These questions and the concerns that stand behind them are not new; they have a very long history. What has changed is the growing sophistication in how we ask and answer these questions. Stimulated in part by feminist, anti-foundationalist, and post-colonialist theories and by the newer approaches to the study of how power is created and used, there is now an immensely fertile literature that has begun to strongly influence the ways critically-oriented scholars place themselves into their research and place their research into the wider relations of power. This book shows the fruits of their efforts.

The aim of the volume is put very clearly in Andrew Gitlin's own words: "For those writing in this volume the central question is not how researchers of different orientations can learn to get along so that we can maintain the discipline and continue doing research in accustomed ways, but how the whole enterprise of research, both qualitative and quantitative, can be reconceptualized so that it can more powerfully act on some of the most persistent and important problems of our schools, namely those surrounding issues of race, class and gender."

Too often, the idea that educational research must be politically engaged is reduced to a slogan. It is a purely rhetorical point in which researchers assert their organic connections with various oppressed groups but then go about their business in ordinary ways. Some researchers go further than the rhetorical level. They actively seek to deconstruct and reconstruct the ways in which research goes on, the ways in which its means and ends are generated, and who counts as a "researcher" in the first place. The problems faced here are extremely difficult. Raising the question of the relationship between activism and research, between power and method, immediately brings to the fore a whole set of issues about the social role of research, about the conceptual and epistemological grounding of knowledge claims, about what such knowledge is *for,* and about *who* ultimately benefits from its generation. It ultimately raises intensely personal questions about ourselves—as raced, gendered, and classed actors—and where we fit in to the relations of power, of domination and subordination, in our societies.

Answers to these questions are not settled. As this book indicates, each of these authors is on a journey; each is constantly attempting to create ways of dealing with the complex political, conceptual, educational, and personal dilemmas we confront when we seek to connect our "research" activities to larger social movements. Yet, we should not assume that the mere fact that we are making good faith efforts to do that eliminates the need to be self-critical about what may be lost as well as gained in these efforts. Daphne Patai's critical response to the chapters by Michelle Fine and Patti Lather serves as a case in point. All three articulate a specific politics of research. Each of them is deeply committed to research that challenges existing power relations. Yet Patai's claim that sometimes the politicization of research can go too far—and Fine's argument that in essence it hasn't yet gone far enough—shows the very real tensions that arise once the connections between power and method are taken as seriously as they deserve. The debate between Fine and Patai, and the difficult issues that are raised by their respective positions, is itself worth the price of admission.

Some of the essays included here are abstract and theoretical; some are written with a sense of gritty reality. Yet all, in the words of the noted feminist philosopher Nancy Fraser, "evince an accent of urgency that bespeaks engagement" (Fraser, 1989, p. 3). Thus, they are *interventions.* They want to interrupt our common sense both about what we do and about the artificial separation we usually make among the professional, political, and the personal. Think of the distinctions educators often make between cognitive, affective, and psychomotor behaviors. Few of us know anyone who "cognates," then "affects," and then "psychomotes." The distinction itself is a construction, a fiction that we tell to make our lives as educators simpler. Yet, it just as often does damage. It is based on a "regime of truth" that sorts out the world in artificial baskets of discrete characteristics to be kept separate from each other. For the authors in this book, the simplifying practices that organize the world of the educational researcher are based on similar regimes of truth. The world is politically complicated. For them, the very idea that we should separate our political lives from our actions as researchers is part of the problem, not part of the solution. It too does damage—to educators, to students, to those we too often refer to as "research subjects."

Think for a minute about the politics of the last word of that sentence. The concept of the subject speaks to the politics of this, for there are two senses of this concept in our ordinary language. A person can be *subjected*— studied, controlled, manipulated, ruled. Yet she or he can also be the *subject of* history, can build and participate in social movements aimed at transforming the institutions and social relations that deny us the values we most prize. It is their opposition to the former and their conscious embrace of the latter that sets the authors in this book apart from so much of the existing research community.

It is wise to reflect on what could be added to the chapters here. Many of these contributions are partly based in post-modern and post-structuralist intuitions. These theories have been immensely productive. Yet, there are dangers here as well: going too far in this direction may lead us to underestimate the realities of economic and political power, of the gritty materiality of class dynamics and the material conditions people experience in their daily lives (Clarke, 1991; Apple, 1993). But this does not in any way diminish the significance of what is illuminated in this book.

Foucault reminded us that if you want to understand how power works, look at the knowledge, self-understandings, and struggles of those whom powerful groups in this society have cast off as "the other" (Best and Kellner, 1991, pp. 34–75). The conservative alliance and its allies have created entire groups of these "others": people of color, women who refuse to accept external control of their lives, histories, bodies, gays and lesbians, the poor; and, as I know from my biography, the vibrant culture of working class life. The list could go on. What the conservative restoration embargoes— the knowledge of the margins, of how culture and power are indissolubly linked—becomes a set of indispensable resources here (Apple, 1993; Apple, in press; Education Group II, 1991). How we think about "research" in a politically tense time will be dramatically altered to the extent that we take these points seriously.

No one book can provide answers to all of the questions surrounding what are and should be the relations between politics and research. In fact, it is probable that such answers, if they exist, can only be found in the crucible of practice as we work them out in our daily lives (Fraser, 1989, p. 3). Yet, *Power and Method* brings together people whose struggles with these questions cannot help but inform us about what is necessary and possible in making this connection.

Michael W. Apple
The University of Wisconsin-Madison

References

Apple, M.W. (1993). *Official Knowledge: Democratic Education in a Conservative Age*. New York: Routledge.

Apple, M.W. (Forthcoming). The politics of official knowledge. *Teachers College Record*.

Best, S., and Kellner, D. (1991). *Postmodern Theory*. New York: Macmillan.

Clarke, J. (1991). *New Times and Old Enemies*. London: Harper-Collins.

Education Group II (1991). *Education Limited*. London: Unwin Hyman.

Fraser, N. (1989). *Unruly Practices*. Minneapolis: Univ. of Minnesota Press.

Introduction

THE SHIFTING TERRAIN OF METHODOLOGICAL DEBATES

Andrew Gitlin

Qualitative research in the field of education, even by the late 1970s, was largely discounted. Published reports were often seen as soft or not rigorous and always subjective. Qualitative dissertations were seldom attempted, and when they were, authors were put on the defensive as they tried to justify this "unconventional" methodology. The beginning of the 1980s, however, brought some dramatic changes, not the least of which was a begrudging acceptance of qualitative research. As it gained a degree of legitimacy, a plethora of qualitative studies and dissertations appeared. With this tremendous flood of qualitative research, a shift in methodological debates occurred that changed the central question from the legitimacy of the qualitative paradigm to the issue of compatibility: Are quantitative and qualitative methods incompatible because they represent fundamentally divergent assumptions about the nature of knowledge, or are these approaches different but complementary? One renowned scholar who has taken up the cause of the latter position is Nate Gage (1989). In a dramatically worded essay on the compatibility question, Gage lays out three scenarios about where methodological debates can go in the future. The first scenario turns the historical hierarchy of quantitative and qualitative methods on its head. Here, the insistent criticisms leveled against positivism and quantitative research in general win out. "Scientific" studies disappear and are replaced with more interpretive and critical-theory approaches to research. In the second scenario, social science researchers realize that

> programs of research that had often been regarded as mutually antagonistic were simply concerned with different, but important, topics and problems. There was no essential incompatibility between process-product research on teaching . . . and research that focused on teachers' and students' thought processes and meaning perspectives. The two kinds of researchers were simply studying different important topics. (Gage 1989, 141)

In the third scenario, the paradigm war continues and nothing really changes. The qualitative folks continue to attack positivism and scientism of all sorts. The quantitative folks strike back, and in the end social science research

1

begins to slip into chaos. Gage suggests that this war may lead to the demise of social and educational research as we know it. Clearly, Gage would like social science researchers to come to their senses, save the discipline, and realize that our differences are of a kind and are not antagonistic in any fundamental way.

In many ways this edited volume is a response to Gage. Our response is that not only has he ignored an essential prior question but also by doing so he has obscured a radically different scenario. For those writing in this volume, the central question is not how researchers of different orientations can learn to get along so that we can maintain the discipline and continue doing research in accustomed ways, but how the whole enterprise of research, both qualitative and quantitative, can be reconceptualized so that it can more powerfully act on some of the most persistent and important problems of our schools, namely those surrounding issues of race, class, and gender. Put simply, from our view, traditional qualitative and quantitative methods may be compatible, but this compatibility primarily centers on what both approaches to knowledge production have failed to do. Pointing to their common failure is not meant to suggest that social science research has not made a difference, even on critical issues. Rather, as Clifford and Guthrie (1988) point out, the difference made seems to have more to do with researchers achieving professional status than with an impact on policy and practice. If research is to do more in terms of making a difference in our schools, then the starting point cannot be an analysis of compatibility, which in many ways is about maintaining the legitimacy of current research approaches. Instead, what is needed is rigorous scrutiny of the assumptions that shape the meaning of research itself. This examination of the meaning of research points to a fourth scenario that Gage does not consider: the possibility of methodological debates that ask questions that attempt to reorient basic assumptions about research. It is this set of questions that this book begins to address. In particular, we take up such questions as: What role can political activism play in the research process? How can we understand the "other" from an insider's point of view? Can research confront and act upon oppressive structures such as patriarchy and Eurocentrism, and, if so, what does this mean for notions of validity, research relations, and possibilities for change? Finally, how does the research context—the material conditions and constructed divisions of labor—limit and distort our ability to make a difference in the practical world?

What all of these questions have in common, and what links the essays in this volume, is an examination of how power is infused in the research process. While the authors in this text certainly understand power in different ways, it is the lack of attention to issues of power, to how research influences identified aims, relationships, and forms of legitimate knowledge, that holds this text together and has been largely missing from methodological debates.

One of the many problems of examining power and method is that the form of the printed text can often reassert some of the oppressive, silencing relationships that the arguments within the text are trying to challenge. Our intention, for example, is not to provide a new orthodoxy that others will simply follow, to assert power over others in an uncritical and product-oriented way, but rather to create spaces for alternative views and considerations. To do so, our words and ideas must be seen as being in-process as part of an ongoing debate among those who are posing questions about the meaning of research. To move in this direction, this book is divided into three sections: Perspectives on Power and Method, Power and Method in Context, and Power and Method Revisited. The first section views the issue of power of method from various perspectives including feminist, gay and lesbian, and cultural. For each perspective, two manuscripts and a response from an outsider—one outside the educational arena—are included. Section two takes up the issue of power and method by focusing more specifically on the researcher/"subject" relationship found in qualitative methods. Again, two positions are presented on this issue, followed by a response from an outsider. Finally, in section three, the ideas and positions on power and method reflected in this volume are critically assessed. Included are responses to the ideas presented in this text to create space for alternative views and to help establish links between educational scholars and those working in other disciplines such that insight is "offered without serving as a barrier for appreciation" (hooks 1984, 70).

In sum, the intent of this book is not to join hands with those at the center of the dominant discourse. It is not to erase important differences such that, as Ross Perot has urged, we can forget we are Democrats or Republicans (he doesn't even consider other alternatives) and just act as Americans. Instead, we want to talk from the margins and cross the tracks in order to "look both from the outside in and from the inside out" (hooks 1984, 149). By doing so, we may be in a better position to examine the complexity of what it means to do activist research.

The first perspective taken up in section one is the feminist. Two contrasting essays written by feminists struggling to define feminist research are included. The first essay, "Dis-stance, and Other Stances: Negotiations of Power Inside Feminist Research" by Michelle Fine, describes three approaches to research: ventriloquy, voices, and activism. She argues that activism is most likely to enable "feminist researchers to take back our gender, race, and class politics woven through our scholarship." The second essay, "Fertile Obsession: Validity After Poststructuralism" by Patti Lather, argues that traditional discourses of validity no longer are able to "chart the journey from the present to the future." To challenge the bounds of this discourse, Lather describes four frames that rethink validity in ways that explore the space "between the no longer and not yet." It is within this space that we can begin to see "the possibility of what was impossible under traditional regimes of truth in the social sciences." The response to these essays, "When Method Becomes Power," by Daphne Patai, a professor of women's studies, questions in passionate tones the weaving of politics into method. She asks when enough is enough in the seemingly endless reconsideration of how our positions relate to knowledge production. She goes on to argue that research should not be confused with political activism. "Feminism today, as it conflates politics and education and effaces any distinction between political agendas and protocols of research, is in danger of suppressing . . . any calm reflective stance that sees some strengths in the effort to set biases aside. . . ."

Because this conversation is central to understanding power and method, an editorial decision was made to have Michelle Fine write a short epilogue (included in her essay). This epilogue further clarifies the relation between politics and research.

The second perspective from which power and method is viewed focuses on gay and lesbian researchers who debate the problems and possibilities of doing research that addresses issues critical to the gay and lesbian community. The first essay, "Queer Relations With Educational Research," by Glorianne Leck, pushes us to think about educational research not simply as analyses of institutional schooling but also as education that takes place in a broader context. Using a Queer Nation "educational event" at the Cracker Barrel restaurant, Leck points to the "absurdity of the traditional (essentialist) way of addressing generalization as an act with meaning embedded in some modernist claim for rationality." She asks the reader to let go of the "fear of error, of disapproval, of fitting in." The second essay, "On Method and Hope," by William Tierney, wrestles with the question of what it means to engage in research with a friend who wants his story told and is dying of AIDS. This emotional essay suggests that research can be part of a project of hope; "the hope that Robert would somehow magically get better, but also a hope for a community that would accept and honor difference rather than marginalize individuals." The response to these essays, "Red Ribbons at the Cracker Barrel" by Roger Platizky, an English professor, talks about the very different ways Leck and Tierney address the institutional silencing of gay and lesbian voices. In contrasting Tierney's literary stance with Leck's wild interpretive dance, Platizky raises issues about public space, collective solutions, and the possibilities of dialogue, among others. He concludes by suggesting that both authors are united in a struggle to move from the margins of the text and as such "help us remove signs of exclusion and hatred from our books, from our buildings, from our blackboards, and eventually from our minds."

The final part of section one looks at power and method from a cultural perspective. Two essays are included that investigate the problems of doing research with and on people of color. Michèle Foster in "The Power to Know One Thing Is Never the Power to Know All Things," explores the dilemmas of doing "insider" research. Drawing largely on autobiographical data and reflections on her work with black teachers, Foster seeks to offer "new if disturbing insights and alternative and disquieting ways of thinking." She also points out that research unfortunately still "subjugates the voices of people of color to further prevailing paradigms and to fit the requirements of a caste society." Margaret LeCompte and Daniel McLaughlin, in "Witchcraft and Blessings, Science and Rationality: Discourses of Power and Silence in Collaborative Work with Navajo Schools," give a striking account of the problems and difficulties that Western scholars face when they attempt to enter into collaborative research projects that force them to critically assess their Western ways of knowing. They conclude that it is essential to understand and value Navajo explanations of behavior and practice, for to deny these explanations, even if they appear outside the norms of Western reason, is "to participate in the same dominant cultural practices which made the programs (studied) problematic." John Stanfield, a sociologist, in "Empowering the Culturally Diversified Sociological Voice," responds to these papers by pointing out that there is a relation between the ideas presented in these chapters and the breakdown and breakup of white male hegemony. "It is no coincidence or accident then that the human sciences and humanities and the American academy have been in the midst of the eye of the storm in hotly contested claims regarding orthodoxy and diversity in debates regarding what knowledge is and what knowledge should be." While praising these papers for suggesting new areas of critical inquiry about the politics of racialized ethnic hegemony, Stanfield also reminds the reader that there is a "steady stream of profound contradictions and paradoxes characteristic of structuring educational institutions in an historically plural nation-state which gives little real political and economic legitimacy to cultural differences, particularly when it comes to people of color."

Section two shifts from considering power and method from various perspectives to looking at this issue in terms of constructed relationships *within* qualitative research. Two essays that in one way or another take a critical look at the roles and relationships formed through the doing of qualitative research are included. The first essay, "Alternative Methodologies and the Research Context," by Andrew Gitlin and Robyn Russell, explores how material conditions and ideological assumptions push alternative methodologies that try to reconstruct research relationships back toward the center. Using their experience with Educative Research, they argue that alternative methodologies are unlikely to make a difference unless they are accompanied by ideological and material changes. They conclude by stating that "the challenge for those working on developing alternative methodologies is to work simultaneously at the level of method and within the community." The second essay, "Distance and Relation Reconsidered: Tensions in the Ethnographic Text," by Don Dippo, explores the possibilities of altering the traditional relationships formed through doing ethnographic research. Such a change, according to Dippo, requires researchers to abandon their attempts to make the strange accessible and instead to try to make the comfortable strange and disconcerting. He refers to this stance as the dilemma of distance and relation: "Simply put, the question is this: How does one provide the details of concrete social relations in a manner which renders them familiar and sensible yet simultaneously calls their taken-for-granted character into question?" Dippo concludes the essay with some examples of current texts that begin to challenge the dilemma of distance and relation. Louise Lamphere, a white, female, feminist anthropologist (her own words) responds to these articles in "Expanding Our Notions of 'Critical Qualitative Methodology': Bringing Race, Class, and Gender into the Discussion" by suggesting that they have largely overlooked issues of race, class, and gender. "I realize that these themes (race, class, gender, sexual orientation) are the focus of other papers in other sections, but we must be careful not to ghettoize each of these attributes, putting the feminist papers in one section, those that deal with ethnicity in another, and those on sexual orientation in a third, leaving the papers on 'ethnographic method' to a section where authors may feel they do not have to deal with those issues." She concludes by suggesting that these articles promise less hierarchical research but need to press further to "take account of difference as it enters the relationship between the researcher and the subject and among the subjects themselves."

Section three presents an essay by James Ladwig and Jennifer Gore, "Extending Power and Specifying Method Within the Discourse of Activist Research," that revisits the ideas presented in this volume and raises a number of important concerns about the project in general. One such concern is what these authors refer to as the "paradox of non-difference." This paradox results in a fundamental oversight where the question "What is different about studying with this oppressed group as opposed to studying with that oppressed group?" is entirely overlooked. These authors also raise fundamental questions about the way power is understood in this text. They identify three major approaches to the study of power and method and suggest that the focus in the volume is primarily on the researcher/"subject" relationship. By paying scant attention to other views ("power as a problem of the utility of methods and power as a problem of academic discourse"), the volume tends to skirt the contradiction of being an academic and an activist and avoids a detailed specification of method. As a consequence, "the book provides minimal guidance to researchers seeking assistance with, for instance, questions of truth, authorship, reality, objectivity, validity, and generalizability".

The conversation that flows throughout these essays would not be possible without the important work of many others who have paved the way to

rethink the relationship between power and method. One particularly influ-
ential work was Willis's (1977) well-known essay on how working-class
kids get working-class jobs. By using a cultural frame that placed schools
within a broader economic/class context, Willis developed a methodological
approach that could examine power both within schools and in its relation
to wider societal structures. This methodological approach encouraged qualitative researchers in the field of education to rethink many of the realist
claims still lingering with the qualitative paradigm and pointed to the limita-
tion of viewing the school as a cultural context unto itself. In essence, Willis's
work was one of the first ethnographic studies in the field of education to
introduce the issue of power into methodological debates and to consider
the interests that research can serve: "No matter how modified, participant
observation and the methods under its aegis, display a tendency towards
naturalism and therefore to conservatism. . . . The method is also patronizing
and condescending—is it possible to imagine the ethnographic account up-
wards in a class society" (194).

The issue of power also emerged in Willis's concern with the relationship
between researcher and "subject." He was aware of the way subjects stand
"too square in their self-referenced world" (194) and how this false unity
results in political silences. In fact, this silence was commented upon by one
of the lads who noted that Willis should "speak for yourself when you say
we, say 'you' " (emphasis added) (195).

The ideas presented in this text try to take up some of the challenges
Willis posed about the conservative nature of research and the way it silences
those who are objectified by the research process. However, the text also
tries to overcome some of the limits of Willis's approach, including his lack
of attention to the "other," the young women in the working-class schools
who often paid the price for the lads' "resistance" to schooling. In this
regard, this book owes a primary debt to feminists such as bell hooks, Maria
Mies, and Dorothy Smith who have pointed to some of the limits of looking
at social relations solely through the lens of class reproduction. Furthermore,
where Willis felt trapped by the methodological approaches available at the
time, we hope to create some space for alternative ways to do research that
acknowledge the way power infiltrates method and the process of knowledge
production.

References

Clifford, G., and Guthrie, J. (1988). *Ed school.* Chicago: Univ. of Chicago Press.

Gage, N. (1989). The paradigm wars and their aftermath. *Teachers College Record*
91(2): 135–50.

hooks, b. (1984). *Feminist theory: From margin to center.* Boston: South End.

Willis, P. 1977. *Learning to labour: How working class kids get working class jobs.*
Westmead, UK: Saxon House.

Section One

Perspectives on Power and Method

Feminist

DIS-STANCE AND OTHER STANCES:
NEGOTIATIONS OF POWER INSIDE FEMINIST RESEARCH

Michelle Fine

[F]eminist politics is not just a tolerable companion of feminist research but a necessary condition for generating less partial and perverse descriptions and explanations. In a socially stratified society, the objectivity of the results of research is increased by political activism by and on behalf of oppressed, exploited and dominated groups. Only through such struggles can we begin to see beneath the appearances created by an unjust social order to the reality of how this social order is in fact constructed and maintained.

—Sandra Harding, *The science question in feminism*

Throughout the 1980s and into the 1990s, feminist researchers have been chatting busily in the kitchen of the social sciences, delighted by the vivid and disruptive possibilities of our scholarship on women's lives. Voyeurs, often, to the deep and radical transformations washing through the humanities and theoretical work in the social sciences. And dis-stanced witnesses to the breaths of feminist activism still alive. As we sit we worry, collectively and alone, about how best to unleash ourselves from our central contradiction—being researchers and being activist feminists (Crawford and Gentry 1989; Crawford and Marecek 1989b; Fine and Gordon 1989; Flax 1990; Hare-Mustin and Marecek 1990b; Kahn and Yoder 1990; Lykes and Stewart 1986; Morawski 1990; Parlee 1990; Payton 1984; Russo 1984; Smith and Stewart 1989; Unger 1990; Wittig 1985). We document at once the depths of violence and discrimination embedded in the lives of women (Amaro & Rousso 1987; Belle 1990; Blackman 1989; Brown 1987a; Gilkes, 1988; Lykes 1989; D. Smith; and the complex maneuvers by which women deny such oppression (Crosby et al. 1989; Gilligan 1993; Majors 1994; Miller 1976; Taylor 1983). (Harvesting substantial evidence of gender-, race/ethnic-, class-, disability-, and sexually-based oppression, we also know how meticulously women take care, make nice, and rarely, in our research, express outrage at the gendered politics of their lives (Brodbey and Fine 1988).

Many—not all—feminist social researchers report these stories, girdled in by now-stretched-out, but nonetheless intact, notions of neutrality and positivism, reliability, and truth. In narratives parallel to some of the women we study, some of us still smuggle our knowledge of social injustice into a discourse of science that fundamentally contains, and painfully undermines, the powerful politics of activist feminism. As is often the case with moments of social containment, feminists in the social sciences carry weighty evidence for a passionately disruptive transformation of our disciplines. And yet, as relatively new kids on the academic block, we also carry domesticating responsibilities to keep this social science appearing dispassionately detached. And we manage these responsibilities differently. Valerie Walkerdine (1986) narrates this problem when she writes:

> I want, therefore, to demonstrate that women, positioned as teachers, mothers, carers and caring professionals . . . are held absolutely necessary for the moral order: they are responsible. This responsibility places women as at once safe, yet potentially dangerous (the bad mother). It places them as responsible for ensuring the possibility of democracy, and yet as deeply conservative. . . . My argument is that, quite simply, women of all classes have been placed as guardians of an order from which it is difficult to escape. (63)

Traditional social sciences have stubbornly refused to interrogate how we as researchers create our texts (see Becker 1986; Brodkey 1987; Reinharz 1988; Rosaldo 1989; Semin and Gergen 1990). Most particularly, this is the case for psychologists, where it is presumed that psychological theories and methods simply neutralize personal and political influences. When we write about "laws" of human behavior, our political stances may evaporate. That we are human inventors of some questions and repressors of others, shapers of the very contexts we study, coparticipants in our interviews, interpreters of others' stories and narrators of our own, is sometimes rendered irrelevant to the texts we publish. While feminists vary in how we manage this treacherous territory, we all manage it.

Donna Haraway (1988) caricatures the epistemological fetish with detachment as a "God trick . . . that mode of seeing that pretends to offer a vision that is from everywhere and nowhere, equally and fully" (584). Such narrative removal seeks to front universal truths while denying the privileges, interests, and politics of researchers. With Haraway and Sandra Harding (1986), feminist scholars have interrupted the membrane of objectivity across the academy and in their respective disciplines, refusing containment and asking how feminist politics can and do play, explicitly and subversively, in our intellectual lives.

Feminist researchers have clearly gained the most ground in the rethinking of our relationships with "subjects" and of the politics of power that loiter between us. British psychologist Sue Wilkinson (1986) characterizes feminist research in the following way:

First, there is its reflexive and self reflective quality . . . an emphasis on the centrality of female experience directly implies its corollary: "ourselves as our own sources." Similarly, du Bois has emphasized the way in which the knower is part of the matrix of what is known; and Reinharz has required the researcher to ask her/himself how s/he has grown or changed in the process of research.

Second, the relationship between the researcher and the re-searched will evidently be very different from that of the traditional "experimenter" and "subject." In feminist research, at the very least, both are to be regarded as having the same status: as partici-pants or collaborators in the same enterprise. . . . (13)

An early advocate of advocacy-based research, psychologist Carolyn Pay-ton has long prodded the field about the bankruptcy of its "professional" social commitments. In the 1980s, she wrote:

Please keep in mind that almost two decades ago the APA grap-pled with the question of the propriety of psychologists as a group advocating social change or taking part in political advocacy, and a process for dealing with such matters are suggested. Yet, here we are in 1983 still denying that we have any responsibility for or obligation to the society in which we live. We behave as if, along with study in this discipline, we inherit a dispensation from consid-ering all matters concerning social consciousness barring those related to guild issues. (1984, 392)

Wilkinson (1986), Tiefer (1990), Payton (1984), and Patricia Hill-Collins, like feminist scholars across disciplines, situate themselves proudly atop a basic assumption that all research projects are (and should be) political; that researchers who represent themselves as detached only camouflage their deepest, most privileged interests (Rosaldo 1989). For instance, Hill-Collins articulates convincingly a political aesthetic that characterizes Black feminist consciousness.

But if feminist research is directed toward social transformations and if practices of "neutrality" primarily laminate deeply conservative interests of the social sciences, then feminist academic researchers face a central di-lemma. That dilemma concerns the self-conscious role our politics can play as we pursue, passionately, our intellectual work. To this dilemma, Donna Haraway offers us passionate detachment through which she believes "men are bound to seek perspectives from those points of view which can never be known in advance, that promise something quite extraordinary, that is, knowledge potential for constructing worlds less organized by axes of domination (1988, 585)." Once full detachment has been revealed as illusory and the stuff of privilege, we can dip into the questions of "stances."

Reflecting on Stances

> Studies which have as their focal point the alleged deviant attitudes and behaviors of Blacks are grounded within the racist assumptions and principals that only render Blacks open to further exploitation. The challenge to social scientists for a redefinition of the basic problem has been raised in terms of the "colonial analogy." It has been argued that the relationship between the researcher and his subjects, by definition, resembles that of the oppressor and the oppressed, because it is the oppressor who defines the problem, the nature of the research, and, to some extent, the quality of interaction between him and his subjects. This inability to understand and research the fundamental problem, neo-colonialism, prevents most social researchers from being able accurately to observe and analyze Black life and culture and the impact racism and oppression have upon Blacks. Their inability to understand the nature and effects of neo-colonialism in the same manner as Black people is rooted in the inherent bias of the social sciences. (Ladner 1971, iii)

Joyce Ladner wrote more than twenty years ago about the inherent racism, bred and obscured, that occurs when researchers elect to stand outside and reify the Self–Other hyphen of social research. Ladner knew then that researchers who sought to invent coherent Master Narratives needed, and created, "Others." The sharp edges of those works were best secured by the shadowed frays of the Other. The articulate professional voices sounded legitimate against the noisy vernacular of the Other. The rationality of the researcher/writer calmed against the outrage of the Other. These texts sought to close contradictions, and by so doing they tranquilized the hyphen, ousting the Other, achieving dis-stance.

This essay here presumes that all researchers are agents, in the flesh (Caraway 1991) and in the collective, who choose, wittingly or not, from among a controversial and constraining set of political stances and epistemologies. Many deny these choices within veils of "neutrality," describing behaviors, attitudes, and preferences of Others, as if these descriptions were static and immutable, "out there," and unconnected to "Self" or political context. They represent these texts as if they were constructed without author(ity). Such texts refuse to ask why one research question or interpretation has prevailed over others, or why this researcher selected this set of questions over others. Such texts render oblique the ways in which we, as researchers, construct our analyses and narratives. Indeed, these texts are written as if researchers were simply vehicles for transmission, with no voice of their own. Such researchers position themselves in dis-stances, as ventriloquists.

Other researchers, in their texts, import to their work the voices of Discarded Others who offer daily or local meanings, which seemingly contrast with and interrupt hegemonic discourses and practices. With "voices" and "experiences" as the vehicles for social representation, these researchers typically claim little position for Self (Scott 1992).

Finally, some researchers fix themselves self-consciously as participatory activists. Their work seeks to unearth, disrupt, and transform existing ideological and/or institutional arrangements. Here, the researcher's stance frames the texts produced and carves out the space in which intellectual surprises surface. These writers position themselves as political and interrogating, fully explicit about their original positions and where their research took them.

I paint these three stances—ventriloquy, "voices," and activism—for feminist researchers to roll around, unpack, try on, discard. It seems crucial in the 1990s that social researchers who seek to be explicitly political (e.g., feminists, African Americans, poststructuralists, neo-Marxists), as well as those who refuse to so acknowledge, should consider aloud, and together, the decisions we have made, through leakage and through pronouncements, in our research.

Ventriloquy

> Once upon a time, the introduction of writings of women and people of color were called politicizing the curriculum. Only *we* had politics (and its nasty little mate, ideology), whereas *they* had standards. (Robinson 1989)

Ventriloquy as a stance relies upon Haraway's God trick. The author tells Truth, has no gender, race, class, or stance. A condition of truth-telling is anonymity, and so it is with ventriloquy. Dramatizing ventriloquy as an academic stance, I offer a snip of institutional biography from an institution with which I've had some intimacy—The University of Pennsylvania.

In 1985, the University of Pennsylvania denied tenure to Dr. Rosalie Tung, then Associate Professor at the Wharton School. While Wharton justified the decision to not tenure Tung "on the grounds that the Wharton School is not interested in China related research," Tung maintained that her Department Chairman had sexually harassed her and that, after she insisted on a professional and not sexual relationship, he submitted a negative letter to the University's Personnel Committee, adversely influencing her tenure decision.

Tung brought the case to the Equal Employment Opportunity Commission (EEOC), which undertook an investigation, requesting documents from Penn. When the University refused to provide these documents, the Commission subpoenaed for Tung's tenure review file as well as those of the five male faculty members who had been tenured just prior to Tung. Penn argued the need to exclude all "confidential peer review information," and failed to provide (1) confidential letters written by Tung's evaluators, (2) the Department Chairman's letter of evaluation, (3) documents reflecting the internal deliberations of faculty committees considering applications for tenure, and (4) comparable portions of the tenure review of the five males. The Commission denied the University's application for these exclusions.

The case made its way to the Supreme Court. Four years after denial of tenure, in a 9–0 vote, the Supreme Court found against Penn in a decision in which the Justice wrote:

> We readily agree with the petitioner regarding that universities and colleges play significant roles in American society. Nor need we question, at this point, petitioner's assertion that confidentiality is important to the proper functioning of the peer review process under which many academic institutions operate. The costs that ensue from this disclosure, however, constitute only one side of the balance. As Congress has recognized, the costs associated with racial and sexual discrimination in institutions of higher learning are very substantial. Disclosure of peer review materials will be necessary in order for the Commission to determine whether illegal discrimination has taken place. Indeed, if there is a "smoking gun" to be found that demonstrates discrimination in tenure decisions, it is likely to be tucked away in peer review files. (*University of Pennsylvania v. EEOC* 58 USLW 4096, 1990)

Penn sought relief on the basis of that well-known precedential exemption for questions of confidentiality—*United States v. Nixon*, with Penn positioning itself with Nixon. Characterizing its First Amendment claim as one of "academic freedom," Penn argued that tenure-related evaluations have historically been written by scholars who have been provided with assurances of confidentiality. Such provisions of confidentiality, they argued, enable evaluators to be candid and institutions to make tenure decisions on the basis of "valid academic criteria." Disclosure of documents or names, Penn continued, would undermine the existing process of awarding tenure, and instigate a "chilling effect" on candid evaluations and discussions of candidates. They wrote:

> This will work to the detriment of universities, as less qualified persons achieve tenure causing the quality of instruction and schol-

arship to decline . . . and also will result in divisiveness and tension, placing strain on faculty relations and impairing the free interchange of ideas that is a hallmark of academic freedom. (University of Pennsylvania, Petitioner v. EEOC, *U.S. Law Week* 1-9-90, #88-493)

To which the Justices responded:

Although it is possible that some evaluations may become less candid as the possibility of disclosure increases, others may simply ground their evaluations in special examples as illustrations in order to deflect potential claims of bias or unfairness. Not all academics will hesitate to stand up and be counted when they evaluate their peers.

Following the Supreme Court decision, Penn submitted to the EEOC a set of redacted documents from the Tung file in which all names and identifiers were removed from the texts. Penn maintained that if faculty were forced to commit their names to their judgments, that they would cower from "true" evaluations. The University took the terrifying position that only when authorship is obscured will truth prevail among academics.

Penn spoke for (but not with) its faculty. The position taken reminded many of Donna Haraway's God trick, in which researchers pronounce "truths" while whiting out their own authority so as to be unlocatable and irresponsible. Penn's position vis-à-vis the Supreme Court embodied institutionally researchers' refusal to acknowledge their personal involvements as they construct the very worlds they write about.

Ventriloquy is perhaps most bold when a university mandates the whiting out of authorship, but can be found in all research narratives in which researchers' privileges and interests are camouflaged. Ventriloquy means never having to say "I" in the text (Clark 1990); means treating subjects as objects while calling them subjects. And, ventriloquy requires the denial of all politics in the very political work of social research.

Voices

It's easy to be glib about the ventriloquism of researchers who seek asylum behind anonymous texts or texts in which they deny their authorial subjectivities. Somewhat closer to home, however, is a critical analysis of the ways in which scholars—critical ethnographers in particular—have used voices to accomplish a subtler form of ventriloquism. While such researchers appear to let the "Other" speak, just under the covers of those marginal, if now "liberated" voices, we hide. As Shulamitz Reinharz has written:

By dealing in voices, we are affecting power relations. To listen to people is to empower them. But if you want to hear it, you have to go hear it, in their space, or in a safe space. Before you can expect to hear anything worth hearing, you have to examine the *power dynamics of the space and the social actors.*

Second, you have to be the person someone else can talk to, and you have to be able to create a context where the person can speak and you can listen. That means we have to *study who we are and who we are in relation to those we study.*

Third, you have to be willing to hear what someone is saying, even when it violates your expectations or threatens our interests. In other words, *if you want someone to tell it like it is, you have to hear it like it is.* (1988, 15–16) emphasis added

Voices offer a qualitative opportunity for scholars interested in generating critical, counter-hegemonic analyses of institutional arrangements. But they also offer a decoy. Through such work, many of us have been fortunate. We've collected rich and multi-situated voices from adolescents—dropouts in my case, teen parents for others (see Lesko 1988; McDade 1988; Sullivan 1990; Tolman 1990; Willis 1981). When I have spoken with adolescents, particularly low-income adolescents, it's consistently easy to gather up their stories of critique, dissent, contradictory consciousness, and quite vivid counter-hegemonic commentary, in order to tell a story. Low-income adolescents easily criticize their schools, challenge the relation of education credentials to labor-market participation, and name the hypocrisies that fuel societal terrors of sexualities (Fine and Zane 1989).

The ease with which such adolescents reflect (somewhat outrageous) versions of my own political stances, has grown more cumbersome, however, as my work has moved from gathering adolescent voices to soliciting those of adults. The stories of adults—be they teachers, parents, students, workers, etc.—constitute a much more dense mass of critical insights cast, typically, within "ruling-class" scripts (D. Smith 1987). A romantic reliance on these voices—as though they were rarified, innocent words of critique—represents a sophisticated form of ventriloquy, with lots of manipulation required. Unlike with teens, here I have struggled in the shadows of the voices of Others.

The complexities of relying upon adult voices are revealed in an evaluation research project involving low-income mothers of sixth-grade students living in Baltimore. Conducted collaboratively with Dr. Donnie Cook of the University of Maryland, this evaluation focuses on a Parent Empowerment Project developed by an advocacy organization for a randomly selected sample of 150 sixth-grade students and their parents or guardians.

The Baltimore women gave us (researchers and project staff) considerable pause about community organizing in the 1990s, but also gave us a chance to consider epistemological troubles with voices as a "raw form" of social science evidence.

Neither monolithic voices of critique nor single voices of institutional praise: These women were multiply situated and their perspectives were stuffed with social contradictions. The braiding of their commentary was rich, but not easily captured with the categories familiar to social analyses. Laced with perspectives of dominant classes, they wanted desperately to believe in public institutions, and at the same time they routinely witnessed the institutional inadequacies of the schools and felt absolutely responsible for the lives of children, who lived at levels of substantial economic disadvantage. These women set forth rich, complex, and hard-to-code voices (Condor 1986). Their experiences did not fit neatly the forms of theorizing available to me without my doing some "violence" to their raw narratives.

As Joan Scott has written on the topic of "experience," the presumption that we can take at face value the voices of experience as if they were the events per se, rather than stories about the events, is to dehistoricize and decontextualize the very experiences being reported. Scott argues that researchers who simply benignly transcribe social experiences fail to examine critically these constructions which seem so real to informants and are in such dire need of interpretation. Scott writes:

> The evidence of experience, whether conceived through a metaphor of visibility or in any other way that takes meaning as transparent, reproduces rather than contests given ideological systems—those that assume that the facts of history speak for themselves and, in the case of histories of gender, those that rest on notions of a natural or established opposition between sexual practices and social conventions, and between homosexuality and heterosexuality . . . the project of making experience visible precludes critical examination of the workings of the ideological system itself. (1992, 25)

Relying on "unadulterated voices" is fundamentally a decoy for an extended version of dis-stance and ventriloquy. Voices are, as Scott would contend, both "an interpretation and in need of an interpretation" (1992, 37). While researchers, particularly White feminists, need to worry about the imperialistic history of qualitative research that we have inherited and to contain the liberal impulse to "translate for" rather than "with" women across chasms of class, race, sexualities, politics, living arrangements, etc. (see Patai 1992), the refusal to theorize reflects either a form of theoretical condescension or hyper-protocol reserved only for Others with whom serious intellectual work and struggle are considered somehow inappropriate.

The interviews with the Baltimore women forced us to come clean; I had to reinsert consciously my interpretive self into my writings, with, but not through, the rendition of their voices. Researchers cannot write about/with/ through adults' (or adolescents') voices as if the researchers had "said it all."

Social research cast through voices typically involves carving out pieces of narrative evidence that we select, edit, and deploy to border our arguments.

The problem is not that we tailor but that so few qualitative researchers reveal *that* we do this work, much less *how* we do this work.

A second dilemma arises when we rely on individual voices to produce social interpretations of group behavior. This often means repoliticizing perspectives narrated by people who have tried hard to represent themselves as nonpolitical. Our interpretations as researchers often betray the very concerted "individualism" and "apolitical nature" insisted on by narrators (Fox-Genovese 1991). This betrayal may well be essential analytically, but it nevertheless reflects the usually unacknowledged stances of researchers who navigate and camouflage theory through the richness of "native voices."

A third issue involves the popular romancing of the voices of women in poverty. Those of us who work to unearth personal stories tend to privilege contradiction, polyvocality, and subjugated voices. And then we often reproduce these voices as though they were relatively uncontaminated, free of power relations. Jill Morawski (1990), reminds feminists that, as we listen to the voices of Others, our work as psychologists is to critically interpret what we hear.

This critique of voices is by no means advanced to deny the legitimacy of rich interview material or other forms of qualitative data. On the contrary, it is meant for us to worry collectively that when voices—as isolated and innocent moments of experience—organize our research texts, there is often a subtle slide toward romantic, uncritical, and uneven handling, and a stable refusal, by researchers, to explicate our own stances and relations with these voices.

Before we leave voices, consider a most complicated instance of scholarly translation located at the hyphen of Othering—the brilliant work of Julie Blackman. A White social psychologist who works as an expert witness for White, Latina and African American battered women who have killed their abusers, Blackman enters courtrooms and retells the stories these women have told her—this time in standard English. She psychologizes and explains away the contradictions. She makes them acceptable. Blackman's project is to get these women a hearing from a jury of their peers. She has an impressive success rate for keeping these women out of jail (Blackman 1989).

Draped in white colonizing science, Julie and I and many Others have cut a deal. We invite the public to listen to the story because the teller is not the Other. Cut with the knives of racism and classism. Should we refuse?

Do we merely reproduce power by playing to power? Do we regenerate the Other as we try to keep her from going to jail? Do we erase and silence as we trade on White/elite privilege?

As these scenes of scholarly translation vividly convey, feminist researchers are chronically and uncomfortably engaged in ethical decisions about how deeply to work with/for/despite those cast as Others and how seamlessly to represent the hyphen. I would differ with Judith Stacey when she writes:

> So, too, does the exploitative aspect of ethnographic process seem unavoidable. The lives, loves and tragedies that fieldwork informants share with a researcher are ultimately data-grist for the ethnographic mill, a mill that has a truly grinding power. More times than I would have liked, this study placed me in a ghoulish and structurally conflictual relationship to personal tragedy. (1991, 113)

To dis-stance is not to avoid the ethical complexities, or negotiations over power.

Activist Feminist Research

Activist research projects seek to unearth, interrupt, and open new frames for intellectual and political theory and practice (Fine and Vanderslice 1991). Researchers critique what seems "natural," recast "experience," connect the vocal to the structural and collective, spin images of what's possible. In such work, the researcher is clearly positioned (passionate) within the domain of a political question or stance, representing a space within which inquiry is pried open, inviting intellectual surprises to flourish (detachment). The text itself is conceived and authored with a critical eye toward "what is," attending seriously to local meanings, changes over time, dominant frames, and contextual contradictions. Within these texts, researchers carry a deep responsibility to assess critically and continually our own, as well as informants', changing positions. The strength of feminist activist research lies in its ability to open contradictions and conflicts within collaborative practices. Essential to an "activist" stance, then—be it feminist, African American, socialist-feminist, educational, or postmodern—is that researchers, activists, informants, and other audiences be engaged as critical participants in what Donna Haraway (1988) calls "power-sensitive conversations."

> Above all, rational knowledge does not pretend to disengagement: to be from everywhere and so nowhere, to be free from interpretation, from being represented, to be fully self-contained or fully formalizable. Rational knowledge is a process of ongoing

critical interpretation among "fields" of interpreters and decoders. *Rational knowledge is power-sensitive conversation.* Decoding and transcoding plus translation and criticism; all are necessary. (590)

Below, I try to capture some images of feminist activist scholarship, all of which share three distinctions. First, the author is explicit about the space in which she stands politically and theoretically—even as her stances are multiple, shifting, and mobile. Second, the text displays critical analyses of current social arrangements and their ideological frames. And third, the narrative reveals and invents disruptive images of "what could be" (Lather 1986).

BREAKING THE SILENCE

A move to activism occurs when research fractures the very ideologies that justify power inequities. In such work, researchers pry open social mythologies that others are committed to sealing. In the pieces of such scholarship cited below, we can hear the costs of breaking the silence for researchers at the margins.

In "Silence: Hispanic and Latina Women and AIDS," Ana Maria Alonso and Maria Teresa Koreck (1989) wedge open a political analysis of women and AIDS in the Latina community. They write about their contradictory loyalties to multiple intellectual, political, and cultural communities:

> The implications of denial are particularly deadly for Latina women. . . . Because of every way in which gender and sexuality are constructed, Latino men are not held accountable. . . . We almost did not write this paper. After much discussion, we decided that maintaining the silence is to cede terrain . . . is to let dominant discourse define the politics of ethnicity, disease, sexuality and morality. . . . We can contest the power of the dominant discourses to define not only who we are and how we live, but also how we die. (57)

These women publicly resist in their narrative the cultures that both threaten and protect them. As border crossers themselves, holding membership in multiple communities (Rosaldo 1989) Alonso and Koreck refuse to collude in cultural or gendered betrayal. But as they remind us, while their project seeks to interrupt those silences which assault the lives of Latinas, the work of de-silencing is costly and dangerous to them.

Scholars interested in race, class, gender, sexuality, and disability know how quickly biological explanations seem to satisfy questions of perceived differences. These explanations float within an almost uninterruptible language of the "natural." If there is no other task that feminist activist researchers can accomplish, we can provoke a deep curiosity about (if not an intolerance for) that which is described as inevitable, immutable, and natural. Two examples may capture the work of splicing "what is" from "what must be."

Frigga Haug in a coauthored text *Female Sexualization,* writes with a German Marxist Feminist women's group committed to "collective memory work" on the sexualization of their bodies (1987). Sexualization, for the collective, involves the reduction and subjugation of women's bodies to a constant requirement to arouse male desire and, at the same time, to be normal. Haug and colleagues write the stories of their bodies with chapters focusing on hair, thighs, buttocks, cleavage, and parts that have grown to be sexually charged. These women track the sexual reconstruction of body parts once considered asexual. They spin histories of their social bodies and, by doing so, denaturalize that which appears to be so natural, so female, so in the body, and not the body politic. Their work forces a re-look at the social production of gender, sexuality, "nature," and, finally, desire.

Moving from bodies to classrooms, but still inside the unpacking of the natural, Patti Lather in *Getting Smart* (1991) invites researchers to look multiply at how we construct the stories we tell about others' data. She seeks to "explore what it means to write science differently" (xx) by framing and reframing interviews, reports, journal entries, and personal musings from her introductory women's studies course. Interested in why women resist feminism, Lather refuses to tell the one natural story about these women. Instead, she spins four possible tales from her data:

> Each of the four tales I shall spin will be grounded in words generated via journals and interviews from students across varied sections of this introductory women's studies class. Borrowing loosely from Van Maanen (1988), I call these a realist tale, a critical tale, a deconstructivist tale, and a reflexive tale. By "realist," I mean those stories which assume a found world, an empirical world knowable through adequate method and theory. By "critical", I mean those stories which assume underlying determining structures for how power shapes the social world. Such structures are posited as largely invisible to common sense ways of making meaning but visible to those who probe below hegemonic meaning systems to produce counterhegemonic knowledge, knowledge intended to

challenge dominant meaning systems. By "deconstructivist," I mean stories that foreground the unsaid in our saying, "the elisions, blind-spots, loci of the unsayable within texts" (Grosz 1989:184). Deconstruction moves against stories that appear to tell themselves. It creates stories that disclose their constructed nature. And, finally, by "reflexive," I mean those stories which bring the teller of the tale back into the narrative, embodied, desiring, invested in a variety of often contradictory privileges and struggles. (128–29)

By forcing readers to recognize the promiscuity of intellectual frames, within which we pour our data, Lather invites researchers and educators to "begin to understand how we are caught up in power situations of which we are, ourselves, the bearers [and to] foreground the limits of our lives and what we can do within those boundaries" (25). By text end, we can enjoy the freshness of Lather's questions: Who speaks? For what and to whom? Who listens? And we can recognize the partiality of any one interpretive frame, even if it is offered as the most natural or essential understanding.

Braiding Haug with Lather, whether the text is armpit hair or the story of women's resistance to feminism, both writers ask researchers/educators to engage critically in the process of interrogating how we have settled on the stories we tell; how else these stories could be told; how we can organize disruptively for "what could be."

ATTACHING WHAT IS TO WHAT COULD BE

Today there is a flurry of writing on "what could be," deepening social critiques of what "has been." By pressing readers to imagine what could be, a collection of writers has taken readers to the boundaries of current intellectual debates in order to conceive beyond, in order to provoke political possibilities. Such work is best exemplified by Lois Weis, in her text, *Working Class Without Work* (1990), and by Derrick Belle in his text, *And We Are Not Yet Saved* (1987). Work that disrupts ideological and theoretical "inevitables" must be recognized as deeply activist for social transformation.

In her text, *Working Class Without Work: High School Students in a De-industrializing America,* Weis describes an ethnography of White male and female students who attend a high school located in a recently deindustrialized working-class town. Weis analyzes working-class White male development as it is carved in opposition to young White women and adolescents of color, and she examines working-class White female development as an instance of incipient feminist awareness. She connects adolescent consciousness (male and female) to the erosion of labor markets and movements, and she anticipates theoretically that these young White working-class men could find comforting political respite within the New Right, while these young

White working-class women could nestle comfortably within an emergent feminist politic. In so doing, Weis attaches her analyses of adolescent development to activist movements past and future. She achieves enormous theoretical advance by repoliticizing psychological development and by inviting readers to see how systematically schools depoliticize individuals from collective social movements that have shaped their lives.

As a talented critical ethnographer, Weis documents closely the ways in which schools not only reproduce but actually refuse to interrupt oppositional white male development. As a theorist of possibility, Weis advances these insights toward a rich melding of "what is" with a powerful sense of "what could be." She breaks silences and denaturalizes what is but, even further, she provokes readers to imagine multiple, postmodern possibilities of what could be, nurturing the social responsibilities among educators and readers to create that which is not yet.

Like Weis, Derrick Belle reframes what has been, and what could be, through a radical jolt of perspective. In *And We Are Not Yet Saved,* a series of legal chronicles, Belle writes through the voice and wisdom of fictitious Geneva Crenshaw. Each chronicle revisits a "racially based" judicial decision and shifts the historic discourse by forcing readers to tour U.S. history through a self-consciously African-American vantage point. The chronicles on desegregation, housing, and affirmative action force multiple readings of these decisions that were rendered ostensibly *for* people of color.

In the final chronicle, Belle describes the dystopia of the "Black Crime Cure." A group of young Black boys find some rocks that they eat, and in so doing they stop participating in criminal activities. Now, he notes, Whites can no longer reason that Blacks don't have housing, education, health care, or adequate living conditions because Blacks bring crime and poverty on themselves. With the Black Crime Cure, the White liberal explanation is removed. And he is relieved. These young boys pass the rocks onto their friends. All indulge, and pass them onto their children. Belle writes:

> Time does not permit a full recounting of how the Black Crime Cure was distributed across the country. While the stones seemed to give indigestion to whites who took them, they worked as they had in the cave for anyone with a substantial amount of African blood. Black people were overjoyed and looked forward to life without fear of attack in even the poorest neighborhoods. Whites also lost their fear of muggings, burglary and rape.
>
> But, now that blacks had forsaken crime and begun fighting it, the doors of opportunity, long closed to them because of their "criminal tendencies," were not opened more than a crack. All-white neighborhoods continued to resist the entry to blacks, save perhaps a few professionals. Employers did not hasten to make

jobs available for those who once made their living preying on individuals and robbing stores. Nor did black schools, now models of disciplined decorum, much improve the quality of their teaching. Teachers who believed blacks too dangerous to teach continued their lackadaisical ways, rationalized now because blacks, they said, were too dumb to learn.

Moreover, the Black Crime Cure drastically undermined the crime industry. Thousands of people lost jobs as police forces were reduced, court schedules were cut back and prisons closed. Manufacturers who provided weapons, uniforms and equipment of all forms to law enforcement agencies were brought to the brink of bankruptcy. Estimates of the dollar losses ran into the hundreds of millions.

And most threatening of all, police—free of the constant menace of black crime and prodded by the citizenry—began to direct attention to the pervasive, long neglected problem of "white collar crime" and the noxious activities of politicians and their business supporters. Those in power, and the many more who always fear that any change will worsen their status, came to an unspoken but no less firm conclusion: fear of black crime has an important stabilizing effect on the nation (1987, 246–47)

Belle, throughout this text, assumes a disruptive narrative stance, unhooking the past, present, and future from the traditional, taken-for-granted notions. The text opens a series of social contradictions and unravels a powerful sense of activist possibility. Working backward (like Haug) and forward (like Weis and Austin), Belle explodes "common sense" (White?) notions of justice, entitlement, and progress and forces readers to reconsider explanations that have for so long suited, legitimized, and even perpetuated, racist hierarchies.

Both Weis and Belle position narratives inside intellectual spaces heretofore uncharted. They capture readers' imaginations with portrayals of adolescent identity and racial history cast in terms of what could be—impending with doom, and rich in possibilities.

ENGAGING IN PARTICIPATORY ACTIVIST RESEARCH

The fourth strategy for feminist research concerns participatory activist research. In the tradition of Kurt Lewin (1948) and Carolyn Payton (1984), this fourth strategy assumes that knowledge is best gathered in the midst of social change projects; that the partial perspectives of participants and observers can be collected by researchers in "power sensitive conversations" (Haraway 1988, 590), which need to be transformative—they cannot be just a pluralistic collection of voices but need to be a struggle. This work is, at once; disruptive, transformative, and reflective; about understanding and about action; not about freezing the scene; but always about change (Gitlin, Siegel, and Boru 1989).

To illustrate: For over a decade, feminist psychologist Brinton Lykes (1989) has been engaged in political activism/research with Guatemalan Indian women in their struggles against political repression. Splicing activist politics with psychological research and a feminist commitment to collaboration, Lykes has woven a piece of work with these women in which

> we . . . shared an interest in better understanding the conditions under which people come to understand themselves as actors constructing their future, as active participants in the social and political development of their people. We agreed that a project that documented the processes by which women, beginning with their immediate concerns, develop a political consciousness that is accompanied by action and gives social meaning to their activity, would contribute both to a better understanding of Guatemalan women's resistance efforts and, more generally, to our knowledge about the development of political self-consciousness among women. The project was conceived thus as a concrete resource for existing Guatemalan communities, as a vehicle for exploring a more theoretical problem of interest to theorists and to breaking the silence surrounding Guatemala's recent history. (171)

This group of women has collaborated with Lykes on the design for gathering, interpreting, and protecting the oral histories of women in refugee communities.

In her writings, Lykes is the exemplary poststructuralist narrator. Positioned multiply, and often contradictorily, she describes herself as an activist, collaborator, and researcher; as a native North American, a critical psychologist, and an overly "ethical" researcher (Lykes documents some telling negotiations over her construction of an "informed consent" form); a reflective interviewer and an anxious interviewee. Engaged over a decade with a set of activist refugees and psychologists, Lykes considers her project to be explicitly about liberatory struggle and its documentation. And she writes, beautifully and reflectively, about the consequences of such an agenda for psychological research practices.

One particularly compelling essay from this project concludes with a detailed analysis of the politics of collaborative research:

> The decision to engage in collaborative research does not *de facto* resolve competing interests. Nor does it minimize the importance

of developing strategies for ensuring, for example, the anonymity of our informants, concerns that are even more critical in research with members of oppressed groups than in university-based work with college sophomores. Rather it affirms a commitment on the part of both researcher and participant to engage the research process as subjects, as constructors to our own reality (Lykes 1989, 179)

With Lykes, social research constructs a gendered archive of political resistance that would otherwise be buried within the deep history by the repression that characterizes these women's lives.

Reflecting Backward and Forward

I use this space to foreshadow a debate I am about to have with Daphne Patai, whose essay responds to my chapter and Patti Lather's. As you will see, Patai worries about the methodological and political implications of our chapters. I won't dispute her remarks except to explore an epistemological space in which we disagree profoundly; a space in need of conversation.

Patai writes for what she calls "intellectual independence." Deeply offended by researchers who nest, inside our scholarship, reflections on biography, position, and politics, she's right to conclude that we fundamentally part ways. *Dis-stance* was written explicitly to provoke conversations about the messy zones between and within politics and social research. I neither seek nor believe in "intellectual independence." I do yearn for any chance to talk, openly, with friends, colleagues, and activists about how to invent research for, with, and on social change.

Scholarship on school reform, racism, community life, violence against women, reproductive freedom . . . sits at the messy nexus of theory, research and organizing. The *raison d'être* for such research is to unsettle questions, texts, and collective struggles; to challenge what is, incite what could be, and help imagine a world that is not yet imagined.

Done critically and collectively with graduate students, community activists, educators, high-school students, and dropouts, this work trespasses borders of class, ethnicities, sexualities, genders, and politics. The collection of data, its interpretation, and our writings spin through a fragile, exhilarating, always tentative "we." "We" as Patai notes, is a utopian marker for a collective of differences in constant negotiation. "We" is not, as Patai suggests, an imperial net thrown over the bodies and minds of Others from my ivory tower. "We" is a political and intellectual stance; a wish worth aspiring toward; a fantasy never coherently achieved. "Our" work is a montage, and it is anything but intellectually independent.

I offer no apologies for the belief that intellectual questions are saturated in biography and politics and that they should be. I do want to be clear, however, about a point raised by Patai and by critics from the New Right. Researchers on the Left may begin with a set of intellectually and politically charged questions, but this does not mean that we force "ideological alignment." When we listen closely, to each other and our informants, we are surprised, and our intellectual work is transformed. We keep each other honest to forces of difference, divergence, and contradiction.

I set out, in *Dis-stance,* to begin a conversation with friends and colleagues about the messy borders of research self-consciously drenched in activism. Throwing a wide net around work I would consider activist, I tried to unroll some of the bumpier aspects of this work, reveal some of the more troubling questions, and slice open some of the more finely scarred tissues in this intellectual arena. I do this because my work, and many others', boils in a delicious but troubling stew of theory, politics, research, and activism, and because I believe intellectuals carry a responsibility to engage with struggles for democracy and justice.

As for "intellectual independence," I've never seen it, I don't believe in it, and I have no desire to share in the illusion. Collective democracies of difference, struggling over authority and validity at the hyphen between activism and research—now there's an illusion worth having.

References

Alonso, A., and Koreck, M. (1989). Silences: Hispanic and Latina women and AIDS. *Sexual Practices* 1 (1):101–124.

Amaro, H. (1989). *Women's reproductive rights in the age of AIDS: New threats to informed choice.* Article drafted from paper presented at the 97th Annual Convention of the American Psychological Association, August XX, New Orleans, LA.

Amaro, H., and Russo, N. F. (1987). Hispanic women and mental health: An overview of contemporary issues in research and practice. *Psychology of Women Quarterly* 11:393–408.

Austin, R. (1989). Sapphire Bound! *Wisconsin Law Review* 3; 539—578.

Becker, H. (1986). *Writing for social scientists: How to start and finish your thesis, book or article.* Chicago: Univ. of Chicago Press.

Belle, D. (1987). *And we are not yet saved: The elusive quest for racial justice.* New York: Basic Books.

Belle, D. (1990). Poverty and women's mental health. *American Psychologist* 45:385–89.

Blackman, J. (1989). *Intimate violence.* New York: Columbia Univ. Press.

Brodkey, L. (1987). *Academic writing as social practice.* Philadelphia: Temple Univ. Press.

Brodkey, L., and Fine, M. (1988). Presence of body, absence of mind. *Journal of Education* 170:84–99.

Brown, L. (1987a). Lesbians, weight, and eating: New analysis and perspectives. *Lesbian psychologies*, 294–309. Chicago: Univ. of Illinois Press.

Brown, L. (1987b). New voices, new visions: Toward a lesbian/gay paradigm for psychology. *Psychology of Women Quarterly* 13:445–58.

Caraway, N. (1991). *Segregated sisterhood.* Knoxville: Univ. of Tennessee Press.

Clark, M. (1990). The difficulty of saying "I": Identifying , analyzing and critiquing voices of self, difference, and discourse in college students' reading and writing about literature. Unpublished Ph.D. dissertation, Univ. of Pennsylvania, 1990.

Condor, A. (1986). Sex roles and "traditional" women: Feminist and intergroup perspectives. In S. Wilkinson (ed.), *Feminist social psychology: Developing theory and practice,* 97–118, Philadelphia: Open Univ. Press.

Crawford, M. (1989). Agreeing to differ: Feminist epistemologies and women's ways of knowing. In M. Crawford and M. Gentry (eds.), *Gender and thought: Psychological perspectives,* 128–45. New York: Springer-Verlag.

Crawford, M., and Gentry, M. (1989). *Gender and thought: Psychological perspectives.* New York: Springer-Verlag.

Crawford, M., and Marecek, J. (1989a). Psychology reconstructs the female, 1968–1988. *Psychology of Women Quarterly,* 13:147–66.

Crawford, M., and Marecek, J. (1989b). Feminist theory, feminist psychology: A bibliography of epistemology, critical analysis and applications. *Psychology of Women Quarterly* 13:477–92.

Crenshaw, K. Whose story is it, anyway? In T. Morrison (ed.), *Race-ing Justice, En-gendering Power,* 402–440. N.Y. Patheon.

Crosby, F. (1984). The denial of personal discrimination. *American Behavioral Scientist* 27 (3):371–86.

Crosby, F., Pufall, A., Snyder, R.C., O'Connell, M., and Walen, P. (1989). Gender and thought: The role of the self-concept. In M. Crawford and M. Gentry (eds.), *Gender and thought: Psychological perspectives,* 100–127. New York: Springer-Verlag.

Fine, M., and Gordon, A. (1989). Feminist transformations of/ despite psychology. In M. Crawford and M. Gentry (eds.), *Gender and thought: Psychological perspectives,* 146–74. New York: Springer-Verlag.

Fine, M., and Vanderslice, V. (1991). Qualitative activist research: Reflections on politics and methods: In E. Posavac (ed.), *Methodological issues in applied social psychology.* New York: Plenum.

Fine, M., and Zane, N. (1989). On bein' wrapped tight: When low income females drop out of high school. In L. Weis (ed.), *Dropouts in schools: Issues, dilemmas and solutions,* 23–54. Albany, NY. State Univ. of New York Press.

Flax, J. (1990). *Thinking fragments: Psychoanalyses, feminism and post-modernism in the contemporary west.* Berkeley: Univ. of California Press.

Fox-Genovese, E. (1991). *Feminism without illusions.* Chapel Hill, NC: Univ. of North Carolina Press.

Gilkes, C. (1988). Building in many places: Multiple commitments and ideologies in Black women's community work. In A. Bookman and S. Morgan (eds.), *Women and the politics of empowerment,* 53–76. Philadelphia: Temple Univ. Press.

Gilligan C. (1993). Joining the resistance: Psychology, politics, girls and women. In L. Weis and M. Fine (eds.), *Beyond silenced voices,* 143–68. Albany, NY: State Univ. of New York Press.

Gitlin, A., Siegel, M., Boru, K. (1989). The politics of method: From leftist ethnography to educative research. *Qualitative Studies in Education* 2:237–53.

Grosz, E. (1988). The in(ter)vention of feminist knowledges. In Barbara Caine, E. Grosz, and M. deLepervanche (eds.), *Crossing boundaries: Feminisms and the critique of knowledges,* **etc. 92–104. Sydney: Allen and Unwin.**

Grosz, E. (1989). *Sexual subversions: Three French feminists.* Sydney, Aust.: Allen and Unwin.

Hare-Mustin, R., and Marecek, J. (1990a). Toward a feminist post-structural psychology: The modern self and the post-modern subject. Paper presented at the American Psychological Association, August 20. Boston, MA.

Hare-Mustin, R., and Marecek, J. (1990b). *Making a difference: Psychology and the construction of gender.* New Haven, CT: Yale Univ. Press.

Haraway, D. (1988). Situated knowledges: The science question in feminism and the privilege of partial perspective. *Feminist Studies* 14(3):575–97.

Harding, S. (1986). *The science question in feminism.* Ithaca, NY: Cornell Univ. Press.

Haug, F. (1987). *Female sexualization: A collective work of memory.* London: Verso.

Hill-Collins, Patricia (19xx). *Black feminist thought.* New York: Routledge.

hooks, b. (1991a). *Yearning.* Boston: South End.

Kahn, A., and Yoder, J. (1990). Domination, subordination and the psychology of women: A theoretical framework. Paper presented at the American Psychological Association, August 20, Boston MA.

Ladner, J. (1971). *Tomorrow's tomorrow.* Garden City, NY: Doubleday.

Lather, P. (1986). Research as praxis. *Harvard Educational Review* 56(3):257–77.

Lather, P. (1990). Staying dumb? Student resistance to liberatory curriculum. Paper presented at annual conference of the American Educational Research Association, April, Boston, MA.

Lather, P. (1991). *Getting smart: Feminist research and pedagogy with/in the postmodern.* New York: Routledge.

Lesko, N. (1988). The curriculum of the body: Lessons from a Catholic high school. In B. Roman (ed.), *Becoming feminine: The politics of popular culture,* 123–42. New York: Falmer.

Lewin, K. (1948). *Resolving social conflicts: Selected papers on group dynamics.* New York: Harper.

Lykes, M. B. (1989). Dialogue with Guatemalan indian women: Critical perspectives on constructing collaborative research. In R. Unger (ed.), *Representations: Social constructions of gender,* 167–84. Amityville, NY: Baywood.

Lykes, B., and Stewart, A. (1986). Evaluating the feminist challenge to research in personality and social psychology, 1963–83. *Psychology of Women Quarterly* 10:393–412.

Majors, B. (1994). From social inequality to personal entitlement: The role of social comparisons, legitimacy appraisals and group membership. *Advances in Experimental Social Psychology* 26:293–355.

McDade, L. (1988). Ethnography and journalism: The critical difference. Paper presented at the Urban Ethnography Forum, February 19, University of Pennsylvania, Philadelphia, PA.

Miller, J. B. (1976). Toward a new psychology of women. Boston: Beacon.

Morawski, J. (1990). Toward the unimagined: Feminism and epistemology in psychology. In R. Hare-Mustin and J. Marecek (eds.), *Making a difference: Psychology and the construction of gender,* 159–83. New Haven, CT: Yale Univ. Press.

Patai, D. (1988). *Brazilian women speak: Contemporary life stories.* New Brunswick, NJ: Rutgers Univ. Press.

Patai, D. (1992). U.S. academics and third world women: Is ethical research possible? *In* S. Gluck and D. Patai (eds.), *Women's words,* 137–53. New York: Routledge.

Parlee, M. (1990). Psychology of menstruation and premenstrual syndrome. Unpublished manuscript, City University of New York, Graduate School and University Center, New York.

Payton, C. (1984). Who must do the hard things? *American Psychologist* 39(3):391–97.

Reinharz, S. (1988). The concept of voice. Paper presented at Human Diversity: Perspectives on People Context, June 8, University of Maryland, College Park, MD.

Robinson, L. (1989). What culture should mean. *The Nation* (September): 319–321.

Rosaldo, R. (1989). *Culture and truth: The remaking of social analysis.* Boston: Beacon.

Russo, N. (1984). *Women in the American psychological association.* Washington, DC: American Psychological Association.

Scott, J. (1992). *Experience.* In J. Butler and J. Scott (eds.), *Feminists theory; the political,* 22–39. New York: Routledge.

Semin, G., and Gergen, K. (1990). *Everyday understanding: Social and scientific implications.* London: Sage.

Smith, D. (1987). *The everyday world as problematic: A feminist sociology.* Boston: Northeastern Univ. Press.

Smith, J., and Stewart, A. (1989). Linking individual development with social changes. *American Psychologist* 44(1):30–42.

Stacey, J. (1991). Can there be a feminist ethnography? In S. Gluck and D. Patai (eds.), *Women's Words,* 111–120. New York: Routledge.

Sullivan, M. (1990). The male role in teenage pregnancy and parenting. New York: Vara Institute of Justice.

Taylor, S. (1983). Adjustment to threatening events. *American Psychologist* 38:1161–73.

Tiefer, L. (1990). Gender and meaning in DSM-111 (and 111-R) sexual dysfunctions. Paper presented at the American Psychological Association, August, Boston, MA.

Tolman, D. (1990). Discourses of adolescent girls' sexual desire in developmental psychology and feminist scholarship. Qualifying paper, Harvard University, Graduate School of Education.

Unger, R. (1990). Sources of variability: A feminist analysis. Paper presented at the American Psychological Association, August 24, Boston, MA.

Van Maanen, J. (1988). *Tales of the field: On writing ethnography.* Chicago: Univ. of Chicago Press.

Walkerdine, V. (1986). Post-stimulated theory and everyday social practices: The family and the school. In V. Wilkinson (ed.), *Feminist social psychology: Developing theory and practice,* 57–76. Philadelphia: Open Univ. Press.

Weis, L. (1990). *Working class without work: High school students in a de-industrializing economy.* New York: Routledge.

Wilkinson, S. (1986). *Feminist social psychology: Developing theory and practice.* Philadelphia: Open Univ. Press.

Willis, P. (1981). *Learning to labor: How working class kids get working class jobs.* Aldershot, England: Gower.

Wittig, M. A. (1985). Metatheoretical dilemmas in the psychology of gender. *American Psychologist* 40(7):800–811.

FERTILE OBSESSION:
VALIDITY AFTER POSTSTRUCTURALISM

Patti Lather

Poised at the end of the twentieth century, the human sciences are in search of a discourse to help chart the journey from the present to the future. Withering critiques of realism, universalism, and individualism take us into the millennium (Borgmann 1992). Conferences are held to explore the End of Science;[1] others argue for science as rhetoric (Nelson, Megill, and McCloskey 1987; Simons 1989), narrative (Polkinghorne 1988), and/or social practice (Woolgar 1988). Regardless of terms, each is part of some move "to grow up in our attitudes toward science" in an antifoundational[2] era characterized by the loss of certainties and absolute frames of reference (Fine 1986).

This article comes out of such ferment and is written against "the merely deconstructive and the endlessly prefatory" (Borgmann 1992, 2). Believing that "science is a performance" (Fine 1986, 148), my effort is to anticipate a generative methodology that registers a possibility and marks a provisional space in which a different science might take form. Seeking answers to such a project in inquiry as it is lived, the article works at the edges of what is currently available in moving toward a science with more to answer to in terms of the complexities of language and the world.

In pursuit of a less comfortable social science, I continue my seeming obsession with the topic of validity: the conditions of the legitimation of knowledge in contemporary postpositivism. Over the last decade or so of postpositivism, the boundaries surrounding the issue of research legitimation have been constructed from many angles: naturalistic and constructivist (Lincoln and Guba 1985; Guba and Lincoln 1989), discourse theory (Mishler 1990), ethnographic authority (Clifford 1983; Gordon 1990), poststructuralism (Cherryholmes 1988; Kvale 1989), forms of validity appropriate to an emancipatory interest (Alcoff 1989; Alcoff 1991–92). Long interested in how the core but changing concept of validity is shaped across the proliferation of "paradigms" that so characterizes postpositivism (Lather 1991b), my thoughts on validity are on the move again. While extending my earlier work toward counterpractices of authority that are adequate to emancipatory interests (Lather 1986a; Lather 1986b), my primary desire here is to rethink validity in light of antifoundational discourse theory. Rather than jettisoning "validity" as the term of choice, I retain the term in order to both circulate and break with the signs that code it. What I mean by the term, then, is both mobilizing all of the baggage that it carries and, in a doubled movement, using it to rupture validity as a "regime of truth," to displace its historical inscription toward "doing the police in different voices" (Con Davis 1990, 109).

In this exploration, I position validity as "an incitement to discourse," much like how Foucault saw sexuality in the attention it receives within the human sciences (Gordon 1988, 23). Validity is a "limit question" of research, one that repeatedly resurfaces, one that can neither be avoided nor resolved, a fertile obsession given its intractability (Fraser 1989, 80). Cornel West (1991) notes that antifoundationalism has displaced concerns about relativism with disagreement over the importance of appropriate restraints and regulations. He cautions that attempts to settle such disagreement by appeals to something outside of practice is to revert to foundationalism. Instead, West argues, such debates would be more fruitful if framed "as a way of rendering explicit the discursive space or conversational activity now made legitimate owing to widespread acceptance of epistemic antifoundationalism" (25).

I brood on these sentences as my interest grows in a reconceptualized validity that is grounded in theorizing our practice. I write out of a feminist poststructural frame where "getting smarter" about theory/practice issues valorizes practice: "In periods when fields are without secure foundations, practice becomes the engine of innovation" (Marcus and Fischer 1986, 166). This entails a reflexivity that attends to the politics of what is and is not done at a practical level in order to learn "to 'read out' the epistemologies in our various practices" (Hartsock 1987, 206). Yet, as Spivak writes, "The field of practice is a broken and uneven place," heavily inscribed with habit and sedimented understandings (1991, 177).

"Where, after the metanarratives, can legitimacy reside?" Lyotard asks (1984, xxv). This article addresses Lyotard's question via a dispersion, circulation, and proliferation of counterpractices of authority that take the crisis of representation into account. What are the antifoundational possibilities outside the limits of normative framings of validity in the human sciences? What might open-ended and context-sensitive validity criteria look like? Why is validity the site of such attraction? How much of this obsession with legitimation/validity issues in research methodology is part of the disciplinary nature of our society of confession and conscience? This paper is situated at the nexus of such doubled questions. Fragmenting and colliding both hegemonic and oppositional codes, my goal is to reinscribe validity in a way that uses the antifoundational problematic to loosen the master code of positivism that continues to so shape even postpositivism (Scheurich 1991). My task is to do so in a way that refuses over-simple answers to intractable questions.

The Masks of Methodology

> Now the rhetorically minded seem prescient . . . for the masks of methodology are wearing thin. (Nelson, Megill, and McCloskey 1987, 3)

> Either let Truth carry the day against deceitful appearances, or else, claiming once more to reverse optics, let us give exclusive privilege to the fake, the mask, the fantasy because, at least at times, they mark the nostalgia we feel for something even more true. (Irigaray, quoted in Whitford 1991, 71–72)

The nostalgia Irigaray writes of has something to do with the distinction between viewing ethnographic stories as about "found" versus "constructed" worlds (Simon and Dippo 1986). The effacement of the referent in postmodern culture has made "the real" contested territory. To shift our sense of the real to "discourses of the real" (Britzman 1991) is to foreground how discourse worlds the world. Whether this is an opening for liberatory politics or the end of politics/history is much debated (e.g., Harvey 1989; Hutcheon 1989; Nicholson 1990). Whether to celebrate or lament the felt loss of found worlds depends on how one reads the political possibilities that open up when "truth" is positioned as made by humans via very specific material practices.

In terms of legitimation issues, antifoundationalists argue that the thing itself, in its absence, cannot be witness to a representative validity. In poststructuralist terms, the "crisis of representation" is not the end of representation, but the end of pure presence. Derrida's point regarding " 'the inescapability of representation' " (Arac, quoted in McGowan 1991, 26) shifts responsibility from representing things in themselves to representing the web of "structure, sign and play" of social relations (Derrida 1978). It is not a matter of looking harder or more closely, but of seeing what frames our seeing—spaces of constructed visibility and incitements to see which constitute power/knowledge.

These are all concerns that decenter validity as being about epistemological guarantees. Such postepistemic concerns reframe validity as multiple, partial, endlessly deferred. They construct a site of development for a *validity of transgression* that runs counter to the standard *validity of correspondence*: a nonreferential validity interested in how discourse does its work, where transgression is defined as "the game of limits . . . at the border of disciplines, and across the line of taboo" (Pefanis 1991, 85; see also Foucault 1977).

In the discourses of the social sciences, validity has always been the problem, not the solution (Cronbach and Meehl 1955). Across such qualitative practices as member checks and peer debriefing (Lincoln and Guba 1985), triangulation (Denzin 1989), and catalytic validity (Lather 1986b), various postpositivist efforts have been made to resolve the problem without exhausting it, constantly providing answers to and freeing social science practices from the problem, but always partially, temporarily. More recently and more attuned to discourse theory, Mishler's (1990) reformulation traces the irrelevance of standard approaches to validity through various postpositivist efforts to rearticulate it. Reframing validity as "problematic in a deep theoretical sense, rather than as a technical problem" (417), Mishler surveys some "candidate exemplars" for generating new practices of validation that do not rely on a correspondence model of truth or assumptions of transparent narration.

In the absence of such livable alternatives, agents are constrained to revert to articulable forms—this does not necessarily imply intellectual consent (McGowan 1991, 257). But it does underscore that not to revert to the dominant foundational, formulaic, and readily available codes of validity requires the invention of counterdiscourse/counterpractices of legitimation.

Like Woolgar (1988), my own position is that the most useful stories about science are those that interrogate representation, "a reflexive exploration of our own practices of representation" (98). This entails taking a position regarding the contested bodies of thought and practice that shape inquiry in the human sciences, negotiating the complex heterogeneity of discourses and practices. This ability to establish and maintain an acceptable dialogue with readers about " 'how to go about reality construction' " (Goldknopf, quoted in Conrad 1990, 101) involves making decisions about which discursive policy to follow, which "regime of truth" to locate one's work within, which mask of methodology to assume. What follows is, in effect, a call for a kind of validity after poststructuralism in which legitimation depends on a researcher's ability to explore the resources of different contemporary inquiry problematics and, perhaps, even contribute to "an 'unjamming' effect in relation to the closed truths of the past, thereby freeing up the present for new forms of thought and practice" (Bennett 1990, 277).

Transgressive Validity

Within Derrida's injunction that " 'we extend ourselves by force of play' against the limits of the already said" (quoted in Ferguson 1991, 330), the following "plays"[3] with the question, what do you do with validity once you've met poststructuralism?[4] I proceed via what Deleuze and Guattari (1983) term "activating by invention" in order to move from "yesterday's institutions" to some other place of social inquiry. In this move, I position validity as a space of constructed visibility of the practices of methodology and "a space of the *incitement* to see" (Rajchman 1991, 85), an apparatus for observing the staging of the poses of methodology, a site that "gives to be seen" the unthought in our thought.

In the remainder of this article, I first present four "framings" of validity that take antifoundational discourse theory into account. Within each, I present an exemplar of empirical work which moves discussion from the epistemological criteria of validity as a relation of correspondence between thought and its object to the generation of counterpractices of authority grounded in the crisis of representation. I then flesh out the intelligibility of such practices via an effort toward self-reflexivity in my study of women living with HIV/AIDS. I conclude with some brief thoughts on poststructuralism and the impossibility of science.

Counterpractices of Authority

The following is a dispersion, circulation, and proliferation of counter-practices of authority which take the crisis of representation into account. In creating a nomadic and dispersed validity, I employ a strategy of excess and categorical scandal in the hope of both imploding ideas of policing social science and working against the inscription of another "regime of truth." Rather than the usual couching of validity in terms of disciplinary maintenance, disciplining the disciplines, my goal is to open new lines of discussion about changed conditions and possibilities for a critical social science (Fay 1987) and the discourse theories that so problematize that project. Rather than prescriptions for establishing validity in postpositivist empirical work, like Walter Benjamin, I offer "a forthrightly personal and deliberately ephemeral antithesis" (Werckmeister 1982, 114) to more conventional and prescriptive discourse practices of validity.

FRAME 1: VALIDITY AS SIMULACRA/IRONIC VALIDITY.

Simulacra are copies without originals (e.g., the Virgin Mary, Disneyland, the foetus as constructed by the New Right [Kroker 1983]). The Baudrillardian argument is that we have shifted from a culture of representations to one of simulacra. Simulacra function to mask the absence of referential finalities. Baudrillard's definition of simulacrum comes from Ecclesiastes, "The simulacrum is never that which conceals the truth—it is the truth which conceals that there is none. The simulacrum is true" (quoted in Bogard 1988). In the world of simulacra, "the referent is secondary at best" (McGowan 1991, 18).

The poststructural move foregrounds the difficulties involved in representing the social rather than repressing them in pursuit of an unrealized ideal. Enacting in language a supplementary simulacrum, poststructuralism "breaks all adequation between copy and model, appearance and essence, event and idea" (Young 1990, 82). This disruptive move foregrounds the production of meaning-effects. To quote Cummings:

> Simulacra wreak havoc with an obsessional economy. Unlike good copies, which identify themselves as counterfeit, simulacra [know enough to] keep quiet about their origins and are thus taken for the genuine article. They have this much in common with hysterical symptoms: to the uninitiated, the two are perfect fakes. Both are the bane of metaphysics because they collapse the distinction between original and copy, subtending binary logic and the law of degree. (1991, 108)

Using simulacra to resist the hold of the real and to foreground radical unknowability, the invisible can be made intelligible via objects that are about nonobjecthood. Contrary to dominant validity practices where the rhetorical nature of scientific claims is masked with methodological assurances, a strategy of ironic validity proliferates forms, recognizing that they are rhetorical and without foundation, postepistemic, lacking in epistemological support. The text is resituated as a representation of its "failure to represent what it points toward but can never reach" (Hayles 1990, 261), an ironic representation of neither the thing itself nor a representation of the thing, but a simulacrum. This move into the hyper-real implodes copies via an operation of displacement rather than representation, where the distinction between the copy and the real ceases to have meaning. Ironic validity is a Baudrillardian move of a "cultural guerilla multiply[ing] simulations beyond any possibility of control by a code" (Angus 1989, 346). It is a deconstructive move that avoids simple reversal and simple replacement

> by inscribing heterogeneity within an opposition so as to displace it and disorient its antagonistic defining terms . . . to subvert it by repeating it, dislocating it fractionally through parody, dissimulation, simulacrum, mime, a mimicry that mocks the binary structure, travestying it . . . a doubling that can easily be mistaken for the real thing. (Young 1990, 209)

James Agee and Walter Evan's (1988) *Let Us Now Praise Famous Men*, originally published in 1941 and recently claimed as a postmodern text (Quinby 1991; Rabinowitz 1992), illustrates what I mean by ironic validity. Documenting the devastation of rural America by the economic disasters of the 1930s through the study of three white tenant farm families, the text is prefaced by Evans's uncaptioned photographs which set the stage for the focus on the politics of knowing and being known. Agee's text, which serves somewhat as one long caption for the photographs, foregrounds the insufficiencies of langauge via prose that is meandering, incantational, and deeply inscribed by musical forms. Beginning with three vignettes and concluding with multiple endings. Agee presents his awkwardness and hesitancies where his anxiety about "his relationship to his subjects becomes an anxiety about the form of the book" (Rabinowitz 1990, 160). Both seeking and refusing a center, he combines documentary and autobiography to describe with "words which are 'not words' " (161) as he moves from representations of the tenant families to the disclosure of his own subjectivity. Agee's "self-indulgent, confessional narrative of middle-class seeing" is both redeemed and problematized by Evan's photographs which resist narrative, sentimentality and sensationalism while still "reveal[ing] the ways differences can be organized and contained" (163).

As such, the book both reinscribes familiar "regimes of truth" and narrative and anticipates a much less comfortable social science in its embodiment of the anxiety of voyeurism. Disrupting their intelligence mission, the authors resist both "the claims of disciplinary power to represent objective reality" and obscene prying into the lives of others in the name of science, "the commodification of one set of human beings for the consumption of another" (Quinby 1991, 104–105). Deferring any final saying, the text is an "excursion into the radical unreliability of meaning," the "rupture between language and the world" (Quinby 1991, 108–109), the unrepresentable. Enacting a doubled movement, Agee both uses words and casts doubt on any transparency between the word and its object via a kind of genealogical specificity that is counterespionage data well outside the conventions of social science discourse.

Endlessly shifting the location of the unknowable and ironically using researcher power to undercut practices of representation, Agee and Evans create a text that is dense with the absence of referential finalities. Foregrounding the production of meaning-effects, they nonetheless construct a text of such specificity that the human cost of economics run amuck is made "visible" in ways that are amplified in flesh.

Refusing closure and turning the analytical categories of the human sciences against themselves, Agee and Evans enact the struggle of an "I" to become an "eye" that both inscribes and interrupts normalizing power/ knowledge (Quinby 1991). Fifty years after its original publication, their self-scrutinizing, non-normalizing production of knowledge is generative of research practices that, by taking the crisis of representation into account, create texts that are double without being paralyzed and that implode controlling codes.

FRAME 2:   LYOTARDIAN PARALOGY/NEOPRAGMATIC VALIDITY.

Legitimation by paralogy is "a model of legitimation that has nothing to do with maximized performance, but has as its basis difference understood as paralogy" (Lyotard 1984, 60). It is to legitimate without recourse to either metanarratives or "the hegemony of the performativity principle" of traditional pragmatism that has arisen in the face of the decline of metanarratives (Kiziltan, Bain, and Canizares 1990, 366). Displacing both the criterion of efficiency and the Habermasian drive for consensus, Lyotardian parology is that which "refines our sensitivity to differences and reinforces our ability to tolerate the incommensurable" via "the constant search for new ideas and concepts that introduces dissensus into consensus" (Fritzman 1990, 371–72). Its goal is to foster differences and let contradictions remain in tension, "as opposed to the recuperation of the other into the same that is always imposed at the end (telos) of a traditional philosophy" (McGowan 1991, 106).

Rather than evoking a world we already seem to know (verisimilitude) in a story offered as transparent, the move is toward "attempts to create indeterminate space for the enactment of human imagination" (Lubiano 1991, 177) which introduce "a destabilizing 'obligation to complexity' " (Lyotard, quoted in Smart 1992, 176). Paralogy legitimates via fostering heterogeneity, refusing closure. It entails "knowledge of language games as such and the decision to assume responsibility for their rules and effects" (Lyotard 1984, 66). Part of the current pragmatics of science, paralogy adopts rules within language games that "would respect both the desire for justice and the desire for the unknown" (67). It is about the search for instabilities and the undermining of the framework within which previous "normal science" has been conducted. It recognizes the multiplicity of language games and the "temporary contract" of any consensus. Its goal is something not entirely subordinated to a system's goals, yet not so abruptly destabilizing of a system that it is ignored or repressed.

A recent dissertation on African-American women and leadership positions in higher education gives some feel for the parameters of paralogic validity (Woodbrooks 1991). Woodbrooks's study was "designed to generate more interactive and contextual ways of knowing" (93) with a particular focus on openness to counterinterpretations: "The overarching goal of the methodology is to present a series of fruitful interruptions that demonstrate the multiplicity of meaning-making and interpretation" (94).

In analyzing interview data, Woodbrooks made extensive use of two familiar qualitative practices of validity, member checks and peer debriefing (Lincoln and Guba 1985). Using both to purposefully locate herself in the contradictory borderland between feminist emancipatory and poststructural positions, she attempted to interrupt her role as the Great Interpreter, "to shake, disrupt, and shift" her feminist critical investments (Woodbrooks 1991, 103). Peer debriefing and member checks, both coherent within present forms of intelligibility, were used to critique her initial analysis of the data, her "perceptions of some broadly defined themes that emerged as I coded the transcripts" (132). Reanalyzing the data and her original analysis, Woodbrooks then sent a second draft out to participants and phoned for responses. This resulted in a textual strategy that juxtaposed the voices of the white female researcher with those of the African-American female participants.

In her textual strategy, Woodbrooks first tells a realist tale which backgrounds the researcher's shaping influence and foregrounds participant voices. She interrupts this with a critical tale that foregrounds how her theoretical investments shaped her analysis of the data. Finally, in a third-person voice, she tells a deconstructive tale which draws on participant reactions to the critical tale. Here, she probes her own desire, "suspicious of . . . the hegemony [of] feminism" (140) in her analysis that marginalized both African-American identity as a source of pride and strength (ascribing it totally to gender) and participant concerns with male/female relations. "This strategy [of feminist consciousness-raising] perpetuates feminism as a white middle class project and trivializes the deep emotional ties that black women share with black men" (200).

Holding up to scrutiny her own complicity, Woodbrooks creates a research design that moves her toward unlearning her own privilege and displacing the colonizing gaze. Foregrounding the availability of multiple discourses and how they can be used to decenter the researcher as the master of truth and justice, she enacts her knowledge of language games as she assumes responsibility for the rules and effects of her investments. Such a strategy refines our sensitivity to differences, introduces dissensus into consensus, and legitimates via fostering heterogeneity. Woodbrooks's expanded use of the familiar techniques of member checks and peer debriefing, a using of what is already available "rather than hoping for something else to come along or to create utopia from thin air" (Kulchyski 1992, 192), results in a search for instabilities and a foregrounding of the multiplicity of language games.

FRAME 3: DERRIDEAN RIGOUR/RHIZOMATIC VALIDITY:[5]

Derridean rigour enacts a hard specificity as to what counts as facts and details. It undermines stability, subverts and unsettles from within; it is a "vocation," a response to the call of the otherness of any system, its alterity. It is Derridean play in the face of the absence of the transcendental signified as it supplements and exceeds what order has tried to make stable and permanent. Most important, such rigour is about a "meticulous diffidence" in its refusal of some great transformation (McGowan 1991, 109). Rather than presenting deconstruction as a counterontology, a method, a concept or an origin, Derridean rigour is a nominal counterlogic: it is what it does (122) as it situates itself in the interstices of the no longer and the not yet.

The rhizome is a metaphor for such a reinscription of rigour. Deleuze and Guattari (1983) suggest the tree as the modernist model of knowledge, with the rhizome as the model for postmodern knowledge. The Chomskyan tree of structural linguistics, for example, presents "a limited number of paths along which words can enter a relationship" (Lecercle 1990, 132). Rhizomes are systems with underground stems and aerial roots, whose fruits are tubers and bulbs. To function rhizomatically is to act via relay, circuit, multiple openings, as " 'crabgrass' in the lawn of academic preconceptions" (Ulmer 1989, 185). There is no trunk, no emergence from a single root, but rather "arbitrary branchings off and temporary frontiers" that can only be mapped, not blueprinted (Lecercle 1990, 132–33). Rhizomes produce paradoxical objects, "they enable us to follow an anarchistic growth, not to survey the smooth unfolding of an orderly structure" (134). Rhizomatics are about the move from hierarchies to networks and the complexity of problematics where any concept, when pulled, is recognized as "connected to a mass of tangled ideas, uprooted, as it were, from the epistemological field" (Pefanis 1991, 22). Rather than a linear progress, rhizomatics is a journey among intersections, nodes, and regionalizations through a multi-centered complexity. As a metaphor, rhizomes work against the constraints of authority, regularity, and common sense, and open thought up to creative constructions. They are "on the ground," immanent, with appeal not to transcendental values but to "their content of 'possibilities', liberty or creativ-ity." The "new," however, is not so much about the fashionable as it is the creativity that arises out of social practices, creativity which marks the ability to transform, to break down present practices in favor of future ones (Deleuze 1992, 163–64).

To probe what rhizomatic validity might mean in the context of an empiri-cal study, I draw from the work of an Australian dissertation student, Erica Lenore McWilliam. In a study of "student-needs talk" in preservice teacher education, McWilliam (1992a, 1992b) developed a research design that involved (1) an initial reflexive phase, where researcher theoretical and political investments were put under scrutiny by moving back and forth among various contestatory discourses in a way that resituated the researcher away from the "transformative intellectual" come to "save" the oppressed: (2) an empirical phase that focused on student-teacher constructions of teacher work; and (3) a final reciprocal phase designed as reflection in action and an extended cotheorizing process that contested and reconstructed the researcher's reading of the phase 2 data. Each stage paid particular attention to discrepant data, the facts unfit to fit categorical schemes in a way that both uses and collides poststructuralism and feminist emancipatory discourses. Of note are McWilliam's learnings that research practices that interrupt researcher privilege must be more about constructing "an interrogative re-searcher text . . . a questioning text." Such a text overtly "signals tenta-tiveness and partiality" in decentering expert authority and moving toward practices of cotheorizing (1992a, 271). Paying particular attention to the tendencies of much advocacy research toward inaccessible language and "intellectual bullying" of the researched (1992b, 14), she attempts to create the conditions in which it becomes possible for both researcher and researched to rethink their attitudes and practices.

Ranging across rather standard attitudinal surveys, dialogic, reciprocally self-disclosive interviews, and sustained interaction, McWilliam works to decenter both her own expertise and the participants' common sense about teaching practices. Her "double-edged analysis" breaches both "congealed critical discourse" and the dominant traditional discourses (1992a, 30). She remarks on the "untidiness" of "this straddling of agendas" (1992a, 91) and the "state of tension" (1992a, 257) that exists between feminism and those who unproblematically side with or against Enlightenment projects. As such, her work enacts what it means to let contradictions remain in tension, to unsettle from within, to dissolve interpretations by making them as temporary, partial, invested, including her paradoxical continuing investment in transformative praxis.

More interested in networks than hierarchies and research that gestures toward the problematics of representation, McWilliam fleshes out a rhizomatic journey among intersections, nodes, and regionalizations through a multicentered complexity that is, like Woodbrooks, particularly noteworthy for attending to the creation of interactive social relations in which the inquiry can proceed. Rather than focusing exclusively on textual strategies that disrupt illusory notions of found worlds, both Woodbrooks and McWilliam illustrate how a poststructural focus on textual strategies can go hand in hand with developing interactive social relations in inquiry. Invested not only in the textual foregrounding of new voices but also in creating sites in the inquiry where those voices can hear themselves and one another fruitfully, Woodbrooks's and McWilliam's straddling of both poststructural and feminist agendas is atuned to Whitford's (1991) caution: "Playing with a text, from Irigaray's point of view, is a rather solipsistic activity; it is not a dialogue with the other which includes process and the possibility of change" (48; see also Lutz 1993, 145).

FRAME 4:   VOLUPTUOUS VALIDITY/SITUATED VALIDITY.

My last "framing" of validity posits the fruitfulness of situating scientific epistemology as shaped by a male imaginary. It asks what the inclusion of a female imaginary would effect where the female is other to the male's Other. Irigaray (1985) terms this the maternal/feminine, the residue which exceeds the categories, a disruptive excess which reveals the limits of the hegemonic male imaginary. Her project is to create a space where women in their multiplicity can become—body, nature, maternal, material.

Baudrillard (1987) talks of voluptuousness as a term "which sex and psychoanalysis have succeeded neither in annexing nor in discrediting with their discourse" (32). Serres (1982) writes:

> It's the revolution of voluptuousness, the physics of Venus chosen over that of Mars. . . . The nature of Mars, of martial physics, is one of hard, rigid, and rigorous bodies; the physics and nature of Venus are formed in flows. . . . It is difficult to think of a rigorous and exact science that might have been conditioned by Venus and not by Mars, for peace and not for destruction . . . since Western science has always followed the weight of power. (101–106)

Irigaray argues that "the murder of the mother" is the founding act of Western culture. Embodiment is relegated to the female, freeing the phallocentric idea to transcend the material, creating the deadly split between epistemology and ethics (Whitford 1991). The feminist debates over objectivity are situated in overcoming this split. Haraway (1988), for example, argues that self-conscious partiality is a necessary condition of being heard to make rational knowledge claims. This constructs a politics and epistemology of positionality versus universal/objective claims. The "view from everywhere" (which is the universalized "view from nowhere" of objectivism) is contrasted with explicit incompleteness, tentativeness, the creation of space for others to enter, the joining of partial voices (Kirkpatrick 1991). Authority then comes from engagement and self-reflexivity, not distanced "objectivity," and the bugaboo of relativism is displaced, positioned as a foundationalist concern (Cherryholmes 1988; Alcoff 1989; Lather 1991a).

Whether it is possible to produce the maternal/feminine and be heard in the culture raises the issue of the politics of excess. The eruption of the mother in feminist discourse was the unthought that was originally perceived as unreadable. This exceeds Lyotardian paralogy in exploring "the potent marginality" (Kristeva 1978–79, 6) of feminist critique, a deliberate excessiveness, what Fraser (1989) terms "leaky" or "runaway": practices "which have broken out of discursive enclaves . . . a species of excess . . ." (169). This sort of going too far "is always some variety of the marginalized, unwilling to stay out of 'the center,' who transgresses . . . who behaves, in this moment, as though she or he has a right to lay claim to a place in the discursive spotlight" (Lubiano 1991, 150). As an example, I have played with calling the license that feminists have taken to theorize from the body "clitoral validity/pagan validity".[6] Such a term constructs an antifoundational field of possibility for opening up to that which is outside the limits of the normative framings of validity in a language so excessive as to render the term unthinkable/unreadable. Such a term marks the "emergent but not yet 'readable' discourse of women" (Con Davis 1990, 106) as some other to Lyotardian neopragmatism, something more akin to "risky practice" in terms of "the politics of uncertainty" that underlies feminist praxis in an antifoundational time (Sawicki 1991, 103).

An example of "going too far" is Richardson's (forthcoming) essay about her larger interview study of unmarried mothers. "Consciously self-revelatory" in probing the lived experience of the researcher (125), Richardson cheekily hopes that she has not "ventured beyond improper" as she "breache[s] sociological writing expectations by writing sociology as poetry" (126). First presenting "a transcript masquerading as a poem/a poem masquerading as a transcript" (127), her primary goal is "to create a position for experiencing the self as a sociological knower/constructor—not just talking about it, but doing it" (136). Speaking autobiographically in order to provide "an opportunity to rethink sociological representation" (133), Richardson writes of her need to break out of the "dreary" writing of " 'straight' sociological prose" (131). The part of her that had written poetry for eight years is called on to "provide a new strategy for resolving those horrid postmodernist writing dilemmas" (131). Deliberately choosing a transcript from a woman quite different from herself in order to encounter the "postmodernist issues of 'authorship'/authority/appropriation," she works toward a text that is "bounded and unbounded closed and open" (132).

Richardson concludes with five consequences to herself of the experience of producing and disseminating the story-poem of *Louisa May*. We hear about changed relations with children; spirituality; Richardson's integration of "the suppressed 'poet' and the overactive 'sociologist' " (135), including her return of the advance from the book contract as she is no longer able to write conventional sociology; her increased attunement to differences in others and herself, including more caution "about what 'doing research' means" (135); and, finally, some disillusionment at "the hold of positivism on even those I consider my allies" as she has presented this work (135). "I experience isolation, alienation, and freedom, exhilaration. I want to record what they are saying; I want to do fieldwork on them. Science them" (136).

Richardson exemplifies a disruptive excess that brings ethics and epistemology together in self-conscious partiality, an embodied positionality and a tentativeness which leaves space for others to enter, for the joining of partial voices. Authority comes from engagement and reflexivity in a way that exceeds Lyotardian paralogy via practices of textual representation that, by hegemonic standards, "go too far" with the politics of uncertainty. This effect is achieved by blurring the lines between the genres of poetry and social-science reporting. Theorizing out of autobiography where her "leaky" practice collapses the private/public distinction, Richardson is mother, wife, scholar, and poet in her desire to move toward some way of doing science more in keeping with her feminist-poststructuralism.

Offered as more problem than solution, my scandalous categories and the exemplars I have recruited as provocateurs of validity after poststructuralism are performances of a transgressive validity that works off spaces already in the making. Situated in the crisis of authority that has occurred across knowledge systems, my challenge has been to make productive use of the dilemma of being left to work from traditions of research legitimacy and discourses of validity that appear no longer adequate to the task. Between the no longer and the not yet lies the possibility of what was impossible under traditional "regimes of truth" in the social sciences: a deconstructive problematic that aims not to govern a practice but to theorize it, deprive it of its innocence, disrupt the ideological effects by which it reproduces itself, pose as a problem what has been offered as a solution (Rooney 1989). Derrida terms this "a 'science of the possibility of science' . . . a nonlinear, multiple, and dissimulated space. . . . Thus we discover a science whose object is not 'truth,' but the constitution and annulment of its own text and the subject inscribed there" (Sollers 1983, 137, 179).

Researching the Lives of Women with HIV/AIDS: A Small Narrative Toward Self-Reflexivity

In this section, I flesh out the intelligibility of validity after poststructuralism via my in-process study of women living with HIV/AIDS (Lather 1992). A Lyotardian "small narrative," the following story about the early phases of my inquiry offers a situated context for fashioning a field of possibilities that is not yet. Methodologically, my primary interest in this study is the implications of researcher/researched positionings for practices of inquiry, a nexus of issues Foucault (1980) has coded with the phrase, "the politics of the gaze." In this study, I see an opportunity to wrestle across the "deconstructive excesses and extreme forms of social constructionism" characteristic of some poststructuralisms via the political responsibility to "real bodies and political rage" (Stockton 1992, 114, 117).

My particular interest in this study is "the unnoticed dangers in the precise techniques we employ to conceive and resolve our problems" (Rajchman 1991, 141). The origin of this curiosity is not from a world view one wants to convert others to, but rather from "an experience of 'deconversion,' from a loss of assurance or certainty as to who we are and may be, opening up spaces in which no one is as yet the master" (141). Questioning the emergent rules or norms of feminist inquiry (Patai 1991; Fine 1992; Opie 1992), my goal in this study is to be required to invent other practices out of the methodological issues that I bring to this study.

Growing out of my immersion in a study that feels both urgent and as something about which I want, at this time, to speak softly and obliquely, I am wrestling with a myriad of questions grounded in the crisis of representation. How does a researcher work not to see so easily in telling stories that belong to others? Does s/he try hard to understand less, to be nudged out of positions we customarily occupy when viewing "the Other" (Brown, 1992)? Who are my "others"? What binaries structure my arguments? What hierarchies are at play? How can I use Irigaray's concept of the "We-you/I" to disrupt those very oppositions, to create a constantly moving speaking position that fixes neither subject nor object, that disrupts the set boundaries between subjects (Game 1991, 88)? What is the role of autobiography here? For example, what does my getting tested for HIV mean within this context? I am considering when to do this: now? at the end? midway through writing? There is a methodological interest here. Is this instrumental? exploitative? What does it mean to position these women and this project as a Gramscian historical laboratory in which to explore a science marked by practices of productive ambiguity that cultivate a taste for complexity?

In terms of a methodology that "comes clean" about how power shapes an inquiry, how do I use disruptive devices in the text to unsettle conventional notions of the real? How do I foreground the dilemmas involved in researcher struggles with the anxiety of voyeurism without entangling myself in an ever more detailed self-analysis, an "implosion" into the self? What is my goal as a researcher: empathy? emancipation? advocacy? learning from/working with/standing with? What is the romance of the desire for research as political intervention? How is this work tied into what Van Maanen (1988) refers to as the by no means trivial "demands of contemporary academic careers" and disciplinary logics (53)? What is this fierce interest in proving the relevance of intellectual work? To what extent is my work tied to "the pretensions of sociology toward politics? (Riley 1988, 54)?

Such questions assume that, in generating counterpractices of authority, the new canon is reflexivity (Rajchman 1985). As Anderson (1989) notes, while this is a common enough point, there are few guidelines for how one goes about the doing of it, especially in a way that both is reflexive and, yet, notes the limits of self-reflexivity. To attempt to deconstruct one's own work is to risk buying into the faith in the powers of critical reflection that places emancipatory efforts in such a contradictory position with the poststructuralist foregrounding of the limits of consciousness. Johnson (1981), too, draws attention to the inadequacies of immediacy, of belief in the self-presentation of meaning which "seems to guarantee the notions that in the spoken word we know what we mean, mean what we say, say what we mean, and know what we have said" (viii). Rather than take refuge in the futility of self-critique, however, I want to attempt it as aware as possible of its inevitable shortcomings, all that which remains opaque to myself. There is much in my performance as a researcher that I cannot reach, much that eludes the logic of the self-present subject. But situated so as to give testimony and witness to what is happening to these women with HIV/

AIDS, my methodological desire is to probe the instructive complications of this study in order to generate a theory of situated methodology that will, hopefully, lead me to a place where I do *not* conclude that "I will never do research this way again" (Marienthal 1992).

How might "transgressive validity," as set out thus far in this paper, help me in such an effort toward generative methodology? Can the scandalous categories heretofore enunciated be of use? To continue the scandal, let us imagine a checklist.

Transgressive Validity Checklist: A Simulacrum

IRONIC VALIDITY

_____ foregrounds the insufficiencies of language and the production of meaning-effects, produces truth as a problem

_____ resists the hold of the real; gestures toward the problematics of representation; foregrounds a suggestive tension regarding the referent and its creation as an object of inquiry

_____ disperses, circulates, and proliferates forms, including the generation of research practices that take the crisis of representation into account

_____ creates analytic practices that are doubled without being paralyzed

PARALOGICAL VALIDITY

_____ fosters differences and heterogeneity via the search for "fruitful interruptions"

_____ implodes controlling codes, but remains coherent within present forms of intelligibility

_____ anticipates a politics that desires both justice and the unknown, but refuses any grand transformation

_____ concerned with undecidables, limits, paradoxes, discontinuities, complexities

_____ searches for the oppositional in our daily practices, the territory we already occupy

RHIZOMATIC VALIDITY

_____ unsettles from within, taps underground

_____ generates new locally determined norms of understanding; proliferates open-ended and context-sensitive criteria; works against reinscription of some new regime, some new systematicity

_____ supplements and exceeds the stable and the permanent, Derridean play

_____ works against constraints of authority via relay, multiple openings, networks, complexities of problematics

_____ puts conventional discursive procedures under erasure; breaches congealed discourses, critical as well as dominant

VOLUPTUOUS VALIDITY

_____ goes too far toward disruptive excess; leaky, runaway, risky practice

_____ embodies a situated, partial, positioned, explicit tentativeness

_____ constructs authority via practices of engagement and self-reflexivity

_____ creates a questioning text that is bounded and unbounded, closed and opened

_____ brings ethics and epistemology together

Rather than actually evaluating my small narrative using this checklist that mimics checklists, my interest is in a return to Cornel West's argument at the beginning of this paper that practices are perpetually becoming available if we render explicit the spaces opened up by the growing acceptance of epistemic antifoundationalism. Moving the discussion of validity from epistemological criteria of truth as a correspondence between thought and its object to criteria grounded in the crisis of representation, the practices I have sketched are "micro-becomings" (Deleuze and Guattari 1983, 70). Defined by a dispersal, circulation, and proliferation of becomings from what has been proceeding obscurely underground, they function rhizomatically, foraging across/between middles, "the area where things take on speed" (58). A supple line, a flux, a "line of fight . . . where the thresholds attain a point of adjacency and rupture," my ephemeral practices of validity after poststructuralism are "an arrangement of desire and of enunciation" (107) rather than a general recipe. My intent has been to forge from a scattered testimony a methodology that is not so much prescription as "curves of visibility and enunciation" (Deleuze 1992, 160). Experiments "that baffle expectations, trace active lines of flight, seek out lines that are bunching, accelerating or decreasing in speed . . . " (Deleuze and Guattari 1983, 111), my evocation is the "horizons toward which experiments work" (Ormiston 1990, 239) as we try to understand what is at play in our practices of constructing a science "after truth."

Conclusion: Poststructuralism and the Impossibility of Science

> To make the thought possible, one occupies the place of the impossible. (Althusser 1990, 209)

While I have by no means exhausted the range of counterpractices of authority that can become possible, my reflections on how we are constituted through certain practices, certain ways of going on, foreground how new practices are perpetually becoming available (West 1991). Derrida posits "the impossible" as the source of invention that creates a space " 'to think the unthought,' 'to say the unsayable,' 'to see the unseeable,' or 'to represent the unrepresentable' " (quoted in Rajchman 1991, 159). Deleuze, in writing about Foucault, helps us grasp this idea via a move into a virtual multiplicity, "a disparate set of things of which we cannot yet have the concept; and its 'actualization' therefore involves the invention of something which, by the lights of our concepts, is impossible" (quoted in Rajchman 1991, 160). Impossibility, then, serves not as a logical concept but as an historical one: "the impossibility of what is not yet or no longer possible for us to think. . . ." Foucault's project was to ask how we might " 'inhabit' those moments of 'actuality' in which we are becoming something else than what our history has constructed us to be, those heterotopic moments of our current historical 'impossibility,' the moments of invention" (161).

  This article posits that the conditions of possibility for validity are also its conditions of impossibility. It is my hope that such a disjunctive affirmation of incommensurates has rendered contradictory claims productive in finding a way of putting into play the loss of the possibility of science and of opening its practice to other possibilities, other histories, the "continent of thought just beyond the horizon" (Pefanis 1991, 138). Such an effort is more about "the changing shape of the thinkable" (Gordon 1991, 8) than it is about the actually existing practices of validity. My strategy has been to move from what Derrida refers to as " 'a novelty of the same' " which invents " 'the possible from the possible' " to "an architecture of 'the impossible', the 'altogether-other' of our invention, the surprise of what is not yet possible in the histories of the spaces in which we find ourselves" (Rajchman 1991, 162–63).

Notes

This is an abridged version of the same essay, published in *The Sociological Quarterly* 34(4) (1993):6.

1. In 1989, at the Twenty-fifth Nobel Conference at Gustavus Adolphous College in St. Peter, Minnesota, on the End of Science, feminist philosopher Sandra Harding put it this way:

    As we study our world today, there is an uneasy feeling that we have come to the end of science, that science, as a unified, objective endeavor, is over. . . . This leads to grave epistemological concerns. If science does not speak about extrahistorical, external, universal laws, but is instead social, temporal and local, then there is no way of speaking of something real beyond science that science merely reflects. (Quoted in Kiziltan, Bain and Canizares 1990, 354)

2. The antifoundational claims of this article are in contradistinction to Michael Hardt (1993), who argues that poststructuralism is much more about imma-nent, material, and open foundations (rather than the transcendental, given, and teleological foundations of Hegel) than it is about the claim that we can do without foundations. Using Deleuze to investigate "a new problematic for research after the poststructuralist rupture" (xv), Hardt is particularly useful in terms of understanding Deleuze's anti-Hegelianism and the ontologically foundational role that difference and constitutive practice play in his thought. I use the term "antifoundational" to signal not that we stand on/act out of nothing, but that the historical space in which we find ourselves is "after truth," after certainties, and absolute frames of reference.

3. McGowan (1991) explicates Derridean "play" as about the difference that opens up language and thought and undermines the stability of identity. "There is much to suggest that the play of substitutions in Derrida is never very free, can always be recuperated within a tradition. . . . 'Stabilization is relative, even if it is sometimes so great as to seem immutable and permanent. It is the momentary result of a whole history of relations of force. . . .' " (103–105). Derridean "play," then, is like the "play" in a machine, to move "freely" within limits which are both cause and effect.

4. Distinctions between postmodern and poststructural can be made in various ways. The former raises issues of chronology, economics (e.g., post-Fordism), and aesthetics, whereas poststructural is used more often in relation to academic theorizing "after structuralism." They are often used interchangeably, driving some cultural theorists to distraction. Whole books have been written on this topic. See, for example, Rose 1991. I am much more interested in distinctions between the postmodern and the postcolonial, e.g., Adam and Tiffin 1990.

5. My thanks to David Smith (1988) for alerting me to the importance of rhizomes via what he termed "rhisomatics."

6. For more on paganism and epistemology, see Lyotard 1989 and Ormiston 1990. Morton (1989) introduced me to the idea of "clitoral theoretics" in a review of Naomi Schor. A symptomatic reading of his review exemplifies the

very point I am making in this section about the general unreadability of the maternal/feminine. For a very different exploration of "the discourse of the clitoris in the mucous of the lips" in Irigaray's work, see Spivak 1992.

7. This sentiment comes directly out of my experience of presenting a talk on my research project to a small gathering of women at the research retreat of our dreams in Wisconsin, August 7–8, 1992. It is also spurred by Paul Marienthal's dissertation experience with "participatory research" and "member checks," where he concluded that "I will never do research this way again" (1992).

References

Adam, I., and Tiffin, H. ed (1990). *Past the last post: Theorizing post-colonialism and post-modernism.* Calgary, Alberta: Univ. of Calgary Press.

Agee, J., and Evans, W. (1988). *Let us praise famous men.* Boston: Houghton-Mifflin.

Alcoff, L. (1989). Justifying feminist social science. In Nancy Tuna, ed., *Feminism and science,* 85–103. Bloomington: Indiana Univ. Press.

Alcoff, L. (1991–92). The problem of speaking for others. *Cultural Critique* 20 (Winter): 5–32.

Althusser, L. (1990). *Philosophy and the spontaneous philosophy of the scientists.* London: Verso.

Anderson, G. (1989). Critical ethnography in education: Origins, current status, and new directions. *Review of Educational Research* 59 (3): 249–70.

Angus, I. (1989). Media beyond representation. In Sut Jhally and I. Angus, eds., *Cultural politics in contemporary America,* 333–46. New York: Routledge.

Baudrillard, J. (1987). *Forget Foucault.* New York: Semiotext(e).

Bennett, T. (1990). *Outside literature.* London: Routledge.

Bogard, W. (1988). Sociology in the absence of the social: The significance of Baudrillard for contemporary social thought. Paper delivered at the Pacific Sociological Association annual conference, April, Las Vegas, Nevada.

Borgmann, A. (1992). *Crossing the postmodern divide.* Chicago: Univ. of Chicago Press.

Britzman, D. (1991). *Practice makes practice: A critical study of learning to teach.* Albany: State Univ. of New York Press.

Brown, K.M. (1992). Writing about "the Other." *Chronicle of Higher Education* (April 15): A56.

Cherryholmes, C. (1988). *Power and criticism: Poststructural investigations in education.* New York: Teachers College Press.

Clifford, J. (1983). On ethnographic authority. *Representations* 1 (2): 118–46.

Con Davis, R. (1990). Woman as oppositional reader: Cixous on discourse. In S. Gabriel and I. Smithson, eds., *Gender in the classroom: Power and pedagogy,* 96–111. Urbana: Univ. of Illinois Press.

Conrad, C. (1990). Rhetoric and the display of organizational ethnographies. In J. Anderson, eds., *Communication Yearbook 13,* 95–106. Newbury Park, CA: Sage.

Cronbach, L. and Meehl, P. (1955). Construct validity in psychological tests. *Psychological Bulletin* 52 (3): 281–302.

Cummings, K. (1991). Principles pleasures: Obsessional pedagogies or (ac)counting from Irving Babbitt to Allan Bloom. In Donald Morton and M. Zavarzadeh, ed., *Texts for change: Theory/pedagogy/politics,* 90–111. Urbana: Univ. of Illinois Press.

Deleuze, G. (1992). What is a Dispositif? In *Michel Foucault Philosopher.* Translated and edited by T. Armstrong. New York: Routledge.

Deleuze, G., and Guattari, F. (1983). *On the line.* Translated by J. Johnston. New York: Semiotext(e).

Denzin, N. (1989). *The research act,* 3rd ed. Englewood Cliffs, NJ: Prentice-Hall.

Derrida, J. (1978). Structure, sign and play in the discourse of the human sciences. In *Writing and difference,* translated by A. Bass, 278–93, Chicago: Univ. of Chicago Press.

Fay, B. (1987). *Critical social science.* Ithaca, NY: Cornell Univ. Press.

Ferguson, K. (1991). Interpretation and genealogy in feminism. *Signs* 16 (2): 322–39.

Fine, A. (1986). *The shaky game: Einstein, realism and the quantum theory.* Chicago: Univ. of Chicago Press.

Fine, M. (1992). *Disruptive voices: The possibilities of feminist research.* Ann Arbor: Univ. of Michigan Press.

Foucault, M. (1977). *Language, counter-memory, practice:* Selected essays & interviews by Michel Foucault. Edited by Donald Bouchard. Ithaca, NY: Cornell Univ. Press.

Foucault, M. (1980). *Power/Knowledge: Selected interviews and other writings, 1972–1977.* Translated and edited by C. Gordon. New York: Pantheon.

Fraser, N. (1989). *Unruly practices: Power, discourse and gender in contemporary social theory.* Minneapolis: Univ. of Minnesota Press.

Fritzman, J. (1990). Lyotard's paralogy and Rorty's pluralism: Their differences and pedagogical implications. *Educational Theory* 40 (3): 371–80.

Game, A. (1991). *Undoing the social: Towards a deconstructive sociology.* Toronto: Univ. of Toronto Press.

Gordon, D. (1988). Writing culture, writing feminism: The poetics and politics of experimental ethnography. *Inscriptions* 3–4: 7–26.

Gordon, D. (1990). The politics of ethnographic authority: Race and writing in the ethnography of Margaret Mead and Zora Neale Hurston. In M. Manganaro, eds., *Modernist anthropology: From fieldwork to text,* 146–62. Princeton: Princeton Univ. Press.

Gordon, C. (1991). Governmental rationality: An introduction. In G. Burchell,

C. Gordon, and P. Miller, eds., *The Foucault effect: Studies in governmentality,* 1–51. Chicago: Univ. of Chicago Press.

Guba, E., and Lincoln, Y. (1989). *Fourth generation evaluation.* Newbury Park, CA: Sage.

Haraway, D. (1988). Situated knowledges: The science question in feminism and the privilege of partial perspective. *Feminist Studies* 14(3): 575–99.

Hardt, M. (1993). *Giles Deleuze: An apprenticeship in philosophy.* Minneapolis: Univ. of Minnesota Press.

Hartsock, N. (1987). Rethinking modernism: Minority vs. majority theories. *Cultural Critique* 7: 187–206.

Harvey, D. (1989). *The condition of postmodernity.* Oxford: Basil Blackwell.

Hayles, N. K. (1990). *Chaos bound: Orderly disorder in contemporary literature and science.* Ithaca, NY: Cornell Univ. Press.

Hutcheon, L. (1989). *The politics of postmodernism.* New York: Routledge.

Irigaray, L. (1985). *The sex which is not one.* Translated by C. Porter and C. Burke. Ithaca, NY: Cornell Univ. Press.

Johnson, B. (1981). *Translator's introduction.* In J. Derrida, *Dissemination,* vii–xxxiii. London: Athlone.

Kirkpatrick, L. (1991). Feminist research and pedagogy and talking social work. Unpublished manuscript. Ohio State University.

Kiziltan, M., Bain, W., and Canizares, A. (1990). Postmodern conditions: Rethinking public education. *Educational Theory* 40 (3): 351–70.

Kristeva, J. (1978–79). Postmodernism and periphery. *Third Text* 2: 1–8.

Kroker, A. (1983). The disembodied eye: Ideology and power in the age of nihilism. *Canadian Journal of Political and Social Theory* 7 (1–2): 194–234.

Kulchyski, P. (1992). Primitive subversions: Totalization and resistance in native Canadian politics. *Cultural Critique* 21 (Spring): 171–96.

Kvale, S. (1989). To validate is to question. In S. Kvale, ed., *Issues of Validity in Qualitative Research,* 73–92. Sweden: Studentliterature.

Lather, P. (1986a). Research as praxis. *Harvard Educational Review* 56 (3): 257–77.

Lather, P. (1986b). Issues of validity in openly ideological research: Between a rock and a soft place. *Interchange* 17 (4): 63–84.

Lather, P. (1991a). *Getting smart: Feminist research and pedagogy with/in the postmodern.* New York: Routledge.

Lather, P. (1991b). *Within/Against: Feminist research in education.* Geelong, Australia: Deakin Univ. Monograph Series.

Lather, P. (1992). Feminism, methodology and the crisis of representation: Researching the lives of women with HIV/AIDS. Paper presented at the annual conference of the *Journal of Curriculum Theorizing,* October, Dayton, OH.

Lecercle, J. (1990). *The violence of language.* London: Routledge.

Lincoln, Y., and Guba, E. (1985). *Naturalistic inquiry.* Newbury Park, CA: Sage.

Lubiano, W. (1991). Shuckin' off the African-American native other: What's "po-mo" got to do with it? *Cultural Critique* 18: 149–86.

Lutz, C. (1993). Social contexts of postmodern cultural analysis. In J. Jones, III, W. Natter, and T. Schatzki, eds., *Postmodern contentions: Epochs, politics, space,* 137–64, New York: Guilford.

Lyotard, J. (1984). *The postmodern condition: A report on knowledge.* Translated by G. Bennington and B. Massumi. Minneapolis: Univ. of Minnesota Press.

Lyotard, J. (1989). Lessons in paganism. In A. Benjamin, ed., *The Lyotard reader,* 122–54. Oxford, NJ: Blackwell.

Marcus, G., and Fischer, R. (1986). *Anthropology as cultural critique.* Chicago: Univ. of Chicago Press.

Marienthal, P. (1992). *The dissertation as praxis: An encounter with liberatory methodologies and the emergence of an educator.* Ph.D. dissertation, Ohio State Univ.

McGowan, J. (1991). *Postmodernism and its critics.* Ithaca, NY: Cornell Univ. Press.

McWilliam, E. L. (1992a). *In broken images: A postpositivist analysis of student needs talk in pre-service teacher education.* Ph.D. dissertation, Univ. of Queensland, Australia.

McWilliam, E. (1992b). "Educative research in pre-service teacher education: Post-positivist possibilities." Unpublished manuscript. Univ. of Queensland, Australia.

Mishler, E. (1990). "Validation in inquiry-guided research: The role of exemplars in narrative studies." *Harvard Educational Review* 60 (4): 415–42.

Morton, D. (1989). "The body in/and the text: The politics of clitoral theoretics," *Reading in Detail: Aesthetics and the Feminine,* by N. Schor. *American Journal of Semiotics* 6 (2–3): 299–305.

Nelson, J., Megill, A., and McCloskey, D. eds. (1987). *The rhetoric of the human sciences: Language and argument in scholarship and public affairs.* Madison: Univ. of Wisconsin Press.

Nicholson, L. ed. (1990). *Feminism/Postmodernism.* New York: Routledge.

Opie, A. (1992). Qualitative research, appropriation of the "other" and empowerment. *Feminist Review,* 40 (1): 52–69.

Ormiston, G. (1990). Postmodern differends. In A. Dallery and C. Scott, eds., *Crisis in Continental Philosophy,* 235–83. Albany: State Univ. of New York Press.

Patai, D. (1991). U.S. academics and third world women: Is ethical research possible? In S. Gluck and D. Patai, eds., *Women's words: The feminist practice of oral history,* 137–54. New York: Routledge.

Pefanis, J. (1991). *Heterology and the postmodern: Bataille, Baudrillard, and Lyotard.* Durham, NC: Duke Univ. Press.

Polkinghorne, D. (1988). *Narrative knowing and the human sciences.* Albany: State Univ. of New York Press.

Quinby, L. (1991). *Freedom, Foucault, and the subject of America.* Boston: Northeastern Univ. Press.

Rabinowitz, P. (1992). Voyeurism and class consciousness: James Agee and Walker Evans, *Let Us Now Praise Famous Men. Cultural Critique* 21 (Spring): 143–70.

Rajchman, J. (1985). *Michel Foucault: The freedom of philosophy.* New York: Columbia Univ. Press.

Rajchman, J. (1991). *Philosophical Events: Essays of the 80's.* New York: Columbia Univ. Press.

Richardson, L. (Forthcoming). The consequences of poetic representation: Writing the other, rewriting the self. In C. Ellis and M. Flaherty, eds., *Windows on Lived Experience,* 125–40. Newbury Park, CA: Sage.

Riley, D. (1988). *"Am I that name?" Feminism and the category of "women" in history.* Minneapolis: Univ. of Minnesota Press.

Rooney, E. (1989). *Seductive reasoning: Pluralism as the problematic of contemporary literary theory.* Ithaca: NY: Cornell Univ. Press.

Rose, M. (1991). *The post-modern and the post-industrial: A critical analysis.* Cambridge, UK: Cambridge Univ. Press.

Sawicki, J. (1991). *Disciplining Foucault: Feminism, power, and the body.* New York: Routledge.

Scheurich, J. (1991). The paradigmatic transgressions of validity. Paper presented at the annual conference of the *Journal of Curriculum Theorizing,* October, Dayton, OH.

Serres, M. (1982). *Hermes: Literature, science, philosophy.* Edited by J. Harari and D. Bell. Baltimore, MD: Johns Hopkins Univ. Press.

Simon, R., and Dippo, D. (1986). On critical ethnographic work. *Anthropology and Education Quarterly* 17 (4): 195–202.

Simons, H., ed. (1989). *Rhetoric in the human sciences.* London: Sage.

Smart, B. (1992). *Modern conditions, postmodern controversies.* London: Routledge.

Smith, D. (1988). From logocentrism to rhisomatics: Working through the boundary police to a new love. Paper presented at the annual conference of the *Journal of Curriculum Theorizing,* October, Dayton, OH.

Sollers, P. (1983). *Writing and the experience of limits.* Translated by P. Barnard and D. Hayman, edited by D. Hayman. New York: Columbia Univ. Press.

Spivak, G. (1991). Theory in the margin: Coetzee's *Foe* reading Defoe's *Crusoe/Roxana.* In J. Arac and B. Johnson, eds., *Consequences of Theory,* 154–80. Baltimore, MD: Johns Hopkins Univ. Press.

Spivak, G. (1992). French feminism revisited: Ethics and politics. In J. Butler and Joan Scott, eds., *Feminists Theorize the Political,* 54–85. New York: Routledge.

Stockton, K. B. (1992). Bodies and God: Poststructuralist feminists return to the fold of spiritual materialism. *Boundary* 19 (2): 113–49.

Ulmer, G. (1989). *Teletheory: Grammatology in the age of video.* New York: Routledge.

Van Maanen, J. (1988). *Tales of the field: On writing ethnography.* Chicago: Univ. of Chicago Press.

Werckmeister, O. K. (1982). Walter Benjamin, Paul Klee, and the angel of history. *Oppositions* 7 (1): 103–125.

West, C. (1991). Theory, pragmatisms, and politics. In J. Arac and B. Johnson, eds., *Consequences of Theory,* 22–38. Baltimore, MD: Johns Hopkins Univ. Press.

Whitford, M. (1991). *Luce Irigaray: Philosophy in the feminine.* London: Routledge.

Woodbrooks, C. (1991). *The construction of identity through the presentation of self: Black women candidates interviewing for administrative positions at a research university.* Ph.D. dissertation, Ohio State Univ.

Woolgar, S. (1988). *Science: The very idea.* London: Tavistock.

Young, R. (1990). *White mythologies: Writing history and the west.* London: Routledge.

WHEN METHOD BECOMES POWER
(RESPONSE)

Daphne Patai

There is a hectoring quality to much of the discussion of methodology these days. I fear I have contributed to this tone myself.[1] Hence I write now shamefacedly, chastened by my more recent exposure to the excess of rhetoric and methodolatry we have reached. But behind the voices of self-reflexive scolds, posing as decentered skeptical feminists, lurks a greater problem. It is this:

Feminism today too often demands ideological alignment from its adherents. This pressure to fall into ranks, which in intellectual matters can only be done by means of gross oversimplification and verbal streamlining, is expressed, I believe, in the new feminist mantra of "integrated analysis of race, class, gender, ethnicity, sexuality" and whatever other "social formation" is currently being added to the mix. An expectation of facile alignment also seems to have afflicted the slogan "the personal is political" (initially a useful feminist posture) so that today feminism seems comfortable in an atmosphere in which drawing distinctions—between politics and education, between education and indoctrination, between research and propagandizing, between "survivors" of sexual harassment and survivors of rape—is frowned upon. The image of ideological alignment also sprang to my mind when I read the innocuous-sounding sentence Michele Fine wrote in her essay in this volume: "Our work is to imagine with other communities in struggle the unimaginable braiding of theorizing, studying, interpreting, and organizing for resistance" (p. 36). Quite an order, this. But is it really "our work?" Are "communities in struggle" ("ours" and those of "others") self-evidently real bodies? When "we" "organize for resistance," are "we" all agreed upon what we are resisting and what we are organizing for? How can we distinguish "our" unimaginable braiding" from past endeavors that were first imaginable, then articulated, and then acted upon and—as reading history demonstrates lamentably—ended in disaster? And how shall we be assured that the "situated methodology" sought by Patti Lather in her essay situates us in a place that is worth inhabiting? Does Lather, too, assume that "we" are in fundamental agreement about the content of the "political interventions" our research should, according to this model, be designed to enact?

Of course, in the real world feminists lack the organizational wherewithal that would allow us to impose ideological conformity—it is distressing for me to realize that I am grateful for this! But in no sense does feminists' inability to enforce their views weaken the ideological trend that is glaringly in evidence. Where political muscle is lacking, coercive discourse steps in, its "we"—as "we" always does—creating inclusions and exclusions.[2] Meanwhile, current discussions of methodology, as the two essays I am commenting on reveal, slip smoothly from descriptive and analytical modes to the prescriptive and (by implication) self-congratulatory.

Feminism, today, as it conflates politics and education and effaces any distinction between political agendas and the protocols of research, is in danger of suppressing—it already dismisses—any calm, reflective stance that sees some strengths in the effort (however difficult to achieve) to set biases aside and that still regards research as a valuable and satisfying endeavor not in need of quite so much postmodernist angst. By its refusal to recognize the distinct boundaries that do and, in my view, should demarcate the realms of politics and education, and politics and scholarship, feminism threatens to entirely delegitimize any research effort not hopelessly mired in collective ideological conformity or in individualistic self-reflexive shenanigans.

Acknowledging the fact that politics in a general way always influences education and intellectual work is a far cry from celebrating that influence and intentionally cultivating it. To refuse to draw a distinction here is like saying: As we can never be sure that we are being entirely truthful, we might as well lie all the time. Furthermore, by embracing the politicization-of-everything mode, feminists engage in some major hypocrisy. After all, feminist criticism has had an impact in large part precisely because it has been successful in pointing out the inordinate bias that disfigures much traditional research and education. Such a demonstration suggests that there is a higher standard that ought to be adhered to—the standard in the name of which the feminist critique is pursued. Instead of this higher standard, however, when the moment arrives for feminism to demonstrate its own better-than-that procedures, it too often retreats into a defense of bias (now relabeled "the inevitability of politics everywhere") as if this were a worthy aim in itself.[3] But such a defense cannot be made without a head-in-the-sand attitude. How can feminism today be so insulated that it fails to worry aver the possible connections between its own celebration of the politicization of everything and the primary models of it that in fact exist in this century's history: Stalin's USSR, Nazi Germany, or China's Cultural Revolution? The failure to want to preserve some very real distinctions between these models of a genuine conflation of politics and education and the ideals of a liberal education turns feminist insight into extraordinary blindness. The "braiding" so eloquently evoked in Michele Fine's essay, from this point of view, seems distressingly similar to a forcing of diverse strands into a pattern whose design one presumably knows in advance. The strands may vary; the pattern is always the same.

What postmodernist methodolatry conceals, of course, is that male bias and the traditional, distorted, scholarship with which it is seen to be irremediably linked are evil, while "critical" self-scrutiny and "feminist emancipatory discourses" (to use Patti Lather's recurring phrase) are, presumably, good. But surely such judgments carry troubling implications, troubling at least for cognoscenti of postmodernism, namely that this kind of feminist claim presumes the utter rightness of its own beliefs and its ability to legitimately valorize one discourse over another, and that it can accurately distinguish right political goals from wrong ones. By any definition of feminism, the embrace of complete cultural relativism becomes impossible. It is not surprising, then, that given this ambivalence, feminist writing oscillates wildly, caught between feminist claims on the one hand and postmodernist rhetoric on the other. In practice, however, postmodernist skepticism has done nothing to chip away at the feminist pose of certainty, just as endless talk about the instability and unviability of "I"—as in a unified self-identity—has not lessened the staking out of personal positions, predicated on highly individual "I"s favored by so many contemporary scholars. The oversimplifications of standpoint epistemology, for example, lead Michele Fine to quote with approval Patricia Hill Collins's praise for the natural validity of Black women's consciousness—again, as if each of the terms of this assertion were self-evident and the assertion itself were beyond question. But in the patchwork quilt of modern methodological writings, how does this claim relate to Lather's characterization of our time as "postepistemic?" Apparently it all depends on who "we" are. What can this mean but that the political positions, the pluses and minuses, have all been demarcated in advance so we know whose speech must be considered legitimate, who (including which of "us") is to be questioned at length, and what kinds of assertions should in no circumstances be subjected to scrutiny?

The biases and distortions that characterize prefeminist knowledge, according to feminists, were enacted in the name of a reprehensible male supremacy (never mind that the knowledge so produced was itself varied and contradictory), the whole of which can be dismissed with the monolithic image "patriarchal." Feminist ideological alignment, on the other hand, is expected in the name of the "right"—feminist—values. But, as many people who have spent time in a women's studies program or other feminist endeavor can confirm, conflicts are as prevalent in these circles as in the "masculinist" world outside—and quite as nasty. What distinguishes "us" from past propagandizers but our quite different certitudes (and, of course, our lack of power, thus far, to enforce them)? Happily, one might say, there is no consensus within feminism about either "communities" or objects of "resistance," let alone about the utopias we might each feel we are working to reach. Even such basic concepts as "patriarchy" cause conflict the moment they are made the occasion for more than rhetorical touchstones: in practice, when decisions must be made, feminists range from those who do not consider all men the enemy to others who would exclude even little boys from the feminist events to which mothers are invited to bring their children (this did happen in the 1970s, and it is still happening in the '90s). If feminists could manage to negotiate conflicts better, if postmodernist discourse had any practical effects beyond the printed page, these conflicts (redefined, of course, as lines of tensions or areas of contestation) might prove extremely productive. Instead, self-righteousness and antagonism too often prevail. It is striking that, even in the absence of consensus, the rhetoric of "community," of "we," and of "political intervention" do their work of indoctrination, coercively reinforcing some nonexistent community of right-minded scholars, all of whom are presumably committed to (using Lather's terms) "epistemological antifoundationalism," "engagement and self-reflexivity" (p. 20).

Michele Fine's essay also displays a belief in verbal magic, even as she contests the grounds on which this magic has traditionally been practiced. Critical scrutiny, it appears, is actually aimed primarily at others, not at oneself. For "oneself," the verbal legerdemain of acknowledging one's own "position"—as if this could ever adequately or sufficiently be done—suffices.[4] The three examples Fine judges as praiseworthy are—let us be clear about this—instances of this very gesture. By this I mean no criticism of the three scholars cited but rather of the excessive significance attributed to their words. Astonishing credit is given these days to researchers who discuss their own conflicts as researchers, as if saying "I almost stopped doing this" wipes away the multiple conflicts resulting from doing research with living human beings (though why I should privilege the living might also be queried as long as we're in the endless querying mode). I agree that taking account of our own positions and circumstances is an important thing to do, though in fact it is not nearly as new as some of us have pretended or erroneously supposed. But it is also important for us to realize what our stances are doing in a particular context and historical moment. At present, in my view, we are spending much too much time wading in the morass of our own positionings. It's nice to say that we need to account for ourselves, that we must not hide behind a spurious invisibility or objectivity. But just how much space should we be devoting to self-accounting and to the methodological discourse that has sprouted, like mushrooms, around it? When is enough enough?

Academic fads move with such rapidity these days that I can clearly recollect how recently such a self-critical practice was unpopular in feminist academic circles. In 1986, at a conference in Minnesota, I first presented some reflections on the ethical problems of research involving personal interviews. At the time I gained the distinct impression that I was regarded as something of a killjoy, raising uncomfortable and ultimately ambiguous questions concerning the ethical appropriateness of White academic feminists doing research across racial, class, and national boundaries. When the contributions to that conference were subsequently published, mine was one of the very few papers omitted from the volume, and no explanation was ever offered to me.

As I continued to speak about this subject over the next few years, I was at first surprised to encounter reactions of impatience on the part of some listeners. They told me that my work on Brazilian women had taught them a great deal, and they could not understand why I was flagellating myself with ethical and methodological issues. Over a period of time, I myself got bored with questions that were so much easier to raise than to answer. I recall a particularly enlightening moment, at an Oral History Association meeting several years ago, when I was on a panel entitled "Empowerment or Appropriation: Oral History, Feminist Process, and Ethics." Michael Frisch, himself an oral historian who has done much to demystify oral history methodology (as evidenced by some of the pieces of his book, *A Shared Authority*),[5] spoke from the floor. Listening to his own tapes, he said, had made him aware how often, despite all the road blocks he inadvertently created, speakers returned to their own themes. They seemed determined to tell him what was important to them, even in the face of his interference. Typically, Frisch stated, they would answer politely when he derailed them, and then after a while get back to what was really on their minds. We should not, in other words, anguish quite so much over our own roles.[6]

I have come to believe he is right. In addition, all this emphasis on ourselves simply puts me off. In my view, Patti Lather's essay should be read above all as an academic prose-poem. In a way that calls to mind Roman Jakobson's description of the poetic function, her paper persistently draws attention to its own language. Its principal referents seem to be the formulaic and abstruse words of other scholars. Manipulation of language is clearly both Lather's intent and achievement. I doubt, however, that even intellectuals as embroiled as she is in postmodernist rhetoric really live in the confined worlds of mere words. The "crisis in representation" (to which Lather repeatedly alludes) notwithstanding, babies still have to be cared for, shelter sought, meals prepared and eaten. People who stay up nights worrying about representation should consider what would happen if all the sewers in their city were stopped up, or if garbage collection ceased for three weeks. They should ask themselves whether the crisis in representation is a crisis in the same sense as the crisis in Bosnia, whether the problem of foundationalism is of the same kind as the problem of malnutrition—and if malnutrition would be alleviated by renaming it or by exploring its ideological roots. Such hostile questions are, I should add, intended to demonstrate just how much of a mental game this tiresome self-reflexivity has become. It is inconceivable that this game could be played in a setting in which material want was an incontrovertible fact of life. Scare quotes would disappear as language took on urgency for purposes of essential communication and problem solving. Facticity would be felt in the flesh, not a bad thing to be reminded of now and then.[7] In a similarly curmudgeonly mode, I suggest that we might some time want to test the postmodernist devaluation of the notion of a coherent, unified identity by examining what happens to people with Alzheimer's disease. Lacking memory, are they free to live without the fictions of presence, unrestrained by ossified past selves as they ever reinvent themselves to the rhythms of new desires? Such a test might lead us to question whether we are not playing language games for the amusement of the new semi-leisured class.

But even so, it is one thing when we subject our own practice to critique; it is quite another when these language games are used as one more weapon in the endless academic pursuit of carving out space for oneself. Feminists, in particular, are having quite a go at this game (as some readers will no doubt think I am doing in writing this irascible commentary). And White feminists, without doubt, have been ideally positioned to be perfect targets of such attacks. On the one hand, White feminists are portrayed as the epitome of privilege (never mind that many White women, too, have struggled to get an education, to gain entry into professions, etc.), the latest outrage counted against them being that they have usurped the voices of other women for their own aggrandizement. On the other hand, and a few turns of the screw later, a new criticism has surfaced. It is best articulated in a passage chosen for advertising a new book in 1992:

> Many academic feminists now acknowledge differences among women and accept that white women cannot speak for non-white women. But perceiving the issue as just a matter of who can speak for whom can also offer a way out of dealing with the complexity of women's experience and women's oppression. It permits white women to forget about non-white women since "We have no right to speak for anyone but ourselves." This reading of the political and theoretical critiques of white feminism can be used to justify ignoring the majority of women in the world altogether.[8]

In other words, damned if you do, damned if you don't. Or: await further instructions about precisely which language and method will be acceptable and how to conduct your balancing act. "White feminism" is already perilously close to going the way of "Eurocentric" as a term of instant dismissal. The dismal effects of all this are readily apparent in women's studies classes, in which students have difficulty focusing on the ideas in a book because they are fixated on the author's "identity,"[9] or in which one White student censoriously tells another that it is not appropriate for a White person to criticize a Black writer's metaphors.[10] Or perhaps less significance is an observation reported to me by several students in different classes: the first thing that occurs on the first day of a women's studies class is a general, mutual, "checking out," as students determine which women shave their legs, wear makeup, and so on. This presumably allows the students to "position" one another.

Feminist censoriousness, in other words, seems to be emerging as the norm. Sisterhood is long gone, exposed as mere mystification designed to conceal a White supremacist agenda. Heterosexuality, of course, preceded Whiteness as grounds for suspicion—though, interestingly, it is now permissible for women of color, whose struggle is "with their men." "Privileges" of all kinds have supposedly been exploded (at least in the realm of words)—and, in rapid retreat, as if hoping to ward off attack, feminists are careful to announce their very fixed and unpostmodernist identities: "As a White heterosexual bourgeois woman, I" . . . etc.

What's going on here? The fact is that those of us whose medium is words do occupy privileged positions, and we hardly give up those positions when we engage in endless self-scrutiny and anxious self-identification. In effect, I cannot ever abdicate my privileges as long as I write for publication or in general lead the life of an academic intellectual. Someone will no doubt soon suggest that some of us should just cease to do precisely that. Then, as we move from mere scolding to proscription, at least it will be clear what is being fought over: access to limited resources—journals, presses, publishers, public attention, careers—and, more generally, professional and pseudopolitical legitimacy. The demand for ideological alignment is apparently strong enough in feminism today so that many people hesitate to voice an opinion they believe is not the accepted one.[11] The effects of such an ethos on scholarly endeavors can only be guessed at. But there is still a world out there, much to learn, much to discover; and the exploration of ourselves, however laudable in that at least it risks no new imperialistic gesture, is not, in the end, capable of sustaining lasting interest.

It cannot be coincidental that at the very time such extreme personalization of everything is occurring, academics have reached new heights in their pretense that the world's ills are set right by mere acknowledgment of one's own position. This is one of the oddest—and in a sense most peculiarly North American—practices to come out of postmodernist rhetoric. Taking account of my own position does not change reality. It does not, for example, redistribute income, gain political rights for those who don't have them, alleviate misery, or improve health. Perhaps conscience-stricken with the realization of their own privilege, many intellectuals today (and feminists are amply represented among these) pretend that whenever they write an article they are "doing politics." We seem to be very good at acquiring new rhetorical turns, at ingratiating ourselves in the mode dictated by this year's academic fashions. But ultimately such pretenses wear thin.

I doubt that I am the only person who is weary of all this individual and collective breast-beating, exhausted by ever more impenetrable prose and more deluded moral claims. If we are scholars, let us acknowledge that we have learned something from the sensitivity training, guilt tripping, and self-reflexiveness of the past few decades, and get on with our scholarship. Becoming better human beings—more responsive, more self-aware—may or may not make us better scholars. Embracing bias—in the name of feminist epistemology or in reaction to the shocking discovery that biases have also existed in the past—certainly will not. If we find our work harmful or morally reprehensible, or if it simply does not fulfill our activist commitments and aspirations, let us stop doing it and move directly into political action. Research projects designed with community or advocacy goals in mind may be both interesting and valuable. But why contend that the only scholarship anyone could or should do is that of the political activist kind? Why hamstring ourselves with new imperatives, this year's dos and next year's don'ts? In fact, putting scholarship at the explicit service of politics carries many (and rather obvious) risks and should not be greeted with the facile assumption that *of course* it is what "we" should do.

A good instance of the confusions unleashed by feminist research rhetoric was provided by Kathleen Blee, author of *Women of the Klan*.[12] At a lunchtime address to the Oral History Association meeting in Cincinnati, October 15–18, 1992, Blee provided an ironic counterpoint to the feminist vocabulary of women's "empowerment" through telling their own stories. The Indiana Klanswomen she had interviewed, it turned out, indeed felt empowered by Blee's interest in them and by this chance to get their stories on the record. Blee's critical comments and disclaimers, intended frankly to demonstrate her lack of identification with these women, were met with mere dismissal by them: they understood, she reported, that she had to say these things, but they believed that in her heart she, a White woman, shared their views. I do not see how feminists adopting the vocabulary of "empowerment" or "self-disclosure" in their research methodologies can avoid this sort of conundrum. Blee's work, of course, stands on its own merits, but the new self-reflexive and moralizing agenda would perhaps dictate that she *not* publish it, out of distaste at its real moral ambiguity. Neither the Klanswomen's agenda nor her own very different one need in fact become a defining characteristic of the work. Once again, as in Michael Frisch's comments cited earlier, a certain sense of our relative lack of power can be salutary. At least it should relieve some of the pressure and also some of the egocentricity involved in our constant self-appraisals.

The insistence on interminable analysis reveals a preoccupation with power in another sense, however. It reflects an overly inflated belief (or is it merely a pretense?) in the significance of our intentions, regardless of our actual accomplishments. Again, I cannot suppress the thought that such a claim of importance is really a substitute for nitty-gritty political work, for which the rewards are far smaller than they are for high-flying academic discourse. But I do not want to be misunderstood on this issue. I am by no means exhorting anyone to stop writing and get out and organize instead. Leaving aside those relatively few projects that seem capable of fulfilling both scholarly and political commitments without compromising either, much other research remains to be done. There is, of course, no reason why a given individual may not engage in both scholarly work *and* political work. Or why preference, at a particular moment, should not be given to one or the other. My criticism is directed merely at the pretense that scholarship necessarily *is* (and ought to be) politics, or that those whose loyalties are first of all to scholarship are ingenuous, or reactionary, or immoral, or—heaven forfend!—unaware of their own positioning and unwilling to give public account of it. Is there no one left on the Left still prepared to argue that scholarship is valuable in and of itself? And capable of recognizing that the impact it makes invariably escapes the control of the scholar, however self-critical and self-reflexive he or she may be?

The thinking behind the disdain for scholarship implicit in the demand that it be transubstantiated as political activism or at the very least as a praxis of critical discourse (complete with the politically requisite statements of identity) once again shows that the spirit of ideological alignment is alive and well. But who are we to demand or pretend that the multiple facets of a life fit together so neatly? That all our activities weave a seamless web? Why impose on ourselves, as Laurel Richardson does in Lather's description of her work (in this volume), a straightjacket we would denounce if applied by a researcher to a "subject"?

Interestingly, one question that the new methodological self-absorption seems not to ask is: Does all this self-reflexivity produce better research?[13] Instead, the researcher seems to be setting out, by implication at least, moral credentials of which a postmodernist vocabulary is to be taken as a significant guarantor. And why not? After all, as Thorstein Veblen might have said, "Vocabulary is the intellectual's form of conspicuous consumption." Clearly the people most successful at word slinging and at the moral one-upmanship of correctly positioned scholarship are members of a class that has time, energy, and incentives for precisely such activities. Like other games, lucid self-reflexivity is in large part an end in itself. It cannot be coincidence that the more arcane the vocabulary, the louder the claim of intellectuals to be engaging in "political," "contestatory," or "destabilizing" work. The jargon changes; the boasts lurking within it do not. How gratifying to redefine politics so that it is what "we," situated in what used to be called (pejoratively) our ivory towers, are doing. (Lather refers, accurately, to the "romance of the desire for research as political intervention"—but succumbs to this romance nonetheless, as does Michele Fine.) It is astonishing that so few people on the Left think an independent academy is worth defending or are prepared to argue that if it has not in fact existed in the past, it is important to try to help it come into being. Quite the contrary, what we see is the reverse—the embrace of politics, even make-believe politics. Why? Perhaps because of some perceived credit to be gained, some higher importance or greater vitality that academics think they will embody if they can construe their work as "inherently political."

The ever spreading quality of the term "political" provides an interesting example of what the sociologist Joel Best calls "domain expansion," a process by which initial claims, once validated, draw into their orbit numerous additional claims. According to Best, "claims-makers present the new, peripheral issues as 'another form of,' 'essentially the same as,' 'the moral equivalent of,' or 'equally damaging as' the original, core problem."[14] Although Best uses the term to explore what happens when social problems—in the negative sense—are identified, the elasticity of the term "political" in the hands of academics demonstrates that domain expansion can also occur when claims are made that are seen to be positive. In this case, once "politics" is judged valuable, important, something "we" should all be doing, our professional activities (both teaching and scholarship) are reconceptualized so as to conform to the new definition, and academics rush to claim this new definition as an accolade for their own work. Such an expansion of the domain of "politics," so that its ingestion of education is taken for granted, obscures important distinctions and thwarts discussions of where to draw the line.

A failure to defend intellectual independence, a blurring of the problems that ensue when education is blatantly politicized, when exploration and analysis give way to advocacy and even indoctrination, are only conceivable in a country such as ours in which a large measure of academic liberty has in fact been enjoyed by the very people who now dismiss this freedom as a facade. Where intellectual freedom has been lacking or curtailed, where dispassionate inquiry is a mere pretense to mask a partisan agenda, we should challenge this attack on liberal values, not embrace it as a model for all education. An inherent irony pervades the gap between the reality and the rhetoric regarding the place of politics in the academy.

The current fetish of questioning oneself and one's standpoint until they yield neatly to the categories of our theorizing cannot overcome the messiness of reality. We do not escape from the consequences of our positions by talking about them endlessly. Nor can methodolatry satisfy our longing for moral or political purity. What it does do is to exhibit the strength, within intellectual life today, of the vocabulary wars and the enormous jockeying for status and approval that seems to motivate them. How long will Lather's "transgressive validity" remain transgressive once it is validated?

There is, however, an important sense in which the vocabulary wars exceed their own bounds and indeed burst through them into the material world. Like athletic contests, these orgies of abstraction—better exemplified by Lather's scavenger-style of profuse quotation than by Fine's more restrained and focused prose—in fact constitute a demonstration of mastery in the competitive arena of arcane academic discourse. From this point of view, the preoccupation with method becomes an occasion for both a claim to and a display of power, a new and improved version of "How to Do Things with Words." Power and method indeed![15]

Notes

1. See, for example, my essay "U.S. Academics and Third World Women: Is Ethical Research Possible?" in S. Berger Gluck and D. Patai, eds., *Women's Words: The Feminist Practice of Oral History* 137–53. (New York: Routledge, 1991). This essay is, however, at some remove from my earlier "Ethical Problems of Personal Narratives, or, Who Should Eat the Last Piece of Cake?" in *International Journal of Oral History* 8 (1) (February 1987): 5–27.

2. See Herbert Spiegelberg, "On the Right to Say 'We': A Linguistic and Phenomenological Analysis," in G. Psathas, ed., *Phenomenological Sociology: Issues and Applications,* 129–56 (New York: Wiley, 1973), for a valuable discussion of the problems of what he calls the "we of copresence."

3. In many of the interviews conducted for the book I have cowritten with Noretta Koertge, entitled *Professing Feminism: Cautionary Tales from the Strange World of Women's Studies* (New York: Basic Books, 1994), professors who identified themselves as feminists again and again made this move: they attempted to justify their acceptance of an overtly politicized curriculum in women's studies by referring, in contradictorily denunciatory tones, to the poor and biased (i.e., political in the other direction) education they had received in prefeminist universities.

4. Michèle Foster and Linda Williamson Nelson, for example, both write about "endogenous" or "native anthropology," and the shifting "positions" the Black interviewer occupies vis-à-vis the women she interviews. They point to the fact that in a face-to-face encounter, identity is constantly under negotiation. Yet both, paradoxically, also affirm the belief that self-reflexivity can lead to a proper appraisal of the interview encounter. See their essays in G. Etter-Lewis and M. Foster, eds., *Unrelated Kin: Ethnic Identity and Gender in Women's Personal Narratives* (forthcoming), which I read in manuscript.

5. Michael Frisch, *A Shared Authority: Essays on the Craft and Meaning of Oral and Public History* (Albany: State Univ. of New York Press, 1990).

6. Frisch's comments were made at the Oral History Association meeting in Baltimore, MD, October 12–15, 1988.

7. One of the most important—and least remembered—dystopian fictions of the twentieth century is E.M. Forster's long story "The Machine Stops" (1909), reprinted in *The Eternal Moment and Other Stories*, 1–61, (London: Sidgwick & Jackson, 1928), which envisions a society of people living in isolated rooms, the world brought to them through visual and audio technology (i.e., as representation). Forster explores the ensuing horror of the body and of contact with other bodies. In the age of electronic mail and cable broadcasting, Forster's vision is of far more pertinence than those of his more famous dystopian contemporaries such as Orwell and Huxley.

8. This passage is excerpted from H. Bannerji, L. Carty, K. Dehli, S. Heald, and K. McKenna, *Unsettling Relations: The University as a Site of Feminist Struggles* (Boston: South End, 1992). It was reproduced in the South End Press catalogue, Fall 1992, p. 3.

9. I have had this experience myself, and have heard other women's studies professors discuss similar episodes. Additional examples that should be of concern to all faculty members: women's studies students who object to the inclusion of any male writers in a course (this is my own and others' experience), or a student who handed in a paper (the assignment was on Freud) that consisted of one line: "Freud was a cigar-smoking, cancer-ridden misogynist" (told to me by a political science professor).

10. As happened in my women's utopias class in the Fall of 1991. Another White student commented that if more Black writers of utopias could not be found, I should not be teaching this course.

11. On the WMST-List (the women's studies e-mail list, run by Joan Korenman), examples abound of feminists' frightening supposition that their expression of an opinion differing from the general tenor of a discussion will bring denunciations upon their heads. It is heartening that a few souls nonetheless do speak their minds, but the apparent (one cannot tell if it is real, of course) unanimity of opinion on the list, and the tendency to apologize for expressing dissenting views, is distressing.

12. K. Blee, *Women of the Klan: Racism and Gender in the 1920s* (Berkeley: Univ. of California Press, 1991).

13. By contrast, when Ann Oakley advocated a more interactive interview process as the proper methodology for feminist research, she was careful to argue that it both fulfills feminist tenets and produces better research results. See her "Interviewing Women: A Contradiction in Terms," in H. Roberts, ed., *Doing Feminist Research*, 30–61 (Boston: Routledge, 1981). Unfortunately, neither claim is necessarily valid; all depends on the particular research project. In some instances, the self-consciously feminist stance is doomed to backfire, as both Judith Stacey and I have argued in separate essays in *Women's Words*.

14. J. Best, *Threatened Children: Rhetoric and Concern about Child-Victims*, 80 (Chicago: Univ. of Chicago Press, 1990). I am grateful to Kathleen Lowney, professor of Sociology at Valdosta State College, for bringing Best's work to my attention.

15. Many of the perspectives set forth in this essay have been developed through discussions with Noretta Koertge, professor of History and Philosophy of Science at Indiana University, Bloomington. Some parts of this essay have appeared, in brief, in my commentary entitled "Sick and Tired of Scholars' Nouveau Solipsism," *Chronicle of Higher Education,* February 23, 1994, A52.

Gay and Lesbian

Queer Relations With Educational Research

Glorianne M. Leck

For What Are We Standing in Line?

In this essay, I, a dues-paid and employed academic, will attempt, paradoxically, to tease out from the mainstream of these research margins some
queer ramblings and to explore or posit significance to such ramblings
as they may be viewed as connected with concerns educators have about
epistemological issues and method in educational theorizing.

It is my sense that teaching is an active/interactive process that can be
highly distorted by claims that it can be scientized. Both educational research
and teaching are politically active phenomena and both are systematically
made to appear neutral in an institutionalized context. It so happens then
that institutionally sanctioned educational researchers frequently make
claims that teaching and learning have essential characteristics and can be
studied for the purpose of identifying universal commonalities. Claims for
research generalizability are often made by those who prefer to stand apart
from and/or dominate rather than locate and immerse themselves within
day-to-day interactional and uniquely embedded processes of the politics
and perspectives of acts of educating. I wish to explore some thoughts about
some undesirable by-products of institutional educational research and
teaching as it is perpetuated in and around schooling. I will follow that
discussion with a description of a Queer Nation action that represents action-
oriented and less-sanctioned research and teaching. If you wish to go directly
to the action you may forfeit the reading of the more patriarchal academic
discussion, although I hope it too has its action moments in its metaphoric
risks.

A Queer Query in an Essentialist Queue

David Hume observed, writing in the mid-1700s in his *Treatise Of Human
Nature,* that "There is no impression nor idea of any kind, of which we
have any consciousness or memory, that is not conceiv'd as existent; and
tis evident, that from this consciousness the most perfect idea and assurance
of *being* is deriv'd." Hume's sense of how we assume essential existence
alerted me and verbalized for me, even in my earliest undergraduate readings,

my strong sense as to the significance, role and function of culture, experience, perception, and power (politics) in the construction of an existence that would be made to appear "safe," public, and essential.

As scholars, we function in what appears to be a culture in which systematic study (especially that done in the name of science) serves to create an appearance that human behaviors can be classified, objectified, and systematically repeated in other settings. Educational research, as such, is both an artifact and the source of much of the maintenance and dominance of such a belief about teaching and learning behaviors.

Existentialist challenges, and now feminist and postmodernist discourses, have heightened the social occasion and thus the invitation for us to look at the viewers' politics and perspectives, the construction and deconstruction of signs and symbols, and the situations of context of meaning. To discuss knowledge is to construct a set or describe a phenomenon that can be assigned existence and brought to our attention as an object worthy of our study.

The playfulness of romping through epistemological text and margin, of construct and process is here my work and my joy.

There Seems to Be Something Queer Going On Here

Educational research is certainly treated by academics and policy makers as a sanctioned, if not systematized and generally agreed-upon, set of procedures. Educational research is being taught, used, and paid for as productive labor. Ken Kempner states that "when researchers see their theories and research as objectified measures of reality their work is confirmatory. This research accepts the hegemony of the culture of positivism and is reductionist in nature. While it may be possible for a positivist to be an action researcher who is devoted to changing a tacitly accepted reality, phenomenologists, particularly feminists and critical theorists, are researchers whose basic premise is devoted to altering the dominant social reality."[2]

And as Kempner suggests, there are those of us who are quite exasperated by the political manipulations that have served to boost the status that has been assigned to educational research, especially that which is positivistic and perpetuates a notion of common "truth." We have witnessed a political "deal" in which public figures can claim greater expertise for their views about education by using results of standardized educational research processes as a source for their "expert" authority.[3] As politicians get backing from the products of the universities, so the universities and colleges continue to institutionalize research methods and processes so they may appear to "produce" those sought-after educational research results. Such claims result in greater status and gain of public funding for those institutions.

The claim that there is or can be essential knowledge (that which would be measurable, agreed upon, duplicated, reliable, and endurable across contexts) is aided by what now appears to have been a simplifying of what constitutes an agreed-upon and scientized process or method of study. Within the current research models, essential claims of knowledge appear to be directed with a focus on the notion of schooling and in particular to the manner with which teachers convey information, how information is applied, and the testing by which it is retrieved. There is a strange sense in which the study of schooling begs the question of what goes on in educational action. Schooling, much like educational research in its institutionally sanctioned form, hybridizes certain features of what are defined as its operations. In so doing, the fecundity is lost and the situation demands resistance and deconstruction so that certain rhythms of life/death/birth and related struggles can be continued without famine, inbreeding, and violence to the differently conceived.

This focus on institutions and information becomes a kind of definition of education which not only becomes narrowly conceived within the common context of formal schooling but also limits what we look at as education, learning, and teaching. The mythologies about the value of doing research on the focus of information exchange has been carried even unto the belief that ongoing teacher labor is a cause/effect process that can be measured by generic instruments, which place emphasis almost entirely on learning as itself a product of information acquired by students in these essentialist schooling contexts.

Throughout all of the politics of these information production processes, the "deal" is that those with the connections to get the funding from those who want certain kinds of results tend to dominate the teaching, research, consulting, and testing businesses. Ah but, you say, I simply describe a capitalist process of supply and demand. Yes, I do see a market economy nudging the university further from a place of exploration and knowledge inquiry to a center of business in which knowledge, research, and information are considered commodities critical to the overall economy of a postindustrial society. I can attest to the discomfort of education deans who want the faculty to appear before the public as productive corporate clones.

Who among us doesn't know that public demands for teacher accountability has been generated by politicians who need to respond to citizen frustration over a changing job market, and who doesn't see that the accountability measures are being generated and evaluated by university-related psychometricians? And who can't recognize that the outcomes of those instruments are necessarily class based, ideologically bound, gender biased, and racist?

Who doesn't know, if they care to, that there is a reified interactive construction process here that appears to generate a hierarchy of corporate researcher over teacher? In the consulting business, teachers are separated off from the researchers as their students who are to work under and learn from the consultants and the research that they promote. The fact that classroom teachers are overworked and minimally supported by salary, materials, or support staff appropriate to the value of their work and years of practice is blurred by the expertise postures of the corporate- or government-supported "outside consultant" model.[4] Is this simply a wage issue? Is it simply a facade to maintain a power elite? Is it a naive positivist/essentialist notion that life is contained in the symbols we generate to describe aspects of our perceptions?

I must include myself among those queer educational activists who might claim that there appears to be some discrepancy between research on institutionalized schooling and a broader, less contained, and more interesting phenomenon called education. More important, there is a fascinating way in which the institutionalized ways of schooling interact with more basic educational means and meanings of learning to learn and getting to know. The language experience, privilege, perspective, bias, process of schooling, and audience of the researchers may in fact dislocate many well-schooled teachers and researchers from daily contexts of many of the clientele who they perceive as needing or receiving schooling services.[5]

Educational research and methodology are a part of the entire enterprise of "schooling" as it was and continues to be organized and maintained around essentialist assumptions and institutional constructions that were and are grounded in a manufactured psychological time, cultural existence, and critical awareness. For many, to do educational research is to continue to perform labor that perpetuates reified and money-defined power relations, a belief in cause and effect, and a modernist notion of teaching and learning as productive labor.

From another perspective then, as educational activists, some of us talk about "survival" world phenomena and educational needs. We are referring to the vivid presence of homelessness; starvation; addiction, violence, and day-to-day struggles of and for interpersonal control; racial presence; material goods; health care; the needs for caring, love, self-esteem, and nutrition; and the struggle for meaningfulness in work and life.

Francis Schrag recently argued[6] that pluralists who critique positivist research "have placed their work in a context in which the following causal hypothesis may be entertained: Given two communities, one with a monolithic positivist research enterprise and the other with a pluralist one, the latter will be more likely to benefit the development of children." There is no doubt in my mind that Schrag would misunderstand and misrepresent a pluralist critique such as mine if he failed to see that interaction is responsive and not predictably reciprocal.[7] To explain: Schrag chooses an example from chemistry, where he contends that ultimately, e.g., in the study of antibiotics, they have to be tested to see if they do what they claim they can do. The point I understand him to be making is that claims of pluralists would have to help us understand and prove that educational research would necessarily have to produce better understandings that would allow us to serve and manage student learning or at least to curb ignorance. In what Schrag seems to consider a parallel example—the study of antibiotics—one looks at whether the pathology subsides upon the implementation of treatment with antibiotics. The assumption appears to be made that when we teach we should be able to show that students' ignorance of that about which we are teaching subsides. The demand for a causal relationship creates not only accountability but also a linear model for the judgment of value.

Unfortunately, only layers of observation and multiple variations of environments, pathologies, and human attitudinal diversities (to name just a few) give us any sense of the ways antibiotics, the production of antibiotics, and biological and psychological responses to antibiotics create an identifiable phenomenon called "the study of antibiotic treatments." If researchers were to observe the simplified linear cause and effect of introduction of antibiotics and the apparent disappearance of pathological symptoms in the subjects tested, wouldn't that tend to distort the very consideration of interactive responses in and among systems and units of identifiable observable phenomena? No, where in such narrowly focused antibiotic studies would we learn of the processing and changing forms of resistance to antibiotics. Likewise in schooling research, which restricts studies to information inputs and test-taking outputs, there will be no acknowledgement of the role of resistance to imposed attitudes about ignorance and evaluation of authority that may be associated with the flow of information.

While anthropologists and historians, with the support of ethnographers and oral historians, would be more likely to produce an accepted, if not an even more contained, essentialist construct for a—long time after-the-fact—description of "what happened," they too would be stifled by their preconceptions of where and at what to look. I would certainly posit that moving further away from the limitedness of cause and effect (as some ethnographers have attempted to do) would enhance our pleasure, if not our dialogue, by working to define the brackets and the contexts of what we are interacting with. That behavior might offer us a way of showing our openness to discourse and, as such, help us explore a construct and a context of community as well as a chosen way of knowing.

It is perhaps with that comfort that a careful scholar, Schrag, rather brazenly assumes that schooling is supposed to benefit pupils. It is a fair opening assumption. But what if the focus of schooling has been, in spite of its own intentions, another socially/economically/culturally reproductive means to control and limit benefits for particular students?

We can at least suspect that schools as we have come to identify them are related to the power concerns of the cultural managers and opinion makers who have defined and designed schooling within certain ongoing habitual ways of operating. Would those pupils who are being controlled perceive school as of benefit to them? Then what and whose intentions and goals are we evaluating?

What if pluralistic research tells us that what we will learn in nonlinear research is that the more we attend to detail of unique characteristics of response and resistance, the more facile and artistic we might become as teachers/learners who learn to dance with the coconstruction of concepts of meaning? Does this benefit students? Society? For whom and for what would noting interactive responses among individuals and groups be a benefit?

I don't know and can't with any confidence make the claim, for example, that educating someone to value diversity and to respect its place in public is of some particular benefit for them. Perhaps it just makes more sense to me. Perhaps it makes me feel I'm doing something to contribute to a reduction of intergroup intolerance and violence. Perhaps for now it suits my political purposes. How might I know my own intentions, let alone the possible value of my research, as it serves my good intentions?

As has been the case with antibiotic research, perhaps all this empirical positivist research has created an appearance of progress so as to perpetuate a cultural and personal sense of control over disease. Perhaps all this educational research and teaching gives us a sense that we are making personal or social progress through schooling.

Is the issue then getting rid of the diseases which we suppress with antibiotics or the ignorance we sweep away with schooling, or might there be equally significant issues regarding our fears of those phenomena we seem not to be able to understand or control? Does doing research on schooling processes provide some of us with a sense of holding back the tide of encroaching awareness of our ignorance about the more intimidatingly complex phenomena of education outside of schooling contexts? Are my intentions knowable?

Just as we may now sense that the introduction of antibiotics may have contributed in some cultural/biologically interactive way to a more horrendous disease (AIDS), perhaps schooling has contributed interactively to the devaluing of learning, self-education, self-esteem, and self-reliance. Perhaps more than anything else, schooling and its formal systems of studying knowledge may have contributed in some significant way to our sense that we can know and control that about which we know. That learning may then have contributed to a deeper need which may be a "need to control" not only what we know, but also what we "let others know about our knowing" and our sense of fear of that which is not or perhaps cannot conceivably be known.

These queries we "other-than-positivist" thinkers raise may be about the reactions that can be felt by some in response to the manufacturing of an essentialist notion of the importance of a psychological state of "feeling in control" or having "a self" through which we process our knowing about our selves, human life, and human learning needs. What would it mean then for some of us to simply claim to be idly curious about a particular phenomenon? Perhaps our studies don't make claims that imply that they will fit into a nationalized research project or to a useful and fundable teaching application.

Perhaps there is just something very queer about those of us who don't make those claims to know. Perhaps we feel and are viewed as queer as we tend to stand in an outside, or out-of-synchronization, relation to knowing, as margins appear to stand "away from" in relation to text.

Educational research, as I currently understand it, is most often directed to the study of clearly defined phenomena that are steeped in, interlaced with, and usually unchallenged in their service to existing social/political/economic power relations. Having a dominant social construction of (or a solid belief in) both a positive valuing of institutionalized research behaviors and in a sense of the importance of constructing a shared and institutionalized reality is likely an explanation for what has made possible this dominant political/research behavior.

My queer inclination is to suggest that the objects that are constructed by educational research processes, when acknowledged as entangled with modern notions of schooling, may be of some historical interest. Once said descriptions become deconstructed, they will probably become artifacts and not significant participants in ongoing processes of education. Just as Paulo Freire notes the necrophilic nature of what he called the "banking concept of teaching" and curriculum, in a parallel I would suggest here that institutionalized research methodologies and objectives may emit similar death-like odors.[8] I suspect that in this case the death may be part of a life-giving cycle. I wish to offer some queer possibilities.

A Queer Process

To construct a description for discourse among learners may be an agreed-upon part of the responsibility of those who learn in community. In order to create such an object for the interaction of this community, I will serve as a scribe who witnessed, as a participant observer, a complex of events and activities that I will describe. After attempting descriptions that will give some texture to the phenomenon (the defined event), I will then return as one who reconsiders, and paradoxically I will try to create some generalizations about the difficulty of generalization. I hope that in some helpful and interesting way the absurdity of the traditional (essentialist) way of addressing generalization as an act with meaning embedded in some modernist claim for rationality can be demonstrated through this process.

I have selected an event or phenomenon that had educational intentions but that would likely be viewed as existing outside of the institutional construct of a school. I contend, however, that the educational processes that are being attempted are very similar to the teaching efforts that one could find in schools if one attended to the diversity of interests and maintained a commitment to attending to efforts being made by one who is "trying to teach." And while I know some readers may see this as wholly political, I will insist that teaching is for its most part just such a political act both at the Cracker Barrel restaurant and at Jefferson Elementary School.

In an effort to construct out of alienation and diverse perspective I am identifiable as Glorianne M. Leck, speaker of education and a queer activist.

Recorded as a self-appointed Secretary of Education of this particular QUEER NATION event.

Descriptive Entities

EDUCATION AS NEGOTIATION

We were sitting in the nonsmoking section of this business that advertises itself as a "family restaurant." I was dressed in my lavender blazer with my white *Every Dyke's A Hero* tee shirt. Sitting with me was my friend Jean who was lookin good in her blue jeans and cotton blouse. The clientele in the nonsmoking section appeared not to be connecting with our alienation or our sense of "today we aren't going to be invisible." They seemed not to notice us as anything out of their ordinary. There was now and then a quick glance at my tee shirt. Dominating the scene for me was my private emotional residence inside the flesh, inside the tee shirt. That feeling might be expressed as replete with a stupendous self-consciousness and sense of marginality. I was experiencing my own presence as a Queer, as "being in a Cracker Barrel restaurant" and as a "disruptive outsider." (Have I grown up fearful, queer, and alienated, or what?)

When the server arrived at the table, we informed her that we were planning to sit for several hours so we could take up table space, but that we did not want her to have to take a financial loss as a result of our "sit-in" effort. We explained that ours was an expression of anger and objection to the Cracker Barrel restaurant chain's discriminatory policies of not hiring (and actually firing) any suspected lesbian, gay, or bisexual workers. She said she was fine with that, after all one of her best friends was gay.

We wrote out our political explanatory notes for the server, making sure she would understand our position, and then placed those notes and the bonus tip in the envelope. Some other restaurant patrons heard the interaction between us and the server and were in varying degrees beginning to assign us noticeability. The tee shirt now appeared to draw more deliberate looks. There were no overt displays of disgust or horror.

When Jean got up to go to the smoking section to visit with other demonstrators, the woman at the next table asked me if the paper I was reading (*The Village Voice*) had done an exposé on Ross Perot. "What a strange way into the conversation," I thought. Then she said, "I heard what he said about not putting gay people in his cabinet." And with that comment there began a discussion of gay-related politics and the management policy of Cracker Barrel restaurants. She and the man she was with were very uninformed about the particular issue but appeared genuinely interested and said they would express their concern to the management about antigay employment policies as well as the selling of items that tend to perpetuate racial bigotry to which I had directed their attention.

And so, for me, began the series of small acts of—what Maxine Greene might call "teacher as stranger"—informing, educating, creating dissonance, and gathering support.[9] And not insignificantly came the sense that the word "dyke" emblazoned on that tee shirt did have some objective meaning in the American/English language and that here in this interaction I was acknowledged as a "dyke" who was wearing and owning and willing to negotiate conversation as one of that designation. And inside that tee shirt was a person trying to feel like a hero, a beautiful swan instead of an ugly duckling, for claiming her lifelong identity and not hiding as a victim in fear of further rejection from that heterosexist condemnation of sexual difference and diversity in orientation. This interaction of activities constituted what was for me an educational effort that could conceivably serve to construct a shared sense of an appropriate reality that would embrace "dykes" and "fags" as humans with a right to exist in public and to be considered, as we are, part of an effort to be allowed our pursuit of life, liberty, and happiness, but not within the definitions of institutionalized heterosexist community.

EDUCATION AS GETTING THEIR ATTENTION

Meanwhile, in the next room other demonstrators were carrying out their political actions. James, an active participant in QUEER NATION, was bedecked in his long earrings and his multiple "Fucks" and "Sucks" stickers. When he appeared at the door, the management representative immediately asked him to remove his "offensive" stickers or the restaurant wouldn't be able to serve her. As such, James was immediately noticed and patron, as well as management, responses of tension and conflict were swift and obvious. Conversation buzzed with concerns about his appearance partially as "her" presence. Here education was confrontation with the fact that "fags" and "dykes" are in the public! A now familiar QUEER NATION slogan resounded in our internalization, "We're here, we're queer and we're not going shopping."

Another group—Wendy, Sondra, Dave, and John— talked loudly and took up the space of a large table for eight. They were the first table to the right side of the door through which all customers entered to be seated. The very presence of these demonstrators bedecked in gender-bending gay apparel alerted the unsuspecting "wanting to be comfortable" diners. Stickers and buttons warned the customers that something strange (some may even have thought "QUEER") might be going on in this restaurant.

A single demonstrator, Paul, at another table called for the manager and talked very loudly and in a very deep and therefore powerful male (associated) voice about his objections to the restaurant's antigay and racist employment and sales practices. His loud, aggressive, and cantankerous behavior seemed to create a great deal of uncomfortableness for those within hearing range. While some patrons seemed curious, others moved quickly through their breakfast motions as if to hurry to get out of this contested public space.

In yet another section of the restaurant, James, Monalisa, Judy, and Randy were colorful in dress and conspicuously QUEER. With large and easily read stickers that read "I suck tit," "I'm queer and I vote," etc., they drew much attention to their presence.

And we were there, "perfectly QUEER." Our presence defined marginality as we bounced off the reliable mode of hetero/reproductive family, decency, quiet, and anonymous conformity. Our symbolic and our confrontative presence was refusing to be invisible and refusing to conform to prescribed good taste. The existence of a piece of QUEER NATION allowed other patrons to have their fears and imaginings confronted by their own varied reactions. We could become, conceive, and confront any and all prejudices the participants could accommodate through their own sense of defining "the" margins of "the" public community within which their identity had been constructed. Here, their power, their identities, and their definitions of public were challenged and momentarily impaired.

EDUCATION AS INTERACTIVE ASSUMPTIONS: "WHAT WE THOUGHT WE MAY HAVE SEEN" OR "READING THROUGH OUR EXPECTATIONS."

In one incident, this QUEER NATION presence interactively constructed the scene for a "breeder" family foursome where the "mother," wearing the Ross Perot tee shirt, was giving the nonverbals to the rest of the family. Hers appeared to be a look of "maintaining dominance by disgust." She offered her group the look that appeared as if it were meant to be shaming and punishing—"This is why we are for Ross Perot!" "We must take America back!" "Public decency must be reclaimed!"

From some of the elder folks there appeared to be yet another message of, "Look away, this is not something we want to know about or get involved in"; or "I wish they would keep this private stuff to themselves or at least keep it in their own social settings"; or "That behavior and those words don't belong in a *family* restaurant." "Segregate, segregate."

For some of the adolescents who were present with their families, this QUEER presence appeared to be quite a curiosity. I felt a twinge inside of me as I imagined what it might be like for any young persons who might have been exploring their own sexual identity. We might have represented a "reality" presence of both some radical and playful possibilities and some incredible threat to or advertisement for the benefits of nonconformity.

To those closeted lesbian, gay, bisexual persons in that restaurant, we may well have reminded them again of life-style issues and tensions in their own life circumstances. For some we were just a painful reminder of alienation and hiding. For some a reminder of a fling or a risky moment in their own sexual expressions.

To other persons who had gone through recognition of their own oppression or who had found themselves creating presence from the margins, we seemed to pull at those identities with the "other others" strings. One African-American couple conveying numerous symbols of economic stability entered the restaurant and, seeing some of these QUEERS, almost instantly revealed painful expressions of conflict, and that always lurking, "Now what?" "Whose civil rights?" "Must I be more sensitive than these privileged White Folks?" "Why can't I just blend in?" "Is there no getting in and resting?" "Leave me alone, I finally have gotten comfortable in these cracker restaurants and now my being here is threatened by someone else wanting to get in." There were other people of color who seemed to not even acknowledge the "variety" as problem. And then how would I know what they might be feeling or thinking? I reminded myself of my own anti-bigotry work on race consciousness I had worked long and hard to demarginalize race before I worked so directly on my own issues of oppression.

The Setting as the Context for Constructing Consumer Culture

Cracker Barrel restaurants appear to be designed to emphasize very traditional patriarchal and racist European-based values as played out in old social stereotypes of the southern United States. In that vein, the restaurant's symbols appear as a stronghold for and a nostalgia about an unchanging rebel resistance against challenges to traditional hierarchies related to Christianity, class, race, and gender. The design and decor of the store invites that atmosphere of sit on the porch in your rocking chair, watch the children, "shoot the breeze," make your presence felt, and pass on traditional clichés of advice. The symbols, be they verbal or material, appear to be designed to maintain and express values that strongly suggest the keeping of dominance by a Euro-Caucasian, Christian, late nineteenth-century, country, southern tradition.

In the menu in a place meant to capture the reader's attention, a headline reads "A story that goes back over a hundred years." "At the Cracker Barrel, we hold to the idea that hams cured the traditional way have the best taste. And they're the only kind we serve . . . ," etc. Meat and potatoes, European-American traditional food is the feature of the menu. Ham, which is pork, and which is excluded by dietary codes in Judaism and Islam, is the centered and featured symbol of Cracker Barrel's fine old food traditions.

In the building design, the front porch features a long row of rocking chairs. As the chairs are often occupied by older persons, it reinforces the notion of who has earned privilege. It is as if to say that those elders who have done their job, that is to have bred, raised, and supported their children, are the individuals to be valued. The family, headed by a male provider and protector, is emulated as the key to well-being.[10] Respecting older people seems tied to the notion that they have earned the chairs on the porch. And we must assume that they earned that privilege by keeping the traditions of family and hard work.

The available merchandise in the general store, while it varies from restaurant to restaurant, has included Aunt-Jemima–type dolls, rebel flags, Yankee and confederate caps, frilly dressed dolls, kitchen decorations, dried floral arrangements, and penny candy. Traditional—woman as wife, spending her time in the kitchen and decorating the "home" for the family; husband as provider and protector; and children as decorative inhabitants being taught class-based gender and race roles—are the constructs of value that are suggested through the gift shop selection.

Tradition, family, and work-ethic Christian values are the exaggerated symbols conveyed through Cracker Barrel's decor and policies. We are meant to be holding the line, keeping the outsiders out, and rewarding the insiders for their appropriate behavior. The reward is good food and a safe predictable setting.

Power, Knowing, Analysis, and Perspective

What we think we know is that some of the activists who staged this demonstration were seriously engaged in an attempt to reclaim their/our presence and sense of belonging "out in public." For some of us, this was described as an effort to claim the word "queer" from the embedded power relationship in which those not identifying as homosexual have used that word. "Queer" has been a term used to oppress those who are differently sexually oriented and thus has been used to express disdain for those whom heterosexuals have labeled "other." Homosexual/heterosexual is a dualistic social language construct evolved through the efforts of modernity to scientize human emotional/erotic with human biological/sexual identity. As such, much of the shaping of negative and positive values has been constructed by using contrasting reference signs.[11]

"Queer" is being used instead of the dualistic disabling word homosexual to empower participants to accept and value the diversity among our own political grouping. As Lisa Duggan explains in "Making It Perfectly Queer": "During the past few years, the new designation 'queer' has emerged from within the lesbian, gay, and bisexual politics and theory. 'Queer Nation' and 'Queer Theory,' now widely familiar locations for activists and academics, are more than just new labels for old boxes. They carry with them the promise of new meanings, new ways of thinking and acting politically—a promise sometimes realized, sometimes not."[12]

What we were doing was what we labeled QUEER action. The flamboyance of participants, reflecting the diversity among those who have been categorized under one rather simplistic label—homosexual—was visually dramatic. Both the demonstrators and those who responded to the demonstrations of the participants reflected the lack of linear and dualistic predictability that could be forced by two-part labeling of homosexual/heterosexual and text and margin. Just as one could not identify who was heterosexual, one could not identify who was homosexual, and that made every one a QUEER suspect.

THE JUGGLING OF IDENTITY WITHIN THE EDUCATOR

I could not make clearer than has Judith Butler in her article "Decking Out: Performing Identities"[13] my concern about identity and its interplay in construction of meaning related both to what I have described and an analysis thereof. Here's Butler: "To write or speak as a lesbian appears a paradoxical appearance of this 'I,' one which feels neither true nor false. For it is a production, usually in response to a request, to come out or write in the name of an identity which, once produced, sometimes functions as a politically efficacious phantasm. . . . This is not to say that I will not appear at political occasions under the sign of lesbian, but that I would like to have it permanently unclear what precisely that sign signifies. . . . One risk I take is to be recolonized by the sign under which I write. . . ."

The lingering presence within educational research of the goal of constructing a common view or some reliable way of "seeing constantly" can threaten and provoke the mobility of perspective as it intersects with construction of knowledge in relation to identity and meaning. Imagine what our construction processes might be if each of us could come to know ourselves as queer, and move from queer text to queer margin and back to longing for "identity." The meaning of the "personal is political," at this moment in my existence appears as a reflexive longing for "personal" that rebounds and then circles the "political" as a reference for location within hierarchies of oppression and well-being.

THE DEDICATION TO COMMON VIEWPOINT

Antithetical to and essential to learning and "knowing" is the earnestness with which one may find oneself trying to hold down a phenomenon and nail it to a sense of reality by using and describing in fixed symbols the occurrence at hand. For me, the threat is that the fixing of a particular frame of reference creates the prospect for my perspectival prison and as such restricts me from the mobility necessary for my sense of freedom. If I look from "here" as one identified as "this," then I lose, even if for the moment, the mobility, to be "there" and seeing it as "she" might. I struggle, probably because of my sense of being oppressed by others' descriptions of my identity, to remain connected to an identity that purports to be free of identity and permanent location. Being marginal and flowing in and out of text is now a description as well as a construction from my being QUEER. Mobility and traveling about, in, and among my many perspectives is all critical to my construction of meaning, identity, and purpose. And I have learned from the mobility of being a person who has some of her identity tied to being a lesbian and yet a large part of her identity connected to other ways of identifying, which at times make my lesbian identity invisible (in what may be positive or negative ways). That movement and identification with diverse perspectives is my "queer" way of life.

And so the dance of knowing appears to be defined within the person's body movement and its relation to rhythms (discourses) and spaces (contexts). One, two, three and one, two, three when institutionalized into prescribed steps is a way to take the learning of listening (or feeling or seeing), coordinating it and moving through a rehearsal that can be repeated and practiced. A problem, one I am discussing in this paper, is about what happens when the rehearsal is renamed "the" dance. Using educational research and teaching as the simile, it fascinates me to think that some could be dancing even when they are doing "the" dance, while yet others have learned "the" dance so well that they have no idea about what we might be referring to when we talk about dancing as not being "the" dance. For those who are doing the prescribed rehearsal steps as "the" dance, the phenomenon of encountering deconstruction or queer dancing is sometimes the way to unlearn "the" illusion of dance rehearsal as text.

SO HOW THEN OR WHY WOULD EDUCATIONAL RESEARCHERS WANT, SEEK, OR STUDY SOME NOTION OF "WHAT IS"?

In moments of experiencing great tedium as I read or listened to educational research reports, I earnestly asked why would a person, a people, or a culture want to have placed so much emphasis on method and the repetitions (rehearsals) of an authorized, fixed, "written-in-stone" kind of world view (of eliminating disease, dancing or educating)? I accept the value of rehearsals, but I find the elevation of rehearsal to scholarship to be disappointing and wasteful. Sometimes I suspect that the rehearsal may actually blot out some person's uninhibited inclinations toward synchrony. I then find myself asking why would a people on a pulsating and sometimes spherical-appearing planet want a flat earth view? Why would people who have experienced a range of pains, tedium, and joy in experiences called educating, learning, and supporting learning want to scientize, control, predict, and tell others of "efficient" ways to get the essence out of these moving, rich, combusting experiences? I try to understand. I try to identify with what seems a strange, but appropriately named, "straight" venture.

I recognize straight, linear, cause and effect in association with the urge I get when I wish to know in some fixed, firm, and reliable way. That need seems identifiable within me as the location from which I operate when I am fearful. (Just as we might fear that to dance to our own body impulses and good feelings might not look right to those who may be watching.) Fear of being out of control, being controlled, or otherwise put at risk by uncertainty sometimes creates a panic for freeze and control and institutionalized rehearsal. Thus I explain to myself this formalization of educational research and teaching as an effort to know in a context that pushes itself up from a sense of need for power over and control of that which is found or judged to be uncontrolled, threatening, or frightening.

The variation on the rehearsal theme is expressed in my choice to demonstrate at a Cracker Barrel restaurant as a challenge of my assessment skills. I demonstrate to educate, I demonstrate to learn (to do research), to move around perceptions, to disrupt, to create new spaces, and to form alternative junctures for co-construing so I might continue to move freely in and among those I see as trying to generate and/or maintain a flat earth view that would fix figure to a ground and margins to a text. I demonstrate to dislodge the complacency of "the" dance which has become taken for granted.

Dominant job brokers have informed us that we need to study and develop skills if we are to come to some sense of understanding that will permit us queers to move from the margins into and away from the existing textual focus. I assume a desire for such a perceived sense of power is supposed to come from a felt need that generates from the sense of absence of same. In contrast and totally interrelated is the notion of unstilled curiosity, which generates an internal felt rhythm that calls me simply to move about and explore and not to fall into nonconsciousness and essential habits.

PUBLIC AS PLAYGROUND FOR CONSTRUCT

Ah, wonderful constructs of community, society, family, and tribe. Enculturation into the meaning of group membership presents prospects for the meaning of relationship and any related need for power. Being QUEER in a family of proselytizing heterosexual breeder fanatics surely offers an easily understood source for wanting to understand constructs for power. It is amazing to me how much of my life it took for me to realize what the issue was and why I had such a need to behave privately while I learned to understand reflexive expressions of power and control.

Just as the description of the Cracker Barrel demonstration provides us with a texture of diverse views, speculations, and serendipitous moments, so each child's life, each moment in a classroom, each family unit's acting out (dance rehearsal) of their privatized social system (essentialist construction)[14] provides us with a phenomenon for analysis of what we might include under the categories of education and learning. (Family, like "the" dance, is a rehearsal form that is institutionalized and thus often needs to be deconstructed with regard to its purpose, e.g., providing support and nurturance for members of its unit.)

To the extent that we wish or need to understand a phenomenon we call education and the constructs of method and power within that phenomenon, we need the field of political and intentional action. And in this sense I suspect the field of play is our concept of public. That is, to specify public as shared symbols and shared space. This book, these words, when offered up to other readers become public domain. Here I must credit Iris Young, whose significant recent work attempts to clarify and explore definitions related to the place and meaning of public. In *Justice and The Politics of Difference,* Young has offered us a working concept of public as that which is open and accessible and as a place where one should expect to hear from those who are different, whose social perspectives, experience, and affiliations are different.[15]

It seems that the QUEER NATION demonstrations are exactly about that matter. It is a matter of not allowing the public to be made into a reification of a particularly powerful dominant group's notion of their privatized power and controlling views. It is to deconstruct the rehearsal of "public" as a place of polite consensual behaviors that serve to define what will be acceptable to the dominant social and political sources of power.

The owners of the Cracker Barrel restaurant chain appear to wish to limit who and what expressions they allow in public, or perhaps they wish to make their public restaurant a key club, a private place where only conforming family members are allowed to prepare the food or to sit at the table. (Beside the parallel issue in the definition of what is educational research and what constitutes education, which is being addressed in this chapter, there is also an interesting parallel here related to public and private schooling in the United States.)

If educational research focuses on the controlled circumstances of schooling, like family becomes focused on reproduction of heterosexual breeding, then education risks being not about growth and learning, just as family is often not about nurturing and development. From my perspectives, schools and families become dysfunctional when they have reproduction as their goal and control and fear of change as their primary mode of operation. This posture of needing to control alters the freedom to learn and to move into perspectival juxtapositions necessary for free fall and growth spurts.

Thanks to Betty Jean Craig, who has reminded us again:

> What right-wing critics of the academy did not understand in the late 19th Century, and do not understand now, is that the pursuit of truth is inherently disruptive; it is anti-authoritarian. To seek truth is to disbelieve what others take on faith. It was to protect the pursuit of truth that 19th-century American academics—responding to the effort to silence advocates of Darwin's theories—adopted the principle of academic freedom. According to that principle, proven scholars are given tenure to insure their freedom to investigate, publish, and teach ideas that may be unpopular with the general public, governing boards, or the politically powerful.[16]

And what then are we dealing with when researchers and teachers are made to rehearse the method for so long that they forget the purpose of the rehearsal and they all begin to do the two-step and try to eliminate from the dance floor those who would do the wild interpretive dance? Is method a need to define? To critique? To remove?

Researching and teaching are fun. They are play. They are living, seeing, squinting, moving, and risking. And in a very serious sense this is spiritual work. In keeping with the emptiness and sterility of the goals and methods and the motives of modernity, we here move to release, to let go of what, in another realm, would be named fear of error, or disapproval, of not fitting in. It seems we are surrounded by a society wishing to dominate and control. While much of organized religion and upperclass authority have been plundered by their own need to steel their "correctness," there appears to be a safe back-up move wherein the academy moves to substitute claims of rationality, reliability, validity, and science. Each of these sources focused on social control contributes to and fosters a need for order, method, credentializing, and generalization. Here, too, modernity marks its own destruction in its power grab and desire to control and freeze the perspective of knowing.

The frost is on the pumpkin and the jack-o'-lantern is ready to make known its divergent face. The multiple voices and faces move to the nightmares of the fears of those whose power and control seem out of control. The margins threaten to become the center as Eurocentrism, facism, and class-based racism and sexism falter in the realms where material control has previously shaped the words and symbols of power.

Now meaning and essentialism in modernist constructs falter in the face of resounding voices for those who have been marginalized outside of what should have been invited public perspectives. Dancing need not be done in a ballroom or on even ground. Research and teaching need not be limited to the ritualistic processes of university and schooling rehearsals. Some of us have been scolded by the dance instructors (our research instructors, our supervising teachers, our principals, and our deans) and have had to look into the face of the fear that we would forever fry and curl up in the heated work we wanted to do in the margins. Some of us have struggled to claim our place by slipping into a centeredness of the texts and hiding from our marginality. Some educational researchers have become the text. Some researchers will claim their identity from their curiosity and may courageously continue to work to groom the unpredictable, the resistant, the interactive, and the joyful passing of moments that have no concept of moments nitched in spatial relations. Some of us will recognize that QUEER THEORY critiques and models an interactive epistemological perspective. Some of us will always be QUEER because queer is dancing, not rehearsing, and as such relational may be not essentially essential.

And in postscript I might add that the struggle over the meaning of dysfunctional epistemology within dysfunctional modernist capitalism is here, in this text, a reiteration of some of my favorite snitches from the exhumed skepticisms of the likes of David Hume and other articulate eight year olds. And I do mean that in its most positive sense.

Notes

1. David Hume, *A treatise of human nature* (Baltimore, MD: Penguin, 1969), 20.

2. Ken Kempner, "Wolves in Sheep's Clothing: Positivists Masquerading as Phenomenologists," *Educational Foundations* (Winter 1992), 75.

3. See proposed Reagan platform, authored by Ronald F. Docksai, in *Mandate for Leadership,* edited by Charles L. Heatherly (Washington, DC., The Heritage Foundation, 1981), pp. 164. "The establishment of a comprehensive, timely and reliable education information system is a task which ought to be performed at the federal level, and one which is necessary for the improvement of educational quality. Any federal education office which succeeds the Department of Education, should it be abolished, should handle this among its principal tasks." While Reagan seems to have failed to dismantle the Department of Education, he wasted no time in setting up a division within the Department of Education of the U.S. government with the placing of a Czar who could handle the dispensing of funds for educational research. Then look at the politics of the Czar, Chester Finn, and the goals and objectives of the Heritage Foundation (the apparent training grounds for the particular perspective on schooling which was to be developed through the research that was sought and rewarded

by the Reagan/Bush administrations). See follow-up written by Eileen M. Gardner in *Mandate for Leadership II* (1984) as well as later Bush advisory documents.

4. Recent efforts in the City of Baltimore, for example, give private learning businesses the license to prove that they can be more effective than bureaucratically strangled schools and teachers. By authorizing waivers from the usual paperwork and logistical restrictions that have been placed in the way of teaching and learning, that very change in itself (along with the Hawthorne effect operating at its side) might give advantages to a private business so it can do the job better than existing bureaucratic schools. Ah, yes, and then private groups can offer their research component and sell their results in competition with the struggling systems of higher education and the trimming-down State Departments of Education.

5. Life style, discourse field, age, and income level are clearly factors in this matter of understanding the school-age client.

6. Francis Schrag, "In Defense of Positivist Research Paradigms," *Educational Researcher* 21(5): 7 (1992).

7. Note the observation of Patricia Hill Collins in *Black Feminist Thought: Knowledge, Consciousness, and the Politics of Empowerment* (London: Harper Collins Academic, 1990).

   Western social and political thought contains two alternative approaches to ascertaining "truth." The first, reflected in positivist science, has long claimed that absolute truths exist and that task of scholarship is to develop objective, unbiased tools of science to measure these truths. But Afrocentric, feminist and other bodies of critical theory have unmasked the concepts and epistemology of this version of science as representing the vested interests of elite white men and therefore as being less valid when applied to experiences of other groups and, more recently, to white male recounting of their own exploits. Earlier versions of standpoint theories, themselves rooted in a Marxist positivism, essentially reversed positivist science's assumptions concerning whose truth would prevail. These approaches suggest that the oppressed allegedly have a clearer view of "truth" than their oppressors because they lack the blinders created by the dominant group's ideology. But this version of standpoint theory basically duplicates the positivist belief in one "true" interpretation of reality and, like positivist science, comes with its own set of problems. (p. 9)

8. Paulo Freire, *Pedagogy of the Oppressed* (New York: Seabury, 1968), 64.

9. Maxine Greene, *Teacher As Stranger: Educational Philosophy for the Modern Age* (Belmont, CA: Wadsworth, 1973).

10. Cracker Barrel restaurants have a long line of rocking chairs in front of their general store entrance. One actually goes through the general store to get into the restaurant. Rocking chairs are for sale through the general store. During busy meal times clowns and balloons are used to entertain the children of families who are sitting in front of the general store and rocking in the rocking chairs.

11. In her introduction to "Queer Theory: Lesbian and Gay Sexualities" (*Differences: A Journal of Feminist Cultural Studies* 3(2) (1991). iii–xviii), Teresa de Lauretis notes on page x that

    For instance, Sue Ellen Case's essay ["Tracking the Vampire," 1–20] in this issue traces the association of heterosexuality with the natural, the healthy, the living and life-giving, and its consequent thinking of homosexuality with the unnatural, the sick, the dead and deadly, in a discursive chain which, from Golden Age Spanish drama to the modern scientist discourse of pure blood and Hitler's death camps, up to the postmodern dominant discourse on AIDS, binds the sexual with the racial in Western cultures, opposing the purity of lawful, patriarchally-gendered sexuality—and its blood right to money—to the contaminated, impure blood of homosexuals, Jews, and Moors. Throughout the centuries, she argues, queers have resisted these proscriptions with various counterdiscourses ranging from mysticism to reveling in impurity to organized political resistance. But, the queer theorist might ask, could this heritage perhaps undermine our own contemporary counterdiscourse, our own queer thinking, unwilling or unwitting heir to these discursive tropes?

12. Lisa Duggan, "Making It Perfectly Queer," *Socialist Review* 22(1) (1992): 11. And from the editor in introduction to this issue of the journal (p5) "QUEER: It's a controversial term, even—or especially—among gay and lesbian activists. For those whose personal memories of the word as homophobic epithet still sting, its hard to see why anyone would want to turn a relic of hate into a rallying cry.

    But there's more to the logic of the new queer activism than simple linguistic reclamation. Fluid and inclusive, "queerness," at its best, serves as shorthand for a new way of thinking about oppositional identities—and, just maybe, as a new model for social movement politics."

13. This appears in Diana Fuss, ed., *inside/out* (New York: Routledge, 1991).

14. It seems to me the nuclear family is a dysfunctional institution as it is given or takes on both the role of working to control and indoctrinate the child while it also promises to nurture and support the development of individual identity. This task is especially tenuous in the private setting, where conflict in and among values which promote democratic political claims, religious dogmatism, ageism, sexism, racism, classism, parental ownership of biological offspring, and radical individualism stir with power habits. Family unit dysfunctionality may be defined from this, my, perspective as the fixing of text and exclusion of margin so as to deliberately cause loss of flexibility for constructs of diversity. Closing off open dialogue is epistemologically degenerate and antithetical to the prospects for fluidity in knowing. Interactions between claims for public values and privacy rights are often most severely felt in the lives of children who are afforded minimal public protection or voice.

15. Iris Marion Young, *Justice and The Politics of Difference* (Princeton: Princeton Univ. Press, 1990), 119–20.

16. Betty Jean Craig, "Point of View," *The Chronicle of Higher Education* (January 6, 1993): A56.

ON METHOD AND HOPE

William G. Tierney

Robert sat on the rattan couch as the sun set and said, "I don't care if you use my real name or a pseudonym. Well, maybe a pseudonym. How about Sunchild? I've always liked that name. It's the name of a friend. You could call me Robert Sunchild." He stretched his legs out on the couch and threw the red blanket over them; he reached for a glass of water with his right hand, and in his left hand he held the ever present handkerchief for his runny nose. His hand unsteadily moved the glass cup to his lips where he took a sip and slowly replaced the glass on the table. He pulled the blanket up around his shoulders; it now covered all of his body except his face. He continued:

> I'd like to talk about the format for the book. It's been on my mind. I don't want to appear as a flunky, as a sellout. I'm pouring out all that has meaning in my life. My whole life, that's all I have. It's not that you'll capitalize on it. I believe in your motives. It's just that I don't want to appear like Black Elk. They used this old man for his knowledge, memories, and vision. It's almost as if they capitalized on him. I don't want to be perceived as someone who sold out. Does that make sense?

Robert had turned forty a few months back, and shortly before his birthday we had begun working on his life history. We agreed to do the history when I visited him in the hospital. It was the second time he had been hospitalized because of AIDS. I originally had not known he was sick because he did not want anyone to know about his illness. Robert later recalled:

> Those first two times I went in the hospital I was real depressed. I guess I thought that I wouldn't be like others, that if I took care of myself, took it easy, I wouldn't have to go in. When we talked about doing this history, I knew that things would never be normal again. Like you said that morning, I'd have ups and downs. I'd be in and out of the hospital.
>
> When you suggested doing the life history I wasn't sure what

to think. I guess I was flattered at first that you thought my story
was worth telling. I wondered about who'd read it. How I'd appear.

Introduction

Social science researchers have long argued over the superiority of different
theoretical frameworks and methodological designs. Indeed, many would
say that the argument has dominated social science research since World
War II. In this chapter, I discuss theory and method by way of my work
with Robert Sunchild, a forty-year-old gay, Native American, university
professor, who died of AIDS in the late spring of 1991. I call upon the
analytical lens of postmodernism and critical theory and argue that we
need to take into account the politics of method, and of consequence, to
reconfigure both the manner in which we conduct research and our purpose
in undertaking research.

My intent is twofold. First, I bring into question the role of the author
in a text. As with other anthropologists who have written about the author/
narrator in writing (Crapanzano 1977; Dwyer 1977; Geertz 1988; Rabinow
1985; Rosaldo 1989), I suggest that the creation of the text exists in a
dialectical relationship between author and "subject" to such an extent that
we must forego analyses that assume the researcher-cum-author is capable
of objectively describing any given reality. Second, I argue that our research
efforts operate within ongoing patterns of contestation and struggle, and
that a central challenge for educational researchers who subscribe to critical
and postmodern assumptions of society must be to enable those with whom
we are engaged to develop voice and to develop a sense of what I shall call
"hope." In addition to my own recent work (Tierney 1989; Tierney 1991;
Tierney 1992), I draw upon the work of Giroux (1988a; 1988b; 1990) and
Gitlin (1989; 1990) in my discussion of the purpose of research.

This chapter has two parts. I first outline a reformulation of the author's
role in a text, and I then delineate the consequences of such an approach.
Although an elaborated discussion of what is meant by "critical theory" or
"postmodernism" is beyond the parameters of this chapter, I begin by offering a sketch of a "critical postmodernist" framework as a way to consider
how we might redefine the nature of the research relationship.

The Politics Of Method: Theoretical Scaffolding

Simon and Dippo have argued that critical postmodern research is "structured in relation to our efforts to construct a mode of learning and a conception of knowledge that may enhance the possibility of collectively constituted
thought and action which seeks to transform the relations of power that
constrict people's lives" (1986, 196). From this perspective, research is meant

to be transformative; we do not merely analyze or study an object to gain greater understanding, but instead struggle to investigate how individuals and groups might be better able to change their situations. Further, researchers appear embedded in the research process; they are not "scientists" who perform their work in a laboratory.

Such a perspective has different assumptions about the nature of knowledge and the nature of research from modernist conceptions, and yet there are ties to modernist notions about reason and equality. As Burbules and Rice note, postmodernism seeks to "reappropriate, redefine and reground modernist categories" (1991, 397). In short, "post"-modernism has a relationship to modernism insofar as it moves beyond a particular theoretical stance, but it also has ties to that model.

The differences between modernism and postmodernism are contested and too numerous to go into here, but I briefly delineate the central points that pertain to the role of the author and the development of the text. The modernist belief is that knowledge can be scientifically studied and analyzed. The use of objective evidence forms the foundation for what modernists accept or reject. The postmodern world, however, is one that rejects the positivist definition of "objectivity" or that one singular "truth" exists that awaits to be discovered. Rather than a Durkheimian concept of reality that synthesizes knowledge and people to abstract norms, postmodernists focus on difference and conflict where competing interpretations of reality are inevitable Thus, the researcher's task is not to discover the "true" interpretation, for none exists; instead, the challenge is to uncover the multiple voices at work in society that have been silenced.

> The postmodern is a world where people are inundated with multiple voices—some harmonious and some alien. The "plurality of voices" vie for the legitimation of their own version of social reality—their own narrative so to speak. . . . In the postmodern condition, the totalizing perspectives offered by grand narratives are replaced by subject-centered pluralist discourses. Societies are seen not as ordered systems highlighted by unity or a totality of beliefs and values, but instead, are marked by differences and opposites. Postmodernists reject the assumption that progress exists, for such a belief is founded on an essentialist definition of knowledge. Indeed, one wonders if progress does not exist, and the search for truth is foresworn, then what is humanity's purpose in a postmodern world? (Tierney and Rhoads 1993)

In large part, that question frames the purpose of this chapter and underscores how I employ "critical postmodernism." The argument that research is subjective, that data is "created" and not simply "discovered," and that the author has particular biases generates a distinctly different framework with which one conducts research. In doing so, I use critical theory not in opposition to postmodernism but as a way to give political purpose to the postmodern project. Critical theorists work from the assumption that oppressive relations must be transformed and that these relations are in some way connected to structural and material constructions. I am advertising a method, then, that combines essential elements of critical theory (i.e., praxis) and of postmodernism (i.e., intersubjectivity) in order to develop the concepts of difference and hope.

My goal is to reorient our work away from modernist assumptions of reality and the purpose of research. Instead, I suggest we assume a postmodern stance informed by critical theory. Such a position takes into account the multiple realities that exist in the world and struggles to come to terms with how we might build educational communities based on these multiple constructions. I am particularly concerned with educational researchers' ability to become more fully engaged with uncovering what Foucault called "the mechanisms of power" (1980) in society and in our organizations, and also in enabling our research subjects to become involved in such endeavors. We must develop research strategies that provide individuals with the ability to come to terms with the "infinitesimal mechanisms" of power that determine their lives. Unlike Foucault, however, I suggest we interrogate these discursive practices as ways to create change and, ultimately, hope, in the postmodern world. What follows is a schema for reconfiguring the author's role.

Author/Subject

"I'd like to talk about this book today, before we go back to the stories," Robert had said during one of our first interviews. He wondered how the book would be configured. Would I be the sole author? Would he? If we were both authors who would come first? Whose words would account for the text? "It's critical for you to talk to people who know me. I'm not good telling stories about myself," he added one day later on in our interviews. "They'll tell you I'm crazy! I can make people laugh hysterically! We need more stories, funny stories about me, perspectives from other people, including yourself."

Robert had responded that he was not good at telling stories because I began most sessions by saying, "Tell me a story." We spoke with one another in a formal interview at least once a week for about six months. In addition to the formal interviews, I also saw Robert constantly in other settings— en route to a doctor, or with his family and friends at the hospital, or at either of our houses where I cooked him a meal.

Robert had suggested that we set aside a specific time once a week for two hours for the interviews; this "rule" was broken more often than it was kept. Either Robert or I continued talking for more than two hours, or some emergency arose that made the interview impossible. One fact I learned over the months was that a person with AIDS must live moment to moment because the macabre twists and turns of the disease force the individual to meet AIDS's timetable and no one else's. Thus, Robert would grow sick and have to be hospitalized again, or he would get an infection in a finger or a toe and have to make an immediate trip to the pharmacy, or he had the opportunity to see a friend who was passing through town and we silently knew that it might be the last time Robert would see the individual. Indeed, one point Robert brought out consistently in his interviews, and demonstrated in his actions, was his concern that he be on good terms with everyone. "People will say that I can walk away from a person who has fucked me over and I may not relent or forgive. I can be real stubborn. But AIDS has changed that. I'm glad to say that there are no individuals who I haven't made peace with," he said toward the end. "I have contacted people I haven't spoken with in years and in my own way, I've said goodbye."

Regardless of the interruptions to our formal interviews, our work took on increased intensity as our time together proceeded. Even with the constant concerns that AIDS brought on, Robert often returned us to his life history. He said at one point, "I can't deal with deadlines anymore. I don't want to go into the office now. I don't feel I can get up and work for even four hours every day anymore. We can still continue this, though. I think about my life and about this illness all the time."

About half of the formal interviews began with Robert reflecting on our previous meeting. "I want to add something to what I said about my family," he commented one winter afternoon. Another day he said, "I think we're concentrating too much on me being gay. That's all we talked about last week." And another time he said, "Right now I want to talk about my changing feeling about AIDS. I think this should be a major portion of the book."

The rest of the interviews either began with my question, "Tell me a story," or Robert prompting me for a question. As he said one late afternoon: "You can't just ask me, 'Tell me a story' today. I'm too tired. I'm dragging. Be more specific and I'll try to respond." He also changed my questions. When I asked him about his first gay experience, for example, he responded: "You don't mean it that way because that makes it sound that I suddenly realized one day I was gay, and I always knew I was gay. From the very start." He then proceeded to talk about his sexuality and how he "knew" he was gay at a very early age. In this light, the researcher/author of the text was not simply myself but Robert as well. He was the one who set the questions, raised reflections that led to revisions, or told me to ask a different question so that we would arrive at a different answer.

At the same time, who I was and my relationship with Robert unalterably set the terms of the text. That is, I was not only a researcher interested in conducting a life history with a particular individual; I entered the situation as Robert's friend. Because I was one of the first individuals to know he had AIDS, and because we were both gay, I also became a confidant. And too, the fact that we shared the same sexual orientation also helped frame the context of our encounter. As Robert commented, "I'm sure you'll want to know about the gay stuff, all the gory details, and I'll tell you. I'm not ashamed of any of it. But then, if you weren't gay, I don't know if I would even bring it up or want to talk about it."

Thus, the development of the text in large part depended on who we were as well as our relationship with one another. Presumably, if two heterosexuals had been involved in this project they would not have formed as immediate a bond with one another as Robert and I had; I suspect, however, that individuals in groups that differ from the norm—lesbians, African Americans, the disabled—may well begin an ethnographic encounter with a specific relationship such as that which Robert and I had. In his work about the *berdache* ("gay men") in Native American communities, for example, Walter Williams suggests that heterosexuals could not have gotten the information he had received from gay Native Americans (1992, 187). More importantly, any two individuals involved in either a loose unstructured interview, or a more intensive structured process such as that which occurred between Robert and myself, have multiple and specific identities that shape how the process takes place and, ultimately, how the text gets developed. Any two individuals have alternative definitions of what counts for knowledge; accordingly, the questions raised, the topics left unchallenged, and the areas accepted as legitimate will be framed by interaction between the two.

The form of the interaction also helps frame the text. A formal interview with a tape recorder—even between two friends—is different from an unstructured conversation between the same individuals. Even though the topics may be the same in both situations, the manner in which they are related will differ. For example, Robert had once explained: "I know I told you that I liked to tease Izetta (his best friend), but I can't tell you how I teased her, because this is different." What was "different" were the parameters within with which Robert and I were talking. He continued:

> If I told you now some of my famous "Izetta stories" it would be like I'm making fun of her, and I wouldn't do that. This is an academic interview and I can't just tell stories spontaneously. "Izetta stories" are ones that I've told in a group. That's how

[Indian people] are, in a group, we laugh, we tease each other, not in an interview like this.

Robert's comment highlights how, in his mind, we were engaged in an intellectual process different from other interactions. Even though Robert related to me the most private details of his life, from his poverty as a child to his coming out as a gay man, he still felt that our encounter was not one where you told stories about a treasured friend. Indeed, Robert's identity as a faculty member helped frame this definition of "academic work" and the sense that he was using his "professional voice" in our encounters.

Again, we return to the question of who is author and who is subject. The week after Robert said he couldn't tell me an "Izetta story," he commented:

I made up a list of people you should talk to. They can tell you the kind of stories you want to hear. I also think it should be your book. My story, your book. But I'll write a preface and introduce myself. I don't care about editorial control. I think you should be the author because your opinion counts too. You've been involved in all of this. I've told you things I haven't told anyone else. And somebody needs to be objective and make sense of all of this. How it all fits together.

Robert thus not only had assumed a professional voice for himself but also had created a traditional role for myself as an author: that of a researcher who had combed through all the pertinent facts; that of an expert who was able to tie the text together; and that of an involved investigator. I raise this point because such traditional assumptions stand in sharp distinction to how Robert and I actually worked together. Each of these "roles" was circumscribed by Robert's imprimatur.

He had given me the list of individuals with whom to talk, and obviously those people would paint a different picture than if I had randomly chosen people with whom Robert had worked. For example, Robert had chosen individuals all of whom knew he was gay, whereas the vast majority of people who came into contact with Robert did not know about his sexual orientation, or rather they made the heterosexist assumption that he was heterosexual.

He also believed that I had a purpose in choosing to work with him on his life history. Indeed, he had written in his journal, "I look back through these pages and wonder what would they reveal to an outside reader? Arrogant of me to think (or have thought) I was living a life so unique that one would find it worth the chronicle." Consequently, Robert and I often discussed at the outset of our interviews why his life was even worth recording, for originally Robert saw himself as a "simple man" whose life was not important enough to write about and have others read. Eventually, he changed his mind:

> I guess it's important if this book is published so that people can learn from my experiences. I don't think I'm unusually strong. I've met a lot of people stronger than I. There are terminal illnesses that are just terrible. But I've learned to accept my fate. I've learned what life is for, why we are here. Life is full of tragedy, but I've learned a larger lesson about people, about myself.

Caring

My initial goal in this text was not to produce a written work but to enable Robert the time and space to reflect on his life during a most difficult period. That is, I did not initially see my role in a traditional manner as an "expert" who conducted research to advance knowledge or to solve an empirical question. Rather, the "research" began as a way for Robert to maintain his own research agenda and to consider his past. Indeed, at the outset I cared very little about the "outcome" of the "research"; my concern was for the individual with whom I was engaged in the research encounter.

Further, in large part my "expertise" derived from Robert. I am assuming that countless others, for example, are familiar with the standardized techniques used to collect interview data and write up notes. Yet the heart of life history research is not merely the verbatim transcription of what an individual says. The basis of our work is in the involvement with the individual; to that extent, Robert enabled me to give voice to his life. Without his voice there would be no text.

And finally, as Robert had assumed, I was an involved investigator. "You would probably call me a social integrationist, rather than a radical critical theorist like yourself," Robert had once teased. Yet Robert knew that my work with him was a passion not for collecting data so that I could make a presentation at a conference, but rather it was a concern for himself. "One of the positive aspects of AIDS is what I've seen in the compassion of the people around me—friends, family, secretaries, students," he said once when he was in the hospital. "People have really rallied around me. The love of people has just overwhelmed me. My family. My friends. You know how much I've come to rely on you and Maria. I've learned a larger lesson about the compassion of people."

My point here is that far too often as researchers we remove ourselves from those we study or the situation in which we are involved so that we can supposedly gain "distance" or "objectivity." As with Gitlin et al. (1989), I am no longer comfortable with that distance. "It is impossible for the researcher to understand the 'subject' ", they write, "unless she/he enters into a dialogue with the 'subject' aimed at mutual understanding" (243). My work with Robert, for example, began with the goal of entering into such a dialogue. In her book, *Caring*, Nel Noddings is helpful in delineating how one might characterize such a relationship:

> Apprehending the other's reality, feeling what he feels as nearly as possible, is the essential part of caring. . . . For if I take on the other's reality as possibility and begin to feel its reality, I feel, also, that I must act accordingly; that is, I am impelled to act as though in my own behalf, but in behalf of the other. (1986, 16)

Although I reject Noddings's overreliance on the essentializing nature of relationships, her notion of "caring" is integral to the critical postmodernist idea I am trying to advance here. That is, the researcher encounter needs to be imbued with more than simply a desire to collect data from a "subject." As researchers, one facet of our research capability must be to exhibit a sense of care and concern to understand the "other's possibility." I am suggesting that our research endeavors need to be reformulated so that they include a capacity for empathy.

Analyzing Texts

I appreciate the problems that go along with advocating for a sense of caring in our research. Research should have an empirical base, be data driven, and provide enough substance so that a reader may come to a different conclusion from that of the author. And there are ways that we can ensure that such checks take place. LeCompte and Goetz (1982), Lather (1986a; 1986b), and Lincoln and Guba (1985), for example, have provided helpful guideposts to use in order to frame one's work.

However, I also want us to move toward a literary stance in our work instead of a scientific one. In essence, I am suggesting that a researcher does not discover "truth" or "reality" from a removed distance. Indeed, the search for such absolutes is mistaken. Richard Rorty is helpful here: "To say that we should drop the idea of truth out there waiting to be discovered," he writes, "is not to say that we have discovered that, out there, there is no truth. It is to say that our purposes would be best served by ceasing to see truth as a deep matter" (1990, 8). To argue for a literary stance means that we need to experience those topics and live with those people we are to study rather than struggle for neutrality.

To call for analyses based on literary criticism denies postmodern researchers any firm rules, for at this juncture the field of literary criticism also encounters fierce debate about how one judges the worthiness of a text. Nevertheless, I offer two provisional suggestions about what I mean by using literary criticism as a way to analyze our texts. The reader might ask what was learned from a text and if a text corresponds with what is believed to be reality. The point here is that asking such questions moves us toward defining "good literature" and enables the reader to reflect on his or her own life. From a postmodern standpoint, texts demand a sense of self-reflexivity on the part of the reader. Langness and Frank have offered a related comment:

> We judge an ethnographic novel by the quality of the authorial voice, by the aptness or pungency of detail, by the consistency of the characters and their culture, and by the plausibility of their behavior as situations develop in which the reader becomes more equipped to assess the characters' attitudes and choices. (1978, 20)

Ultimately, I am suggesting that an author exists as a name on a page and not much more. To be sure, my fingers have pushed the keys that created this text, but this paper is as much a fiction as those works that we commonly call fiction if we assume that reality is constructed and reconstructed rather than that it is "out there" waiting to be discovered. A text is a construction among multiple constituencies—subject, researcher, narrator, author, and, ultimately, reader.

I cannot even say that this text represents Robert and myself, for in it is involved our own life stories, the contexts in which we lived and interacted, and the contexts in which the reader discovers the text. Another individual with AIDS would have responded differently. Robert's life history reflects memories that derived from a particular moment in time; he would undoubtedly have had different reflections at a different point in his life. My work with him would have been immensely different ten years ago, when I would have been more reticent to discuss his sexual orientation and less willing to let the "subject" drive the research process. Moreover, a reader in 1993 will have one interpretation, a reader who happens to be gay will have yet another interpretation, a reader who has AIDS will have an additional interpretation, and so on.

I am not suggesting that we reside in a postmodern world where individuals live within their own microrealities and have little, if anything, in common. Nor am I suggesting that ours is a world of Babel where no one can be understood because of the multitude of languages that exist. To the contrary, I am arguing that out of these different languages we find areas of agreement, commonality, and fellowship. Yet the path to such fellowship cannot be found on an avenue assumed to be constructed by a singular entity. It needs to be based on the recognition and honoring of differences. It is found on another road where the authority of the author is brought into question, and the search for communal intersections becomes paramount.

Tronto offers a feminist analysis of caring that parallels what I am suggesting from a critical postmodern perspective:

> A feminist approach to caring needs to begin by broadening our understanding of what caring for others means, both in terms of the moral questions it raises and in terms of the need to restructure broader social and political institutions if caring for others is to be made a more central part of the everyday lives of everyone in society. (1989, 184)

And as critical/postmodern researchers, we develop a sense of care not as a way to ameliorate differences, as if we were all the same, but rather as a way to accentuate differences and come to terms with one another. Caring, then, is a way to work on an individual level and at the same time relate that care to the broader questions about the structure of society. We employ aspects of critical theory, for we try to create individual and structural change, and we utilize postmodern insights insofar as we bring into question the nature of identity, the public/private distinction, and how to develop voice and difference. In doing so, the project of democracy is at the core. As Mouffe has observed:

> Democratic politics must accept division and conflict as unavoidable and the reconciliation of rival claims and conflicting interests can only be partial and provisional. It is the very characteristic of modern democracy to impede a final fixation of the social order and to preclude the possibility of any discourse establishing a definite closure. There will always be competing interpretations. (1990, 63)

The implications for authors who subscribe to the ideas of postmodernism and critical theory are that in developing our texts we provide some sense of where we are as authors. We must collapse the hierarchical nature of our research endeavors. In so doing, we reframe our assumptions about reality. The author plays a powerful role in the development of the reality of the text, and we prepare ourselves for that power by developing a greater sense of self-reflexivity than we have heretofore shown. As Little argues,

> The aesthetics of life description calls upon our powers of insight and empathy. . . . This kind of vision that the writer must develop is quite demanding. It consists of a critical self-reflection, an inner positioning and recognition of one's self as a living person and an insight into the knowledge that self-reflection brings to the understanding of another life. (1980, 224)

Now that I have pointed out that the author needs to insert him-or her-self into a text in some manner, I also offer one caveat. Although I admire the experimental writing of recent anthropologists, I believe that the degree of self-reflexivity that occurs in Crapanzano's work *Tuhami* (1980), or in Kevin Dwyer's (1982) or Paul Rabinow's (1977) works on Morocco, for instance, have swung too far in the other direction. Our research needs to be more than personal reflections. Essentially, we have a question of balance. I am arguing that one of our challenges with regard to educational research is to come to terms with how we as writers-cum-researchers fit within a text.

The Critical Postmodern Project

Until the last two months of his life, Robert harbored the hope that he would live and be able to edit/author/coauthor the text. Even after he was first hospitalized and he realized that he actually had AIDS, he still believed he would live. "It's strange doing both things," he said one morning. "I worked on my will and I also accepted a speaking engagement next spring. And I want to go to Europe at Christmas, too!"

Little by little, AIDS chipped away at him. He realized that he would be unable to continue to work, and we talked with his department chair about a leave of absence. The conference he had planned to go to in the spring became an impossibility. He was hospitalized in March and had to stop his teaching. All that remained of his "work" was the life history. He commented in the hospital, "I realize now that I don't have much time. Our hope of doing this together isn't going to happen. I'd like to do more, but it's difficult to concentrate. I have lots of images now of my childhood. But ideas come and go so fast, so fast."

Robert left the hospital for a short time. We had a formal interview in mid-April for the last time. He had lost considerable weight by then, and his long black hair had been cut short and had thinned so that there were bald splotches. His feet and ankles had swollen so that he found it difficult to wear shoes or to walk. When he walked, he rolled off the edges of his feet so that the pain would be less than if he had walked firmly on the ground. He felt alternately hot and cold so that he threw the blankets on and off and on again.

> I was feeling miserable yesterday. The doctor told me I had slight anemia, slight dehydration, slight malnutrition. And I was coughing until it was just unbearable. My sides ache I've coughed up so much sputum. I just get the sense, not of giving up, but of coming to accept life. I think my time is very limited. . . . I hate to sound

like a big baby. I know there are people whose condition is worse than mine. But I just don't know how much more I can take.

Three days later he returned to the hospital and almost died. He recovered, but he was near death. His family took him home to his tribal reservation. Before he left we talked again, but this time he was less coherent, utterly fatigued. One point he made pertained to how AIDS was yet another battle he faced in a life of challenges as a gay, Native American.

I've been given the weapons to fight a long life battle. I see myself as a warrior just as a warrior would be in the old days, but it's taken a different form, although in my own way I still have to struggle with the White man. I've had to fight the White man's way, his system, and hold onto my identity as an Indian.

After he returned home, we talked almost daily on the telephone. "We had a sun dance sing the other night," he told me happily one day. "I didn't get out of the van, but everyone came by and said hello. The singers always mentioned me in their songs." Another time he asked, "So how's the book going? I sent you a poem that I want you to look at." Finally, three weeks after he had returned home, Robert died in his sleep.

Developing Voice

I have written elsewhere (Tierney 1993) that Robert held several narrative voices—that of someone who grew up in poverty, that of an American Indian, that of someone who was gay, that of a university professor, and that of someone who was living with AIDS. As it is a fiction to assume that the author of a text is the individual whose name appears on a page, it is also a fiction to assume individuals hold one singular identity to which their self can be defined (Gergen 1991).

But also, many of our voices are denied or overlooked because they are subsumed by the hegemonic voice of the norm. I am not suggesting that we develop voices in our narratives simply so that we have a taxonomy of difference. The liberal notion of multiculturalism adds voice without reconfiguring the parameters of power. Without bringing into question the notion of difference itself—how it is arranged and configured, and whose interests exist within the norm—we will forever doom voices such as Robert's to the border zones of our society.

We also do not engage those individuals with whom we are involved often enough in our own work. I have found it disconcerting, for example, to read life histories and the individual under study seems to be absent from any analysis of the text. Too often we overlook the advice of those under study and we act as if the author's voice were omniscient. Surely we need the advice and suggestions of those specific people in our research—be they students in a classroom, administrators in a study of organizational culture, or a faculty member with AIDS—to understand whether our interpretations are similar to those who have been studied. I do not necessarily believe that the researcher and the researched must always agree on a particular interpretation, but I am troubled if we do not even bother to ask our interviewees what they think about our analyses.

Further, if research is to be praxis oriented, if our purpose is somehow to change the world, then of necessity we must get involved with those whom we study. As Gitlin et al. ask, "To what extent [can] research be conceptualized so that those connected to schools can begin to change schooling in emancipatory ways?" (1989, 238). From a feminist perspective, Weiler gives one answer: "This kind of qualitative research into individual lives rests on certain implicit intentions or goals. One of these is to provide an opportunity for the women who are objects of study to discuss their work and to discuss the researcher's observation and analysis (1988, 70)."

My work with Robert was an attempt to enable someone under study to develop his own questions and to begin to analyze the data. Indeed, in large part the project was undertaken so that Robert would be able to reflect on his life at a time of intense crisis. For myself, such a project meant that any sense of being a dispassionate observer went by the wayside. During my involvement with him I spent considerable amounts of time in ostensibly nonresearch activities such as dealing with social service agencies and hospitals, or driving him to one place or another. The point of all this is that I undertook the research not merely to collect empirical data but also to aid the individual under study.

From this perspective, the role of the researcher/author is dramatically different from the modernist conception of the scientist who works in a vacuum. As Van Maanen has observed, the modernist author assumes the role "of a third party scribe reporting directly on the life of the observed. The tone suggests anonymity, a characteristic of science writing, where the fieldworker is self-cast as a busy but unseen little fellow who is confident that the world as represented in the writing is the real one (1988, 64)."

I am not just suggesting that the role of the postmodern author will differ from previous engagements with research subjects. To be sure, the encounter between researcher and researched will need to be refashioned in a manner suggested here. And in doing so, the way data are presented will differ. But I am taking Gitlin and Weiler's comments about the role of the researcher/author one step further. As noted, they rightfully argue that research ought to enable those under study to change their conditions.

Although I agree, in effect their suggestion does not provide direction for the role of the author outside of the research engagement. What is the author's role in advocating change? From a critical and postmodern perspective, an author's role at times ought to take on an explicitly political stance. The author needs to actively work toward changing inequalities. As Noddings notes, "simply talking about or writing about caring is a poor substitute for caring" (1986, 122).

Thus, I am arguing that the researcher/author has three tasks: the researcher engages the researched in a self-reflexive encounter; the research "act"—the book, article or presentation—brings to light the inequities of power that may exist; and the researcher actively works for care and change. My work with Robert attempted all three roles. The research encounter enabled him a degree of reflection that he may not otherwise have had. My subsequent writing has tried to bring to light the struggles and challenges faced by individuals who have AIDS. And given what I learned from Robert, I have become actively involved in trying to change the inequities that people with AIDS undergo. Such work ranges from developing university policies that provide AIDS patients with adequate medical leave to raising the consciousness of university administrators about how they might better deal with a heretofore silent crisis.

Research and Hope

If our research efforts reject the positivist notion of adding onto rationally conceived definitions of knowledge, than for what reason do we conduct research? We have long since lost the romantic concept of faith in human perfection. And, the modernist faith in rationality and reason has been exploded. If research is not to lead toward a better understanding of human perfection or to a more scientific and precise analysis of the human condition, than why ought we undertake research? To be sure, the professionalization of the academy where research and publications are the path to academic success has brought forth one additional, albeit cynical, reason to undertake research. Indeed, our research efforts should lessen if their central focus is merely to move academic careers forward.

However, I wish to advance a different idea, and that is the concept of "hope." In a world such as ours, beset with oppression and the sense that life cannot change for the better, one constant that might unite us is that of hope. Our research efforts ought to enable our readers to reflect on their own lives and to help us to envision lives for ourselves and our students that exist within communities of difference and hope.

By "difference," I mean that those identities of self with which we have come to define ourselves—race, class, gender, and sexual orientation, for example—ought to be honored and brought into the center of our discourses about education and its purpose. To honor difference, we must reject abstractions and universalized static ideals of concepts such as self and identity. In essence, the researcher struggles not to come to terms with understanding principles such as "truth" but instead strives to understand the reality of the other.

By "hope" I mean the sense that the human potential might be reached where individual and communal differences are acknowledged and where we come together in the expectation that out of difference arises communitas. As employed here, hope is not a rhetorical nor religious device through which we see the pain of the present day and await some future salvation or utopia; rather, the concept of hope I am advancing is grounded in understanding the present conditions and delineating how we might change them. Similar to difference, hope is not the devotion to an abstract principle but rather the commitment to a dimension of human existence that offers meaning across differences.

Unlike the romantic ideal, postmodernism will not allow us to fool ourselves into thinking that a utopia exists where consensual accord and agreement occur. Postmodernism also has shown us the fallacy of the modernist belief that science will lead to human perfection. We have learned that if we are to enable differences to flourish, then disagreement and conflict are inevitable and to be encouraged. Striving for utopias or perfection has led to the rigidification of the norm and the silence of those of us who are different. Yet, because universal beliefs—in truth, in faith, in reason—no longer exist, I am not suggesting that ours is a nihilist age where we have little that binds us together other than despair. In a similar vein, bell hooks speaks of hope as "yearning." She writes, "The shared space and feeling of 'yearning' opens up the possibility of common ground where all these differences might meet and engage one another" (1990, 13). Hope unites us in the belief that out of dialogue we may build transformative communities of difference.

Such communities will be cacophonous, because disagreements over the nature of reality will abound. Yet rather than meet these conflicts as problems to be avoided or overlooked, the challenge is to work out how different realities might be accommodated and understood. Examples of communities of difference exist in society where gay and lesbian people, for example, try to develop an agenda and discover significant differences across race, class, and gender; academic communities of difference exist in institutions such as Evergreen State College where they have developed an explicit commitment to diversity and constantly seek to change what they have built. In general, such communities are hard to find in society and in academe. But simply because we have not yet defined the parameters of what such a community may look like does not mean we must stick with what we have. One role of the researcher is to paint portraits of possibility.

Rorty has noted, "Solidarity has to be constructed out of little pieces, rather than found already waiting, in the form of an ur-language which all of us recognize when we hear it" (1990, 94). My work with Robert was perhaps an example of one of those "little pieces." The work began not as an abstraction but as a desire to care for someone. We engaged in an encounter that sought to enable us to understand one another and to allow others to also understand the challenges of Robert.

Hope occurs and gets defined in the contexts of the dialogues that frame our lives. The task of the researcher, then, is not to develop yet another abstract principle such as "hope"; rather, our work is to create the contexts where communities of difference might be able to come to terms with their own identities and, in doing so, create the conditions for hope in a postmodern world.

Oddly, perhaps, these ideas derive from work with an individual who died of AIDS—a disease whose political, social, and medical ramifications more often smother hope and deny voice. Yet Robert struggled to hope, and in his hope he rediscovered his own voice and his own hidden identities. In a small way, the research in which we engaged enabled hope to arise for Robert, for myself, and between ourselves. Our hope was not only that Robert would somehow magically get better, but also a hope for a community that would accept and honor difference rather than marginalize individuals. As Robert said at the end:

> I'm not interested in any great legacy. I'd like people who knew me to remember me with pleasant thoughts. I want a grave marker—I've said that much—so I can't say I'm totally unconcerned about how people think of me. I know my situation is hopeless, that I don't have long. I don't hope for long-term recovery, but I haven't given up. Do you understand? It's more an acceptance of who I am. I guess that's what I've been thinking and feeling. That's where I'm at. I don't sob and cry because I don't think it's right. I don't have the right. I don't have any regrets. I've lived a good life. AIDS has made me think of me. I'm proud of who I am, who I've been. Gay. Native American. Poor. I'm Robert Sunchild.

References

Burbules, N., and Rice, S. (1991). Dialogue across differences: Continuing the conversation. *Harvard Educational Review* 61 (4): 393–416.

Crapanzano, V. (1977). On the writing of ethnography. *Dialectical Anthropology* 2 (1): 69–73.

Crapanzano, V. (1980). *Tuhami, portrait of a Moroccan.* Chicago: Univ. of Chicago Press.

Dwyer, K. (1977). On the dialogic of field work. *Dialectical Anthropology* 2 (2): 143–151.

Dwyer, K. (1982). *Moroccan dialogues: Anthropology in question*. Baltimore: Johns Hopkins Univ. Press.

Foucault, M. (1980). *Power/knowledge: Selected interviews and other writings 1971–1977*. New York: Pantheon.

Geertz, C. (1988). *Works and lives: The anthropologist as author*. Stanford, CA: Stanford Univ. Press.

Gergen, K. (1991). *The saturated self: Dilemmas of identity in contemporary life*. New York: Basic Books.

Giroux, H. (1988a). Border pedagogy in the age of postmodernism. *Journal of Education* 170 (3): 162–81.

Giroux, H. (1988b). *Teachers as intellectuals: Toward a critical pedagogy of learning*. South Hadley, MA: Bergin & Garvey.

Giroux, H. (1990). The politics of postmodernism. *Journal of Urban and Cultural Studies* 1 (1): 5–38.

Gitlin, A. (1989). The politics of method: From leftist ethnography to educative research. *Qualitative Studies in Education* 2 (3): 237–53.

Gitlin, A. (1990). Educative research, voice, and school change. *Harvard Educational Review* 60 (4): 443–66.

Gitlin, A., Siegel, M., and Boru, K. (1989). The politics of method: From leftist ethnography to educative research. *Qualitative Studies in Education* 2 (3): 237–53.

hooks, b. (1990). *Yearning: Race, gender and cultural politics*. Boston: South End.

Langness, L., and Frank, G. (1978). Fact, fiction and the ethnographic novel. *Anthropology and Humanism Quarterly* 3: 18–22.

Lather, P. (1986a). Issues of validity in openly ideological research: Between a rock and a soft place. *Interchange* 17 (4): 63–84.

Lather, P. (1986b). Research as praxis. *Harvard Educational Review* 56 (3): 257–77.

Lincoln, Y. S., and Guba, E. G. (1985). *Naturalistic inquiry*. Beverly Hills, CA: Sage.

LeCompte, M. D., and Goetz, J. P. (1982). Problems of reliability and validity in ethnographic research. *Review of Educational Research* 52 (1): 31–60.

Little, K. (1980). Explanation and individual lives: A reconsideration of life writing in anthropology. *Dialectical Anthropology* 5 (3): 215–26.

Mouffe, C. (1990). Radical democracy or liberal democracy? *Socialist Review* 2 (90/2): 57–66.

Noddings, N. (1986). *Caring: A feminine approach to ethics and moral education*. Berkeley: Univ. of California Press.

Rabinow, P. (1977). *Reflections on fieldwork*. Berkeley: Univ. of California Press.

Rabinow, P. (1985). Discourse and power: On the limits of ethnographic texts. *Dialectical Anthropology* 10 (1–2): 1–13.

Rorty, R. (1990). *Contingency, irony, and solidarity.* Cambridge, MA: Cambridge Univ. Press.

Rosaldo, R. (1989). *Culture and truth: The remaking of social analysis.* Boston: Beacon.

Simon, R., and Dippo, D. (1986). On critical ethnographic work. *Anthropology and Education Quarterly* 17 (4): 195–202.

Tierney, W. G. (1989). *Curricular landscapes, democratic vistas: Transformative leadership in higher education.* New York: Praeger.

Tierney, W. G. (1992). *Official encouragement, institutional discouragement: Minorities in academe—The Native American experience.* Norwood, NJ: Ablex.

Tierney, W. G. (1993). Self and identity in a postmodern world: A life story. In D. McLaughlin and W. G. Tierney, eds., *Naming silenced lives.* New York: Routledge.

Tierney, W. G. (ed.). (1991). *Culture and ideology in higher education: Advancing a critical agenda.* New York: Praeger.

Tierney, W. G., and Rhoads, R. (1993). Postmodernism and critical theory in higher education. In J. Smart, ed., *Higher education: Handbook of theory and research.* New York: Agathon.

Tronto, J. (1989). Women and caring. In A. Jaggar and S. Bordo, eds., *Gender/Body/Knowledge,* 172–87. New Brunswick, NJ: Rutgers Univ. Press.

Van Maanen, J. (1988). *Tales of the field: On writing ethnography.* Chicago: Univ. of Chicago Press.

Weiler, K. (1988). *Women teaching for change: Gender, class & power.* South Hadley, MA: Bergin & Garvey.

Williams, W. (1992). *The spirit and the flesh.* Boston: Beacon.

RED RIBBONS AT THE CRACKER BARREL
(RESPONSE)

Roger Platizky

Three years ago at a Popular Culture Conference in St. Louis, Missouri, I heard John Leo, an openly gay professor of English at the University of Rhode Island, deliver a paper that contrasted the more moderate and militant strategies, respectively, of the AIDS quilt makers and gay activist groups like Queer Nation and Act Up. In divergent yet complementary ways, these groups have drawn national attention to our gay oppressed minority in America, the land supposedly of the free. The quilters primarily focus on the tragedy of AIDS in a compassionate way—their archetype being the Healer—and make public the "common threads" of this disease in an attempt to awaken social conscience and to promote solidarity in the fight against AIDS. Gay activist groups on the other hand—their archetype being the Warrior—combat heterosexism directly by refusing to be silenced, ghettoized, and victimized by an ideology in this country that brands difference as sinful, unnatural, and illegal. As different in tenor as Martin Luther King was ostensibly to Malcolm X and the Black Panthers, both groups continue to serve the purpose of questioning or directly challenging and disrupting the status quo: the quilters meeting with less overall resistance (but also, arguably, slower progress) than the more iconoclastic activists who demand freedom of voice, space, and justice under the law.

In a somewhat similar way, the thematic pairing of the essays by Glorianne Leck and William Tierney offers antiphonal yet interrelated ideological responses to the institutionalized silencing of gay voices in academia and society. Posing different solutions to the problem of marginality in a postmodern world, both authors see the need to revise methods of research in education and ethnography to make them more interactive and inclusive. Both authors also discredit traditional, positivist methods of research as being invalidly essentialistic, outmoded, and politically repressive of disenfranchised groups like gays or lesbians.

Tierney's essay, an admittedly elegiac tribute to a Native American friend and colleague, Robert Sunchild, who died of AIDS in 1991, is a quilt made of postmodern cloth, the pattern of which includes a diversity of communities—the marginalized and the re-educated mainstream—in what the author believes can be a potential, if difficult, dialogue of hope, caring, and collective healing.

Leck's essay, more radical in ideological positioning and playfully transgressive in tone, deconstructs traditional, "scientized" forms of ethnography in recounting a political sit-in at a Cracker Barrel restaurant by members of Queer Nation, including the author in her roles as scribe, "teacher-as-stranger," and "disruptive outsider." In part, Leck's experimental essay is a wake-up call to heterosexist employers who would actively discriminate against gay, lesbian, and bisexual employees. The essay also poses a challenge to academics who replicate hegemonic norms of racism, sexism, classism, and heterosexism in schools through politically repressive educational methods that not only alienate minorities but also devalue the multivocal search for truth.

Having myself recently lost several friends to AIDS, having taught the stories of survivors in my AIDS and Literature class, and being gay in a predominantly heterosexual society, I was instinctively moved by Tierney's stirring tribute to his friend, Robert, who had died of AIDS while they were coauthoring his memoirs. Like a quilter who is saddened but also empowered and enriched spiritually by so commemorating the life of someone he has lost, with a quilt panel, Tierney interweaves his essay with Robert's voice, his reflections, his presence. In elegiac fashion, the essay begins and ends with Robert's words, and the despair of losing a friend to AIDS is transformed into hope as both the researcher and subject are given voice by the written word and the lasting impression that Robert's story and Tierney's retelling of it will have on the reader. As a reader of this story who believes that men can be more nurturing than society prescribes or often allows, I was impressed by the compassion Tierney shows in regarding Robert not as a subject to be interrogated scientifically but as an individual to be respected, protected, and empowered by an I/thou relationship between researcher and his subject.

Tierney, who argues that postmodern research must not be static and detached but interactive and transformative both for individuals and communities, describes how both his life and Robert's were altered and enriched by their collaboration. Robert, who had been generally closeted both about having AIDS and being gay in academia, would finally be allowed to "speak" openly, unfearfully, and deeply about what it meant for him to be a Native American gay man with AIDS in a country that discriminates against Native Americans, gay men, and people with AIDS. For Tierney, the transformation was personal as well as philosophical and professional. Although scientific purists (especially heterosexual ones) might raise more than one eyebrow at the kind of professional intimacy Robert and Tierney developed in their collaboration, Tierney sees himself as having been humanized as a result of his encounter with Robert: both men could learn more about and from each other because both were gay. Furthermore, Tierney cared enough about his friend's welfare to adjust the method of his research when Robert's illness made adhering to a regular schedule impossible and when Robert chose to set boundaries for the kinds of questions he wanted to answer. Acknowledging his change in methodology, Tierney says, "My work with [Robert] would have been immensely different ten years ago when I would have been more reticent to discuss his sexual orientation and less willing to let the 'subject' drive the research process."

The benefits in this change of methodology—from the more impersonal to the more interactive and mutually respectful—are apparent:

> In a small way, the research in which we engaged enabled hope to arise for Robert, for myself, and between ourselves. Our hope was not only that Robert would somehow magically get better, but also a hope for a community that would accept and honor difference rather than marginalize individuals.

Based on his experience with working with Robert, Tierney offers a possible model, though not a paradigm, of how postmodern ethnographers might revise their research methods so that there is more intersubjectivity and praxis. As an English teacher and a pluralist, I was especially interested in two facets of Tierney's theory: (1) his idea that researchers should "move toward a literary stance in our work instead of a scientific one," and (2) his belief that researchers should not simply write about inequality in society but "actively work for care and change."

According to Tierney, the move toward a literary stance in research would entail living with the people studied and trying to achieve empathy with them rather than struggling "for neutrality." Since much of literature is imagined rather than actually experienced, and many plots, conflicts, and themes are reconstituted rather than original in fiction, I believe Tierney may be referring more to elegies, memoirs, chronicles, and biographies in his appeal to a more "literary stance" in ethnographies, especially since his story about Robert has something in common with these genres. Tierney's appeal seems less radical later in the essay where he asserts that research needs to be empirically based and "data driven," not just a series of personal reflections. Still, while reading the story about Robert, I could not help but be curious about what literary works may have influenced Tierney in his tribute to Robert. Paul Monette's work came to mind, and I also recalled part of Michael Klein's introduction to *Poets for Life: Seventy-Six Poets Respond to AIDS:*[1]

> As it has diminished community after community, AIDS has also strangely united us. As it has summoned still more fear and uncer-

tainty in the way we live, AIDS has revealed more courage and understanding about how we affect each other. . . . AIDS has forced us into a firmer embrace of our lives.

Furthermore, when Tierney mentions that Robert had sent him an original poem he had written from his tribal reservation a few weeks before he died, I was interested in reading the poem not only because it would have made an interesting extratextual, cultural artifact but also because Robert may have also been comforted in his journey by literature—both by what was written about him and by what he read and wrote himself, especially during his time of crisis.

Perhaps what I value most in the solution section of Tierney's essay is his argument for praxis, for far too often postmodern writing does not get beyond intellectual wordplay and theoretical meditation. Tierney believes researchers should not just write about marginalized people but also should actively promote cultural change, which he is trying to do at Penn State by educating administrators about AIDS and by helping to write policy. While achieving this form of praxis might not be easy for teachers—particularly untenured ones—who already have many demands made on their energy and time, being content to reside in ivory towers is counterproductive to the transformative kind of education Tierney espouses. Differing with those theorists who only see a world in which "individuals live within their own microrealities" with no possibility of a common language to unite them, Tierney envisions a community in which "agreement, commonality, and fellowship" can be achieved. Although a feminist might rightly balk at the word "fellowship," Tierney also states that the kind of research he did with Robert and the social concern it reflects could be replicated in ethnographies of other marginal groups, including lesbians, African Americans, and the disabled. Since all of these groups are now being affected directly by AIDS, the implications of Tierney's personal tribute to Robert Sunchild extend to the wider "communities of difference," where there is also the great need "to understand the 'other's possibility.' "

Despite its subversive gay content, Tierney's essay is formally organized with clearly set definitional assumptions, developed examples, manageable thesis boundaries, lucid transitions, an accommodating argument, and a balance of ethos, pathos, and logos. In contrast, Leck's essay resembles what she calls a "wild interpretive dance." From the first page of her work, in which she invites the reader who is bored with "patriarchal academic discussion" to go directly to the "action" section on the Queer Nation sit-in at the Cracker Barrel restaurant, Leck shapes her experimental essay like an asymmetrical haircut and guides her nonlinear argument like a butterfly's flight that resists being pinned down to any one authoritative set of assumptions. She also resists being classified according to any one perception of identity. As with a quick-change artist, her role as the lesbian activist at the Queer Nation sit-in—the one with the "Every Dyke's a Hero" tee shirt— suddenly transforms into the person who has "a large part of her identity connected to other ways of identifying, which at times makes my lesbian identity invisible (in what may be positive or negative ways)." While personal identity is relatively stable in Tierney's essay—Robert is always a gay Native American male with AIDS—and the argument for revising ethnography is authoritative and even prescriptive in places, the most frequently repeated words in Leck's essay—"perhaps," "seemed," "appeared," "might"—emphasize that what Leck calls her "queer ramblings" are speculative and playful in nonessentialist ways.

Finally, whereas Tierney believes that ethnographies should be transformative in ways that bring communities of difference together in a potentially healing form of dialogue, Leck, more ostensibly a separatist, does not appear to share confidence in a collectivist solution (or praxis) that will bring communities together, although she does seem to be searching for ways to give more voice, visibility, and power to marginalized groups:

> I don't know and can't with any confidence make the claim . . . that educating someone to value diversity and to respect its place in public is of some particular benefit for them. Perhaps it just makes more sense to me. Perhaps it makes me feel I'm doing something to contribute to a reduction of intergroup intolerance and violence. Perhaps for now it suits my political purpose.

Despite what seems to be the tentativeness, uncommittedness, evasiveness, and circularity of Leck's argument—the wild formlessness of her "dance"— the iconoclastic, transgressive, irreverent, and antiphallogocentric style of her experimental essay disrupts the normative "rhythm" of ethnographic discourse (the positivist and scientific "rhythm") with the energy of an Act Up break-in at St. Patrick's Cathedral, or a Queer Nation sit-in at a Cracker Barrel restaurant. In her vivid description of the Cracker Barrel sit-in, Leck paradoxically makes two seemingly opposed but interrelated points about (1) how absurdly generalized essentialist ethnographies can become and (2) how politically forceful and, perhaps, even educational a revised ethnography can be when the perspective of the minority ("Queers") is suddenly privileged over that of the heterosexist norm in even momentarily disruptive ways.

In introducing the sit-in at Cracker Barrel, Leck initially makes the disclaimer that she will be using the incident to show "in some helpful and interesting way the absurdity of the traditional (essentialist) way of addressing generalization as an act with meaning embedded in some modernist claim for rationality." Keeping this caveat in mind, one can read the Cracker

Barrel incident deconstructively as a theatrical spectacle, complete with costumes, in which the roles of the heroes ("Queers") and villains (Cracker Barrel Christians, southern Eurocentrists) have been assigned by a supposedly objective scribe who cannot get beyond the subjectivity of turning every tee shirt saying, menu offering, gift-shop souvenir, or even rocking chair into an instant symbol of a heterosexist, oppressive culture. No one asks the patrons whether they are in the Cracker Barrel just to get a quick meal or whether they are knowingly supporting the restaurant's homophobic policies. No one seems to be the least concerned about the stories of the gay, lesbian, and bisexual employees who actually lost their jobs. What we get, instead, is a We/They binary opposition between the Queer avengers and the Cracker Barrel bigoted bullies—an essentialist description masquerading as an objective ethnography. The only difference—and it is a key difference—is that the ones usually observed and judged have become observers and judges and, through this political repositioning, have moved from the margins into the text.

Politically, the effect of this repositioning is somewhat like what happens when an African-American comedian suddenly launches into a series of anti-White racist jokes before a White paying audience. In both cases, to quote Leck, the majority's power, identities, and "definitions of public [are] challenged and momentarily impaired." For gay and lesbian readers, I believe the political force of Leck's description of the sit-in will be directed at the way the Queer Nation activists, even from the nonsmoking section of the restaurant, turn the tables on the Cracker Barrel operatives by temporarily reclaiming the public space, voice, and visibility denied to lesbian, gay, and bisexual employees who were fired there. Despite her philosophical objections to essentialism (if she contradicts herself, so she contradicts herself), Leck, in her "Every Dyke's a Hero" tee shirt, also appears to be empowered at the sit-in:

> And inside that tee shirt was a person trying to feel like a hero, a beautiful swan instead of an ugly duckling, for claiming her lifelong identity and not hiding as a victim in fear of further rejection from that heterosexist condemnation of sexual difference and diversity in orientation.

Leck also considers the educational possibilities of such demonstrations:

> This interaction of activities constituted what was for me an educational effort that could conceivably serve to construct a shared sense of an appropriate reality that would embrace "dykes" and "fags" as humans with a right to exist in public and to be considered, as we are, part of an effort to be allowed our pursuit of life,

liberty, and happiness, but not within the definitions of institution-alized heterosexist community.

Since Leck compares the political act inside the Cracker Barrel restaurant to the politics of teaching "at Jefferson Elementary School," one might regard both of these "educational" settings as linked by the drive of minorities to make their voices heard either through disruption of places of discrimina-tion—including heterosexist, racist classrooms—or through the creative as-sertion of what should be their intellectual and constitutional rights. Leck, in fact, describes herself as a "teacher as stranger" when she gets a sympathetic couple—the exception rather than the rule—at the Cracker Barrel interested enough in the plight of fired gay employees to speak to the management about their discriminatory policies. Although I find the comparison between "education" at the Cracker Barrel restaurant and the Jefferson Elementary School rather strained—the sit-in was a concerted political action by trained (and transient) adult members of a resistance group—the political climates of both settings can be considered analogous: the gay student in a heterosexist classroom might well feel as alienated as a closeted gay worker in a Cracker Barrel restaurant. Leck's solution to this acculturated problem seems not to be one of a healing, collective dialogue, but one of resistance—"a wild interpretive dance" on a flat dance floor where everybody else is doing the two-step. Like Act Up and Queer Nation activists who march into heterosexual strongholds, whether they be churches or restaurants (or class-rooms?), Leck's position seems to be that change will gradually occur from repeated acts of disruption (be they intellectual or physical) that momentarily challenge and impair the mainstream's right to control public space, public voice, public thought, and public authority while excluding all groups that refuse to conform. Leck believes the time and climate are ripe for change, if we only could learn how to put on and feel free in our new dance shoes: "Dancing need not be done in a ballroom or on even ground."

Although Leck's and Tierney's essays are choreographed differently and pose alternate solutions to problems seen in traditional forms of ethnography and education, both authors are united in a struggle for gay and lesbian scholars to move from the margins to the text, from the closets into the classrooms. Their goal in writing these articles recalls Marlon Riggs's state-ment about the need for lesbian and gay writers to reclaim our power and identities:

> When the existing history and culture do not acknowledge and address you—do not see or talk to you—you must write a new history, shape a new culture that will.[2]

As a gay teacher of literature and writing, I am empowered by essays like the ones by Tierney and Leck. Growing up in a homophobic society without any gay or lesbian role models—or any positive mentionings of gay and lesbian accomplishments in the classroom—I would have felt far less alienated if pro-gay and -lesbian literature were even considered in any of my classrooms. Although one's gay identity is only part of one's social identity, it is an important part that needs to be accepted and integrated for a person to feel whole and safe. That is what I want all the students in my classroom— heterosexual, gay, lesbian, or bisexual—to feel: safe and proud of who they are. Having felt alienated and like an outsider myself for so many years, I do not want to replicate that atmosphere by turning my classroom into bipartisan battlefields or fiefdoms of separatism. Finding a balance in a heterogeneous classroom is, of course, difficult, and pretending that a heterosexist culture does not exist will not work for so many of us who are living proof that it does. Whether one chooses, however, to be a quilter or an activist, a healer or a warrior (or a little of each), should be just that— a choice, contingent on one's temperament, skill, position of power, and philosophy of teaching.

Because I was alienated and mistreated as a result (or consequence) of my sexual orientation as a student and a young adult, I try to do what I can to help my students not feel the same way. At the same time, I try to help them understand that the struggle for identity and integrity may help them become more empathetic and committed to justice in the future. When a student of mine wrote in a narrative that he drank until he passed out because he feared someone in his fraternity would discover he was gay, I filled his paper with supportive comments, recommended books that would help him feel less alone, and encouraged him to speak to me or a counselor as he worked on improving his self-esteem. Although the drinking problem continued until he graduated, I received a letter from him from California about two years ago. He had enclosed six original pro-gay poems—more thanks than any teacher could expect. When a formerly battered student told me her family was verbally chastising her because she had just come out to them as a lesbian, I was glad I could come out to her, tell her where to get help, and watch her smile through tears as I added, "Someone once told me that although you can't choose your family, you can choose your friends." I also encouraged her in her decision to attend the 1993 Pride march in Washington with a small group of friends. When she returned and visited me a week later, she not only brought me enthusiastic stories about "Dykes on Bikes" and other radical groups she had discovered at the march, but also several souvenirs from the march since she knew I had not been able to attend. Thus, in empowering a student, I had also empowered myself. As a teacher of a diversity of students, I also feel the need to support the rights of those that I do not agree with. When a conservative religious student in my AIDS and Literature class was baffled that there are Christian gays and lesbians because she had always been taught that "homosexuals will not be admitted into the Kingdom of Heaven," I tried to control my anger of twenty years of facing homophobia because I realized this is a question raised out of conditioned ignorance, not deliberate malice. To avoid alienating either the conservative religious student or others in my class, I deferred the question to a pro-gay student majoring in religion who was doing her research paper on the MCC (Metropolitan Community Church) (a gay-lesbian Christian church). Because dialogue was encouraged between peers, the conservative religious student left the discussion that day having to rethink her position: she could not simply rest assured that her moral viewpoint was still the only sacred one, which she might have done had I immediately challenged her viewpoint or embarrassed her publicly.

There are times, of course, when I am not as patient, sensitive, courageous, or self-aware as a younger generation of politically more active gay and lesbian students might need me to be. Perhaps this is still part of the damage that was done to me by my not being able for so many years to express or take any pride in who I genuinely was without fear of either personal or professional repercussions. But as I try to put together the puzzle of my life as an educator, I am also becoming more able to see the larger picture of what my role has been and will be as an educator in the future. Perhaps this is something other educators could benefit from doing: trying to fit in without making others in their classes feel as though they did not or should not belong. This is not a matter of political correctness; rather it is a matter of common respect and decency for people who may just have been created in a different image than we were. As the spectre of AIDS equalizes us all, can we really afford not to take a long, hard look at all the pieces of that puzzle, all the dance steps (regardless of whether we approve of the rhythms), and all the people in our classrooms who have a right to feel safe and whole and healthy even as we challenge their value assumptions and visions of truth in the world?

Leck's and Tierney's essays are part of a national push by gay-studies scholars to shape a culture in which gays, lesbians, and bisexuals—regardless of age, class, race, and philosophy—are no longer oppressed, marginalized, and mythified in our supposedly democratic classrooms. Essays like these, which prod us all into interesting new directions of thinking, are, indeed, cultural artifacts for times that are changing. To be sure, there may need to be many more marches in Washington—as there have been in other Civil Rights movements—before gays and lesbians are accepted into the military and protected on the streets or against discrimination in jobs at places like the Cracker Barrel. And there will, doubtless, need to be many other educators who say, yes, there is a rich heritage of gay and lesbian accomplishments that our students need to learn about to be considered educated about art, culture, human struggle, perseverance, and faith. Such knowledge is not only essential for gay and lesbian students and faculty but is also important for heterosexual students and educators, for as Warren Blumenthal writes,

> Homophobia prevents heterosexuals from accepting the benefits and gifts offered by the lesbian, gay, and bisexual communities: theoretical insights, spiritual visions and options, contributions to the arts and culture. . . .[3]

These essays by Tierney and Leck are two such gifts that will help us remove signs of exclusion and hatred from our books, from our buildings, from our blackboards, and, eventually, from our minds.

Notes

1. Michael Klein, *Poets for Life: Seventy-Six Poets Respond to AIDS* (New York: Crown, 1989), 16.
2. Marlon T. Riggs, "Ruminations of a Snap Queen: What Time Is It?" *Outlook* 12 (Spring 1991): 15.
3. Warren Blumenthal, "How Homophobia Hurts Heterosuals," *Empathy* 3 (1992–93): 80.

Cultural

The Power to Know One Thing Is Never the Power to Know All Things: Methodological Notes on Two Studies of Black American Teachers

Michèle Foster

In a 1988 novel by Gloria Naylor, a well-educated young man known only as "Reema's boy" returns home from across the river where he had gone to be educated to conduct research among his own people on Willow Springs, a coastal sea island that, according to Naylor, belonged neither to Georgia nor South Carolina. Armed with notebooks and a tape recorder, the indispensable instruments of an anthropologist, Reema's boy begins questioning relatives and neighbors about a commonly used phrase.

> And when he went around asking about 18 & 23, there weren't nothing to do but take pity on him as he rattled on about "ethnography," "unique speech patterns," "cultural preservation," and whatever else he seemed to be getting so much pleasure out of while talking into his little gray machine. He was all over the place—What 18 & 23 mean? What 18 & 23 mean? And we told him the God-honest truth: it was just our way of saying something. Winky was awful, though, he even spit tobacco juice for him. Sat on his porch all day, chewing up the boy's Red Devil premium and spitting so the machine could pick it up. There was enough fun in that to take us through the fall and winter when he had hauled himself back over The Sound to wherever he was getting what was supposed to be passing for an education. And he sent everybody he'd talked to copies of the book he wrote, bound all nice with our name and his signed on the first page. We couldn't hold Reema down, she was so proud. It's a good thing she didn't read it. None of us made it much through the introduction, but that said it all: you see, he had come to the conclusion after "extensive field work" (ain't never picked a boll of cotton or head of lettuce in his life—Reema spoiled him silly), but he done still made it to the conclusion that 18 & 23 wasn't 18 & 23 at all—was really 81 and 32, which just so happened to be the lines of longitude

and latitude marking off where Willow Springs sits on the map. And we were just so damned dumb that we turned the whole thing around.

Not that he called it being dumb, mind you, called it "asserting our cultural identity," "inverting hostile social and political parameters." 'Cause, see, being we was brought here as slaves, we had no choice but to look at everything upside-down. And then being that we was isolated off here on this island, everybody else in the country went on learning good English and calling things what they really was—in the dictionary and all that—while we kept on calling things ass-backwards. And he thought that was just so wonderful and marvelous, et cetera, et cetera . . . Well, after that crate of books came here, if anybody had any doubts about what them developers were up to, if there was just a tinge of seriousness behind them jokes about the motorboats and swimming pools that could be gotten from selling a piece of land them books squashed it. The people who ran the type of schools that could turn our children into raving lunatics—and then put his picture on the back of the book so we couldn't even deny it was him—didn't mean us a speck of good. (Naylor 1988, 7–8)

For those of us doing research in our own communities, this excerpt from Naylor's novel should serve as a cautionary tale. Increasingly, those undertaking fieldwork and conducting life-history research are insiders, members of the subordinate groups they have chosen to study. Social science reveals a growing trend toward "native anthropology" and other insider research, studies by ethnic minorities of our own communities.

Despite this trend and a large literature on ethnographic and anthropological method that treats the involvement, role, and stance that researchers adopt vis-à-vis the communities they are studying, most of these references— contemporary work as well as that from earlier periods—deal with research conducted among others whether the others are the "natives" in "exotic" communities in United States society or abroad. This is not surprising. Traditionally, anthropologists have studied "the other." Thus, anthropology, even as it has promoted cultural relativity, was conceived and nurtured in a colonial world of haves and have-nots, powerful and powerless, self and other. As the ethnographic method became more commonplace and studies grew to include more complex industrial and postindustrial societies like the United States, the power relationship between researcher and researched remained unaltered. For the most part, this research has also been dichotomized, with the self studying the other, the powerful the powerless, the haves the have-nots. However, a distinctive hallmark of the newer literature in ethnographic theory and method, including recent work in education, is its self–conscious examination of the subjective nature of the research endeavor.

Presently it is widely acknowledged that all researchers are influenced by their particular perspectives. But what about the perspectives of ethnic minorities? In what ways do our experiences inform our research endeavors? Many of us are first socialized into the values, norms, and communication standards of our home communities and later, after many years of education, into those of the mainstream culture. Moreover, the subordinate position assigned to our communities in the American social order forces us to see ourselves through others' eyes. This means that we are more likely to understand, if only through our own lived experiences, what it means to be marginalized.

Crossing the cultural borders into the mainstream is often fraught with contradictions. In matriculating into the dominant culture, we are instructed in different paradigms, tutored in new world views, and trained in correct "ways of knowing." Years of schooling teach us to rename, recategorize, reclassify, and reconceptualize our experiences. Like the transition to English, the transition to dominant ways of thinking, valuing, and behaving is often complete and one-way. New values implanted, new voices acquired like the fictional character in Naylor's account; or, like the unfictitious Richard Rodriguez (1982), we may have forfeited the ability to communicate appropriately, may have renounced community belief systems, or embraced an ideology no longer in accord with that of our communities.

But these experiences also contain the potential for developing multiple perspectives that can be brought to bear on our research endeavors. Noted Black feminist bell hooks (1984) maintains that including the experiences of those who have lived on margin and in the center not only can enrich contemporary paradigms but can also invigorate progressive movements as well.

This essay is concerned with the problems and the possibilities that obtain when researcher and researched are members of the same cultural and speech community. It is written from the vantage of a Black woman with eight years' experience conducting ethnographic and life-history research in the Black community. Drawing on my personal autobiography as well as on firsthand experiences accumulated in two separate studies as a researcher studying the lives and practices of Black teachers, this chapter examines some of the political conflicts in which I have become entangled, the methodological dilemmas and ethical issues I have grappled with, and the multiple and often conflicting roles I have had to adopt in order to accomplish my research. The goal of this essay is twofold: first, to compare the competing mainstream and Black value systems at work in my own background and which frequently marked the research settings and resulted in political struggles; and second, to demonstrate the positive effect that a shared identity can have on establishing rapport and recovering authentic accounts, but also to illustrate that even members of the same speech and cultural community are differentiated by other equally important characteristics that make the researcher both an insider as well as an outsider.

Problem, Theory, and Method

A review of the sociological, anthropological, and first-person literature on teachers convinced me that African-American teachers had largely been ignored by the literature; where they had been portrayed, except in a few instances, it had generally been in a negative not a positive light. Most of the negative portrayals of African Americans were written by outsiders and at a time when the rhetoric of equal opportunity made attacks on segregated schools with all their attendant shortcomings, including Black teachers, legitimate targets. These findings seemed to endorse DuBois's comment (1945) that because the fates of Black teachers have been so entangled with the maintenance of segregated schools for Black pupils, it has been difficult to attack segregated schools and at the same time to commend and respect Black teachers.

To my surprise, when Blacks wrote about Black teachers, their descriptions were considerably more flattering and well balanced than those penned by Whites. Finally, though I found several historical accounts that chronicled the fight undertaken by the Black community to secure Black teachers for its children, accounts written by Black teachers themselves, either historic or contemporary, are relatively rare.

The preponderance of negative portrayals of Black teachers written by outsiders, the contrasting more flattering and well-balanced insider descriptions, and the paucity of Black teachers telling their own stories convinced me of the need to augment the literature of Black teachers speaking in their own voices. Voice is a multifaceted concept. On one hand, it may be understood simply as words; on the other the concept of voice can extend beyond mere words to include perspectives and particular orientations. Consequently in developing my research strategy, I had to deal with several other issues—the choice of subjects, the definition of the problem, the source of the analytic categories employed, and the appropriateness of theories applied to interpreting the words—all essential to the concept of voice.

My first consideration was developing a process that would enable me to study those Black teachers whose practice could typify what the Black community thought best about its teachers. To this end, I developed "community nomination," a term and method of selecting the teachers designed specifically for this study. Community nomination builds on the concept of "native anthropology" developed by Jones (1970) and Gwaltney (1980, Gwaltney, 1981) in order to gain what anthropologists call an "emic" perspective, an insider's view—in this case the Black community's perspective of a good teacher. Teachers selected by this method were chosen though direct contact with Black communities. African-American periodicals, organizations, institutions, and individuals provided the names of the teachers.

Another consideration was deciding among the various theoretical orientations. My graduate training had been in the traditions of phenomenology, African-American anthropology and sociolinguistics, and the related field (ethnography) of speaking. Each of these perspectives and a more recent interest in critical theory influenced my understanding and approach to the topic. At the same time, I was mindful of hooks's (1984) caution that just because individuals are unable to articulate a particular position is not evidence per se of their never having embraced it. Her admonition, coupled with my own desire to preserve the authenticity and integrity of the teachers' experience, inclined me to search for explanations that would enable me to meld their interpretations with the theories that guided my work.

Researcher as Subject

The process of the research as well as the subjective experiences of the researcher are currently the subject of intense debate (Peshkin 1988; Lather 1991). In my case, these are important considerations. In a number of respects, my experiences are not unlike those of the teachers whose lives and practices form the basis of my inquiries. Like them I have been a teacher for most of my professional life. And though younger than some, what we all have in common is having belonged to the generations that came of age during the period when separate but equal was a controlling principle of American society.

It was within my family and local community that I learned my first lessons about simultaneously being an insider and an outsider. My family also made sure that I understood the need for individual and collective struggle against the structures of racism. Being both an insider and outsider in the small, predominantly White, New England community where my family had lived since 1857 necessitated not only that I understand mainstream Anglo values but also become proficient in its norms and behavior. It was not only household and community circumstances that dictated these lessons but also my family's expressed desire for me to prepare myself to take advantage of the improved opportunities for Blacks they believed were on the horizon. At the same time, however, my family wanted me to have a strong racial identity, to feel at ease and be a part of the Black community in which we spent the most significant portion of our social lives. Consequently, they expected me to recognize when the values of the separate but overlapping community were at odds and, depending on the context, to demonstrate appropriate behavior. Whether taught explicitly by pointing out where specific transgressions had occurred or more indirectly through family stories, the training was unambiguous and the lessons to be learned unequivocal. For instance, because of my early school success and the prospect of a favorable future in academic pursuits, my mother made sure I internalized the lesson that, while scholarly pursuits were important, they were not more important nor were they to override competence in social interaction. One could never retreat to solitary activities if others desired social interaction; to do so was considered rude and self-centered. Another lesson drilled into me was the community prohibition against self-aggrandizement, a behavior commonly associated with the White community, which my family scorned. It was not uncommon to hear the sarcastic retort "That's damn White of you" addressed to someone for calling attention to some act that was generally expected of them. Correspondingly, it was not unusual for a person who had been complimented for some personal achievement to minimize its importance by responding that "White folks raised me."

In order to establish the fact that our family was both insider and outsider, and to reinforce a responsibility to fight any injustice, my grandmother told many stories. One of her favorites described an incident that occurred when my uncle was a teenager. While walking with friends on the way home from school one day, he was verbally attacked by a group of out of towners, who were in town to work on a construction project. A person who rarely tolerated insults of any kind, my grandmother insisted that the town fathers take action. The mayor, along with other city officials, responded by demanding that the crew leave town "by sundown." Outsiders, they insisted, could not harass any of the townspeople.

While this story can be read as an acknowledgement of my family's insider status, my grandmother told others that it highlighted the family's standing as outsiders. In one story, my grandmother recalled the fierce battle she had undertaken to ensure that my mother and uncle were placed in the high school's college preparatory program instead of the vocational track deemed more suitable to the employment prospects for Negroes. Accompanying my grandmother's stories were my grandfather's anecdotes of his early involvement in founding the Brotherhood of Sleeping Car Porters, one of the first unions to wage a collective struggle for fair treatment of Black workers.

While the perception of limited opportunity can result in developing an oppositional frame of reference with respect to academic achievement (Ogbu 1988; Ogbu 1989; Ogbu 1991) or in developing a raceless persona in order to achieve academically (Fordham 1988), my family's response to limited opportunity was to excel in spite of the limitations and to maintain strong cultural and political affiliations and ties to the Black community in the process. In other words, my family strove to make sure that I would develop what DuBois (1903) referred to as a double consciousness, an awareness of who I was and what I was capable of achieving regardless of the prevailing beliefs of society.

Unwittingly, with its explicit teaching and unambiguous expectations, my Catholic schooling bolstered my family's teaching. Not until college—the locus of my initial socialization into the bourgeois tradition of academia and the culture of the academy, a process that continued in graduate school—did the ambiguities become prominent. Attending a college with fewer than thirty Black students and living away from the confines of family and community obscured the separation between the two worlds. Concomitantly, the coaching that had previously been available about how to negotiate both worlds became more sporadic and less explicit.

After completing college and relocating to Roxbury, Boston's Black community, I began a twenty-year career as a professional educator. Several years as a substitute teacher in the Boston public schools (where, prior to desegregation Black teachers were unilaterally assigned to de facto segregated schools) and a subsequent position as a director of METCO (a voluntary urban-suburban desegregation program that bused Black students to predominantly White suburban school districts) cast me into the role of outsider once more. Most of the substitutes assigned to all-Black schools found it difficult if not impossible to teach in them. Like the students they served, these schools were considered undesirable. Consequently, the students in the schools to which I was assigned typically saw a procession of substitutes, many who endured only one day, others who vanished by recess. Unlike these substitutes, by revisiting and recovering the belief systems, values, and behaviors learned in my childhood, I not only survived but thrived in these schools.

One of my major responsibilities as a METCO director was serving as a cultural broker, which primarily entailed simultaneously interpreting between White suburban teachers and urban Black students. One task was helping White teachers, many of whom were considered effective with White students and appeared to encounter few serious difficulties teaching them, learn how to interact successfully with Black students participating in the METCO program. This task was matched only by the equally difficult one of trying to convince the Black students that they should cooperate with their teachers. My efforts at cultural brokering were only partially successful. Although teachers and students gradually expanded the meanings they attached to specific behaviors, rarely did these expanded interpretations produce any adjustments in their behavior.

Returning to graduate school, I resumed my struggle with the culture of the academy. One of my principal frustrations was the lack of fit between my experiences and the germinal theories being taught in graduate school. African-American conceptions, values, or belief systems rarely figured into analyses or solutions. My insights into characteristics that differentiated the Black and White communities had no forum in the graduate school classroom, nor did the considerable personal information I had accumulated about how to teach Black students. Consequently, I was left alone to try to reconcile what I was learning in graduate school with my own lived experiences. In her forthright discussion about the formulation and distribution of a particular perspective as if it were universal, Smith (1987) writes:

> The forms of thought we make use of to think about ourselves and our society are part of the relations of ruling and hence originate in positions of power. These positions are occupied by men almost exclusively, which means that our forms of thought put together a view of the world from a place women do not occupy. The means that women have had available to them to think, imagine and make actionable their experience have been made for us and not by us. It means that our experience has not been represented in the making of our culture. There is a gap between where we are and the means we have to express and act. It means that our concerns, interests and experiences forming "our" culture are those of men in positions of dominance whose perspectives are built on the silence of women (and of others). As a result the perspectives, concerns, interests of only one sex and one class are directly and actively involved in producing, debating, and developing its ideas, in creating its art, in forming its medical and psychological conceptions, in framing its laws, its political principles, its educational values and objectives. (19–20)

Though in this passage Smith is referring to the absence of women in the construction of the culture, her words apply to the experiences of other subordinate groups as well. Her words represent the voicelessness I felt in graduate school, where faculty strove to ground me in the particular understandings and knowledge that they assumed were generalizable to everyone, a phenomenon that others have described (Murrell 1991). Despite my determination to maintain my racial identity and cultural behaviors, the faculty also undertook with the assistance of my peers to indoctrinate me into a distinctive mind set and, by altering my manner and deportment, to align my behavior more closely with that expected of academics. As typifies the middle class, the power exerted in the academy was hidden, concealed from view (Delpit 1988).

Regardless of academic potential, failure to conform to middle-class norms exacts severe penalties, including exclusion from the "star system," a process whereby early in their graduate education particular individuals are marked for distinguished achievements. Admission into the star system depends principally on the level of comfort and familiarity potential stars communicate to their sponsors, and only secondarily on talent and persistence (Carter 1991). Denied admission to the star system cast me once again into the role of outsider.

The Studies

As mentioned earlier, this chapter draws on my own experiences conducting research in two separate studies on the lives and practices of Black teachers. While both studies are similar with respect to subject matter, there were important differences pertaining to methodology and context. In the first one, I undertook a study of the practice of one Black teacher, whom students had consistently rated as an "ideal type." The dominant approach to gathering data was ethnography—principally sociolinguistic behavior—with only a secondary focus on life history. As I reviewed the notes from informal conversations and the transcripts of the more formal interviews undertaken with this teacher, it became increasingly apparent the extent to which the teacher's philosophy of teaching and her pedagogy had been influenced by and was grounded in her social and cultural experiences in the Black community. Interested in comparing this teacher to others, I expanded my research to include a larger, more geographically diverse and age-stratified group. In this way, the second research project, a life-history study of Black teachers, grew out of the first. While this decision moved me beyond the idiosyncratic nature of a single case study, it shifted the primary focus of investigation from behavioral and sociolinguistic data to information collected in face-to-face interviews. Thus while the subject matter in both studies was similar, the primary method of data collection in the first study emphasized observation over interviews and the second study emphasized interviews, with observations playing only a secondary role. Using Goodson's (1988) analysis of studies of teachers, it is possible to characterize my two studies as emphasizing varying degrees of focus on the "song" or the "singer." Since the research context was a critical variable that both influenced the course of my research and shaped my relationships with the teachers, the next section characterizes the settings.

Setting I: Regents Community College

I undertook the first study at Regents Community College in Massachusetts, a predominantly Black community college in the Northeast, where I had once been on the faculty. It is beyond the scope of this paper to describe in great detail its demographics and setting. A task that is undertaken elsewhere (Foster 1987; Foster 1989). What is important to advancing this chapter is addressing the political situation at the college and providing a brief explanation of the two competing value systems that were at work there.

Founded in 1973 during a period of considerable community activism, the College was the fifteenth community college to be charted by the State Board of Regents. Its founders envisioned it as a Black college with a unique mission: to serve the underprepared students from the local Black community, a task which the other community colleges had neglected. From its inception, Regents was plagued by a series of problems, a succession of presidents and administrators, three temporary sites, high turnover rates among faculty, and, most important, a marked tension between Black and White faculty over the best way to educate its students.

Most often these conflicts arose because Black and White faculty held different ideas about what were appropriate goals for students. In an example from the college's early history, a group of Black faculty, seeking to establish a comprehensive writing program, forced the English department chair, a White woman, to resign for her comment that "their [Black students] was quaint and shouldn't be changed." Although some Black faculty conceded that the chair's comments could have indicated an acceptance and valuing of Black students' language, they were outraged by her suggestion that the Black students did not need to command standard American written English. In a controversial essay, Delpit (1988) provides a detailed analysis and clarification of both points of this controversy.

At the time of my study, an external grant whose overarching goal was to improve teaching and learning, but which was specifically designed "to train teachers to understand students' use of language and other culturally learned behaviors," was underway at Regents. Through a set of training sessions, workshops, and discussions led by experts, the project aimed to introduce the participants to anthropological research techniques through which they might learn how their students as well as they themselves behaved and used language in and outside the classroom. Because I was Black and knowledgeable about the issues the project sought to address, its director, a White woman, had enlisted my support. And although an outsider at the time, the director was aware many faculty still perceived me as an insider.

During the year that the project was begun the tensions between Black and White faculty reached a boiling point. Many Black faculty members were irritated because they believed White faculty were gaining too much power in the college. Two factors—subtle changes taking place in faculty composition and changes in the faculty leadership—lent support to their perception. Though the absolute number of Black faculty had remained constant, over the two preceding years the percentage of Black faculty had dropped from 38 to 33. The fact that the faculties at the other community colleges in the state were overwhelmingly White made the increasing numbers of White faculty at Regents an especially sore point among Black faculty.

At the same time two organizations—the Faculty Union and the Faculty Assembly, part of the college's governance structure—were scheduled to merge. Historically there has been a division of power based on race with respect to faculty leadership. Almost without exception, the Faculty Union leadership had been White and the Faculty Assembly leadership Black. Prior to the merger, the faculty had participated sporadically and rather unsuccessfully in both organizations. For some, then, merging the two organizations seemed a logical solution in a college where faculty were already overburdened. For others, however, the merger represented another attempt by White faculty to dominate the college. All of these factors coupled with the fact that all except one of the project trainers was White fueled the discontent of the Black faculty. Taken together, these facts suggested, if not a diminishing role for Blacks, an increasing one for Whites. The result was that the project became the flashpoint for increased hostilities between White and Black faculty.

From the beginning, the project was embroiled in controversy, the faculty divided over its merits. Faculty, both Black and White, gave similar reasons for refusing to participate. The reasons ranged from the irrelevancy of anthropology over politics in determining power relations and thus education, to the belief that class content—the subject matter taught—was more critical than the process used to teach it. But, for Black faculty especially, the project became entangled in the larger political issues that gripped the campus.

In order to accomplish the project, a series of workshops and seminars was undertaken with the expectation that the faculty would modify their classroom practices. Although fifty faculty, staff, and administrators participated in at least one of the activities, and while a fourth of these participants were African American, the large majority of those who actively participated and all of those that undertook major curricular changes were White.

Consequently, despite the fact that the project's stated goal was improving the education students received and involving faculty in curricular reform by providing release time—goals that the majority of Black faculty deemed inherently worthwhile—many were overtly hostile to the project and its director.

From the beginning the director was on the defensive. One of the first people to challenge the project was Ms. Morris, the teacher I was studying, who demanded that the director explain how "the study of primitive people"—the definition of ethnography she had read in the dictionary—had anything to with teaching Black students. Other Black faculty questioned what Whites could tell them about their own language and culture, which they believed they shared with the students.

Initially I tried to encourage Black faculty participation. Trying to persuade some Black faculty who were not involved in the project to reap some of its benefits became a personal goal. But despite my efforts, Black faculty remained distant. Part of the problem stemmed from the different value systems that were manifest in different styles of communication, which could be detected in the different patterns of interaction and which reflected the typical patterns for Black and White faculty. One of the major differences was Ms. Morris's use of more official channels as contrasted with my dependence on the more informal networks at the college. Although specific rules controlled routine tasks like xeroxing, securing library materials, and other bureaucratic matters, following the guidelines did not guarantee that tasks would be completed. The prevailing but unofficial culture of the school dictated using informal channels to get the tasks accomplished. Related to this was the director's tendency to avoid confrontation, which she did by conducting most of her communication, whether official or personal, by written channels. In contrast, the preferred style of African-American faculty, also my own, was to confront problems as they arose using written correspondence only to arrange face-to-face meetings. Despite the frustration, inconvenience, and roadblocks they faced in getting tasks accomplished and engaging in fruitful interactions, for the most part White faculty declined to take up unfamiliar ways of behaving. Ultimately, the escalating conflict within the project, a microcosm of that extant in the larger college, threatened to jeopardize my relationships with Black faculty and to derail and compromise my study, so I severed my affiliation with the project.

The irony of this project was that while faculty were attempting to understand the community-oriented participation of Regents's Black students, they were unable or perhaps unwilling to recognize the community norms and preferences of Black faculty colleagues. To be sure, the faculty and the researchers associated with the project wanted to understand the effect of cultural diversity on teaching and learning. Unwilling to engage in critical dialogue with Black and other faculty of color, however, they incorrectly assumed they could gain access to this cultural knowledge without seeking authentic renditions of that knowledge.

Setting II: The Construction of Black Teachers' Life Histories

In February of 1988, the active phase of my second research project, a life-history study of Black teachers, began with the interview of my first informant. Unlike the study at Regents, the teachers who participated in this second study resided in many regions of the country. Although all of the teachers I contacted agreed to an interview, there were long periods between initial written contact, subsequent phone conversations, and visits to interview the informants. One of my greatest fears was that when I arrived in an unfamiliar city, the teacher would not be there.

Eager to secure cooperation, but realizing that my informants were being confronted with a complete stranger, I claimed insider status, making sure from the outset to emphasize our shared characteristics in my initial letter and subsequent phone conversations. Whether claiming insider status minimized the social distance and ultimately influenced the informants' decision to participate is unclear. Most were flattered to have been selected to be interviewed; only once was an interview refused and then because of illness. John Gwaltney (1980), an African-American anthropologist who conducted a major life-history study of African Americans, discussed the willingness of his narrators who knew he was a "native" to assist him with his life-history project. My own experiences paralleled those reported by Gwaltney. Without exception, all of the teachers I sought to interview cooperated with my efforts. This generosity was exceptional since all of the arrangements for interviews had been made by letter and telephone.

Arranging and negotiating the details of my interview and visit provided me with some insights regarding the extent to which the teachers accepted my claims of insider status. Two-thirds of the teachers invited me into their homes to conduct interviews, a fact that seemed to acknowledge my claims of insider status. A few picked me up at my hotel, some had their friends drive me to the airport, and at least one insisted that I sleep in a spare bedroom rather than waste money on a hotel. In these informal settings, I interacted with the participants and their families, frequently accompanying and participating with them in activities within their communities. It is possible to interpret these courtesies as mere instances of hospitality; however, in retrospect I believe that they probably served a dual purpose. Watching me interact with family, friends, and other community members allowed them to observe my behavior and assess for themselves whether my claims of insider status were warranted.

My experiences during my first visit with Miss Ruthie illustrate this dual purpose of hospitality and testing that I was subjected to. When I arrived on Pawley's Island, a small community not far from Charleston, South Carolina, I called Miss Ruthie to find out how far my motel was from her house. "Just up the road," she assured me.

"About a mile?" I asked.

"About a mile," she replied.

Not wanting to be late, I set out at 7:30 the next morning to reach her house in time for our 9 o'clock appointment. The walk along the highway toward her house seemed interminable. Only when I arrived and was greeted by the teacher and two of her friends, who laughingly told me that they "didn't expect a city slicker to be able to make it," did I discover that the distance I had walked was over three miles. Once I had passed this initial test, Miss Ruthie and other members of the community were extremely hospitable, though I was mindful of their continuing scrutiny of my behavior.

What I have concluded from this and other encounters is that invitations into their family and community worlds represented an attempt to tip the power balance in their favor.

A third of the participants suggested a more neutral location for the interviews, usually their school, but in some cases my hotel room. Often, but not always, after the initial interviews were over the teachers suggested that the next interview be held at their homes. This happened frequently enough to suggest that these teachers had felt at ease during our first meeting. Whether the interviews took place in homes or a classroom, a meal eaten at home or in a restaurant often preceded the interview.

My claims of insider status notwithstanding, a number of my interviewees were surprised to discover I was Black, claiming that I didn't sound Black over the telephone. Sometimes merely discovering that I was Black modified their expectations of the interview that was to take place. In other cases, teachers seemed genuinely pleased when they saw I was Black. But they gave no overt indication that they expected that our shared background might shape or influence the interview. Ella Jane was one teacher whose expectations were immediately altered when we met. Like all of the other narrators, she had never seen me before we met at her East Texas elementary school at the close of the school day. As soon as she saw I was Black, she excused herself to telephone her husband. When she returned, she explained she had telephoned to tell him she would be later than expected. "As I saw you were Black, I knew the interview was going to be a lot longer than I thought. White folks want to interview you, but they really don't want to hear all that you have to say."

Miss Ruthie, an eighty year old woman who had taught over fifty years in a one-room schoolhouse, had previously spoken with a number of other interviewers. Nonetheless, she was delighted to discover I was Black because as she said, "I've been waiting a long time for somebody Black to come and hear my story."

From my perspective these initial, overt markers of acceptance were insufficient evidence that the conversations were authentic candid versions of my narrators' lives. Therefore, I paid close attention to the ways in which the teachers used language throughout the interviews. Though I did not transcribe the tapes myself, I spent many hours reviewing them because my training in sociolinguistics had taught me that in order to understand completely what was being conveyed I needed to attend to not only what was being said but also the manner in which it was said. Listening to the tapes revealed a consistent pattern. Early in the interviews, the discourse patterns were those of standard English. As the interviews progressed, the language shifted from standard English to include more markers of Black English. There were many morphological, intonational, and discourse features of

Black English later in the interviews, suggesting that my insider status was being negotiated throughout the course of the interviews.

There were other characteristics that separated me from individual narrators, making me an insider and outsider in ways that were intricate and intertwined. I was a northerner when I interviewed southerners, an urban resident when I talked with rural residents, a younger person when I conversed with older teachers, a woman when I interviewed men. Often I was positioned as an outsider on several dimensions simultaneously. These characteristics shaped the interviews in some immediately obvious and less obvious ways. Consider the dimension of generation. Because I had lived through the turbulent time of the 60s, it was easier for me to identify emotionally with the racial struggles of the teachers who came of age during the same period. Conversely, although I had read a lot about the struggles of Blacks during the 20s, 30s, 40s, and 50s, and heard about them from my grandparents who experienced them firsthand, my emotional responses were muted compared to those I'd experienced when interviewing my age mates. This generational disjunction affected my interview with Miss Ruthie, a teacher born at the turn of the century. Throughout her interview she repeated her assertion that during the first and second decades of the twentieth century when she had attended Avery Institute, a private normal school founded by the American Missionary Association, the students regularly put on Shakespeare plays. At first, I missed the significance of her statement. It was only after reviewing the tape several times and hearing her repeat the claim in marked intonation that I understood its importance in her own mind. Not until I had read several books on the education of Blacks in the South, however, did I understand the historical significance of her assertion. What I discovered as I read these accounts was her attempt to convey that she considered the classical and liberal arts education received at Avery Institute to have been a challenge to the social order of the time, schooling that typically consisted of vocational training advocated by Washington and supported by the larger White educational establishment of the time (Anderson 1988). What this experience taught me was that my own outsider status, the result of generational differences, made it difficult for me to perceive easily or appreciate fully the significance of the racial struggles waged by some of the older teachers whose eras I had not experienced.

A comparison of the interviews of men with those of women also provided evidence that the connections that emerged from race were easily overshadowed by those of gender. The interviews with men showed sharply divergent turn-taking patterns compared to those conducted with the women. When I spoke with women, the talk was more conversational. Turn-taking exchanges were more balanced and there were many more instances of overlapping speech to mark comembership. In contrast, in the interviews with men there were considerably fewer occurrences of overlapping speech, and the turn-taking patterns were more asymmetrical, with men speaking for much longer stretches at a time.

The Power to Know

I undertook this research in order to recover part of the cultural knowledge and history of the Black community. By using the personal histories and personal experiences of members of the Black community and framing them in theoretical and conceptual perspectives that gave voice to their realities, it was my hope to contribute to a more complete understanding and empowerment of Black communities and that the work would become part of the collective memory of the Black community as well as part of the scholarship studied within the academy.

Even though there is a substantial and steadily accumulating body of research written by African-American scholars from an African-American perspective, it is too often the case that this work is marginalized from mainstream academic discourse. Let me cite a personal example. My early work on the performative aspects of "sharing time" (Foster 1982) and my subsequent work on the Black tradition of performance that undergirded the study of a successful Black teacher at Regents (Foster 1986; Foster 1987; Foster 1989) (reported earlier in this chapter) remain largely overlooked in scholarly considerations in favor of alternate, more mainstream, and Eurocentric explanations, despite the fact that West (1985) has identified the Black tradition of performance as one of the organic intellectual traditions in African-American life. It was only when the teacher in the Regents study authenticated her reliance on the Black traditions of preaching and performance and the students confirmed its significance that I felt that I had adequately captured her perspective and consequently that this theoretical perspective had merit as an analytic construct able to represent the organic intellectual tradition of contemporary African-American life.

I am convinced that the teachers' acceptance of me as an insider influenced their willingness to participate and shaped their expectations and responses. At the same time, I know that my claims to insider status were continuously tested and renegotiated, and that differences of gender, generation, and geography produced varying degrees of solidarity. Consequently, I make no claim that the information acquired through interviews and observations is absolute. Nor do I claim that the interpretations I have brought to bear on them are the only ones possible.

Research conducted by insiders cannot capture the total experience of an entire community. But neither can research conducted by outsiders. We must be mindful of this fact for, as the title of this paper attests, no one commands the power to know all things.

There were many times when I interacted with my subjects that I heard my own voice in theirs, voices that had waged a continuing struggle against an analysis of their lives imposed by outsiders; voices that had struggled to be heard among the echoes of dissonant interpretive frames seeking to reorder their realities to conform to an external agenda; voices that reflected the complexities of their lives unacknowledged by liberals, conservatives, or progressives speaking from their various camps, but seeking to appropriate them nonetheless. Research undertaken by scholars of color can be revisionist: it can offer new if disturbing insights, alternative and disquieting ways of thinking, can be a means of creating new paradigms and expanding existing ones, and can result in a much needed dialogue between scholars of color and their White peers. Regrettably, it is still the rule rather than the exception to distort and to exclude the realities and to subjugate the voices of people of color to further prevailing paradigms so as to fit the requirements of a caste society.

References

Anderson, J. (1988). *The education of Blacks in the South, 1860–1935.* Chapel Hill: Univ. of North Carolina Press.

Carter, S. (1991). *Reflections of an affirmative action baby:* New York: Basic Books.

Delpit, L. (1988). The silenced dialogue: Power and pedagogy in educating other people's children. *Harvard Educational Review* 58 (3): 280–98.

DuBois, W.E.B. (1903). *The souls of Black folk.* Greenwich, CT: Fawcett.

Dubois, W.E.B. (1945). *The winds of time. Chicago Defender* (13 October), 13.

Fordham, S. (1988). Racelessness as a factor in Black students' success: Pragmatic strategy or Pyrrhic victory? *Harvard Educational Review* (58 (1): 29–84.

Foster, M. (1982). Sharing time: A student-run speech event, ERIC Document Reproduction Service No. ED 234 906.

Foster, M. (1986). Folklore and performance theories: Models for analyzing classrooms. Special qualifying paper. Cambridge, MA: Harvard Graduate School of Education.

Foster, M. (1987). It's cookin' now: An ethnographic study of the teaching style of a Black teacher in an urban community college. Ph.D. dissertation, Harvard University.

Foster, M. (1989). It's cookin' now: A performance analysis of the speech events of a Black teacher in an urban community college. *Language in Society* 18 (1): 1–29.

Goodson, I. (1988). Teachers' lives. *Qualitative Research in Education: Teaching and Learning Qualitative Traditions.* Proceedings from the second annual conference of the Qualitative Interest Group. Univ. of Georgia, Athens, GA.

Gwaltney, J. (1980). *Drylongso: A self-portrait of Black America.* New York: Random House.

Gwaltney, J. (1981). Common sense and science: Urban core Black observations. In D. Messerschmidt, ed., *Anthropologists at home in North America: Methods and issues in the study of one's own society,* 46–61. New York: Cambridge Univ. Press.

hooks, b. (1984). *Feminist theory: From margin to center.* Boston: South End.

Jones, D. (1970). Toward a native anthropology. *Human Organization* 29 (4) (Winter): 251–59.

Lather, P. (1991). Getting smart: Feminist research and pedagogy within the postmodern. New York: Routledge.

Murrell, P. (1991). Cultural politics in teacher education: What is missing in the preparation of minority teachers? In M. Foster, ed., *Reading on equal education, Volume 11: Qualitative investigations into schools and schooling,* 205–225, New York: AMS.

Naylor, G. (1988). *Mama Day:* New York: Vintage.

Ogbu, J. (1988). Diversity in public education: Community forces and minority school adjustment and performance. In R. Haskins and D. Macrae, eds., *Policies for America's public schools: Teachers, equity and indicators,* 127–70. Norwood, NJ: Ablex.

Ogbu, J. (1989). The individual in collective adaptation: A framework for focusing on academic underperformance and dropping out among involuntary minorities. In L. Weiss, E. Farrar, and H. Petrie, eds., *Dropouts from schools: Issues, dilemmas and solutions,* 181–204. Albany, NY: State Univ. of New York Press.

Ogbu, J. (1991). Low school performance as an adaptation: The case of Blacks in Stockton, California. In M. A. Gibson and J. U. Ogbu, eds., *Minority status and schooling: A comparative study of immigrants and involuntary immigrants,* 249–85. New York: Garland.

Peshkin, A. (1988). In search of subjectivity—One's own. *Educational Researcher* (October): 17–21.

Rodriguez, R. (1982). *Hunger of memory: The education of Richard Rodriguez: An autobiography.* New York: Godine.

Smith, D. (1987). *The everyday world as problematic: A feminist sociology.* Boston: Northeastern Univ. Press.

West, C. (1985). The dilemma of the Black intellectual. *Cultural Critique* 1: 109–124.

Witchcraft and Blessings, Science and Rationality: Discourses of Power and Silence in Collaborative Work with Navajo Schools

Margaret D. LeCompte and Daniel McLaughlin

This chapter describes dilemmas that field-workers face when confronting multiple discourses of representation and belief prevalent among teachers and schools in American Indian communities. Our chapter is informed by our work on the Navajo Reservation, as we make sense of the multiple voices we hear and attempt to synthesize them into a coherent whole while attending to traditional ethical concerns about disclosure and protection of human subjects. We also engage in collaborative educational reform efforts while trying to publish analyses of that work. One of the stories we tell in this chapter illustrates the importance of traditional cultural discourse in the Navajo community and how it was perceived and co-opted by members of the educational community. The second illustrates the importance of technical bureaucratic discourse to the innovative teacher education programs we tried to set up in our respective communities. In both cases, interruptions in and silences of discourse complicated our efforts to initiate change and to understand the dynamics of the context in which we worked.

The Role of Collaborative Critical Researchers

Our current work challenges the positivistic epistemologies that once informed and constrained educational research. For us, questions of objectivity have become moot; we cannot be disengaged "others" because collaborative researchers not only observe the acts of others but also are deeply involved in those acts. As critical researchers, we must maintain sensitivity to our own role in the research setting as well as confront both our own biases and the place within relations of power and privilege that our status as researchers confers. While we do tell stories from the field, including in

Grateful acknowledgment is owed to the Metropolitan Life Foundation, which supported LeCompte's research in the Pinnacle School District, and to the cooperation of the many individuals from the Pinnacle and Red Gap communities who, although they must remain anonymous, made this work possible.

them descriptions of our own roles, we cannot wrap ourselves in a mantle of immunity from acts that silence others simply because we pose as objective tellers of holistic stories. Our work is complicated not only by decisions about what to tell to which constituency or audience and how it should be framed (McDade 1985; Schensul et al., 1981) but also by how we make sense of the different world views that the stories from our sites generate.

Our first dilemma is that of audience. It raises questions of privilege and power: by what right do we arrogate the ability to speak to others about yet another "other" (see Geertz 1989)? Early anthropologists answered these questions by treating the practical knowledge of research subjects as quaint or primitive when it conflicted with Western knowledge forms or the knowledge of the researcher. More recently, discrepancies between research and practical knowledge have been treated relativistically so the exotic does not conflict with what are assumed to be more accurate or rigorous forms of explanation. Our work, however, requires working across multiple cultural boundaries and is both applied and collaborative. To us, such "orientalism" (Said 1978) is arrogant, and relativism renders an unsatisfactory solution.

The second dilemma is how to reconcile variations in cultural ideas about what is important, what constitutes a predictor, and how people explain why things happen as they do. We find ourselves addressing competing discourses framing truth and reality, since one of the principle issues we face is not so much disclosure of truth, but deciding which truth to tell, to whom it should be told, and which of the many realities told to us provides the best explanation for any given experience. We cannot ask, "How do you know if the informant is telling the truth?" (Dean and Whyte 1969). Each of the multiple communities which constitute our work/research sites adheres to different metaphysical principles, cultural rules, and truths. The life of each person who works in these school districts overlaps with these multiple communities at the intersection of the work place. This intersection in turn constitutes a unique community affected by the sum of its participant parts and constituting its own truths. However, people who work in the school district also are affected by their rootedness in discrete cultural communities.

Problems of audience, reality, and truth shape, and are shaped by, our understanding of critical ethnography. The ultimate goal of our projects is empowerment; we want to provide access to power and privilege for the people with whom we work. However, as critical ethnographers, what we do is framed within cultural limits, some constituted by the participants within the research setting, while others are created by the ideologies, cultural affiliations, and status positions that we as researchers bring with us to the field. Our work is framed in "particular economies of truth, value, and power" (McLaren 1992, 78). At the most simplistic level, both of us have the ambiguous status of outsiders as well as the power that bringing money and intellectual resources into the community confers. At a deeper level, we participate in larger structures of power and privilege, which, because they are linked to university and government research communities, are not available to our research participants.

In this chapter we discuss how we lived within the various communities in our research work site, worked across their boundaries, and promoted school change while trying to communicate our research and experiences legitimately and ethically to the academic research community. We suggest that critical ethnographers working across cultural boundaries have two tasks. The first is deconstruction of competing discourses within the field site, an ongoing task we partially render in this chapter. The second is the process of sharing insights about these discourses with different constituencies in the research site to promote equity, empowerment, and social justice, particularly with respect to those who traditionally and systematically have been silenced and disenfranchised.

Healing Community Disharmony: The Blessing Way Ceremony

LeCompte and McLaughlin worked, respectively, in the adjoining districts of Pinnacle and Narrow Ridge on the Navajo Reservation.[1] We provided consultation and taught courses to teachers and administrators, wrote grant proposals for the districts, and did critical ethnography. In the past few years, both the Pinnacle School District and Red Gap Elementary School in the Narrow Ridge District have experienced a run of "bad luck." Pinnacle's problems have included the illness and death of some faculty and staff; accidents and deaths among children; construction and structural problems with some of the key school buildings; turnover and conflict among faculty and staff; and dissatisfaction within the community over events in the schools. In Red Gap Elementary School, the performance of students in the school had become worse and worse. Staff morale had plummeted and many teachers and administrators left. Members of both communities attributed the misfortune to witchcraft, which Navajos believe disrupts the normal balance between good and evil in society, producing disharmony, which people experience as illness or community disorder.

Navajos use the Blessing Way Ceremony to restore an ailing person, institution, or community to balance and harmony with the environment. The ceremony also counteracts the effects of witching. Both communities held a Blessing Way for their educational institutions in the hope that a more positive environment could be produced. While Anglos expressed some discomfort at the idea that their schools might be cursed, they all accepted the idea of renewal. As the Anglo principal of Red Gap said, "Witchcraft? Just from a public relations standpoint, it's going to be difficult to get support. But we can approach it from a standpoint of renewal, to bless the school and get rid of any evil associated with it."

Blessing Way Ceremonies last for several days and nights, during which a medicine man performs an elaborate ritual, all portions of which must be executed perfectly. The effectiveness of the entire ceremony is jeopardized if any mistakes or deviations from key aspects of the ritual are introduced. If anyone involved in the ceremony, including the patient, deviates from required patterns of participation, attempts to restore harmony may fail. Pinnacle School District and Red Gap Elementary School chose institutional representatives to serve as the "patients" who were "healed" on behalf of their respective communities. In Pinnacle, the school superintendent, Dr. Sanders, volunteered to be the patient; in Red Gap, the patient was the chapter house president.[2] Both are Navajo.

The Blessing Way requires considerable work for all those directly involved. Participation of the community and the care with which the ceremony is executed determine its efficacy. Certain ritual observances must be followed; one is not supposed to chop wood, have sexual relations, or cross running water. Since several permanent streams bisect both communities, getting to work would have been impossible for some people. The community representatives maintained these more onerous observances for the community. Community members attended the ceremony, participated in the songs and prayers, shared meals prepared by the families most affected, and re-affirmed their membership in the community and their solidarity with all ceremony participants. In both communities, Navajos did all the work. As the principal of Red Gap said,

> The best way to deal with it . . . is to go through our parents. So this was brought up in a parent meeting about a year and a half ago. The parents thought it should be a parent program; they would raise the money for it. The Navajo people [did] the planning for it. And it was probably the only staff meeting dominated by the Navajos.

Despite the considerable religious diversity within Navajo communities, the Blessing Way retains great power. However, Pinnacle School District and Red Gap Elementary School are not homogenous Navajo communities. They are, in fact, constituted of people from a wide range of cultural backgrounds. Although both districts are located in Navajo communities in one of the most culturally traditional parts of the Navajo Nation, and almost all of the students and parents are Navajo, most of the teachers and administrators in Pinnacle are Anglo. The teaching force in Red Gap Elementary School is about 60 percent Navajo and 40 percent Anglo; the principal is Anglo.

Ethnic distinctions alone fail to describe the diversity in the communities; neither Navajos nor Anglos constitute homogenous groups. For both, full- versus part-time employment creates distinctions, as does town or rural residence. Navajo subgroups include traditional Navajos, Navajos who par- ticipate in a variety of traditional and mainstream religious practices, Mor- mon converts, members of the Native American Church, and members of a variety of other Christian denominations. Navajos also are divided by educational attainment and experience; those who have experienced "Mor- mon home placement" or boarding school have different feelings about schooling from those who have attended school on the reservation.[3]

While many Anglos live on the fringes of the reservation, their housing and job opportunities on the reservation itself are limited. In general, Anglos are viewed as transients; they only live on the reservation because they are employed as professionals in the human services industries—such as schools and clinics—or the tourist trade, in which they operate restaurants, hotels, and trading posts. Anglos cannot purchase land on the reservation and even find it difficult to rent. Since Pinnacle is located entirely on the reservation, housing is in short supply because all land on the Navajo Reservation either is already allocated to Navajo families who have historically lived there or is controlled by the Navajo Nation. Although the tiny community sur- rounding Red Gap Elementary School is a nonreservation enclave, Anglos find it difficult to find appropriate housing there. This means that Anglo teachers cannot make a commitment to the communities where they work.[4]

Religious and professional affiliation also distinguishes among people, especially between Mormons and non-Mormons and between professional or certified staff—who are primarily Anglo—and the classified, or nonprofes- sional staff, who are primarily Navajo. Economic distinctions also exist, since, among certified staff, administrators are paid considerably more than teachers. Classified staff, who tend to live permanently in or near the commu- nity, are paid considerably less than certified teachers.

We researchers, who commute from outlying university communities, add complications. Both of us have had considerable experience working in these and similar communities, but we are not part of them. Neither of us is Navajo. We wrote program proposals at the request of our respective dis- tricts for projects of interest to district personnel; these grants funded our presence.

Subcultural distinctions are critical in understanding the impact of the Blessing Way. These established the normative and heuristic discourses in- forming how people interpreted the ceremony, and exemplify the disso- nances among meanings and discourses constructed within our research sites. They are a principle source of discourse conflict, especially with what we call the technical/rational or scientific discourse that educators use. These dissonances in meaning are more than neutral issues of difference or exotica to be treated relativistically. They are the substance of daily life and survival in the communities of Narrow Ridge and Pinnacle. It is ethically problematic for us to portray these discourses to communities outside of the research context without acknowledging the partial and biased pictures we render. These silence some voices while privileging others. In particular, we tend to silence or render absent the voice of community constituencies with whom we have less contact, especially those not involved with schools. We also sometimes silence ourselves, either to honor confidences from our collaborators or, less honorably, to avoid mentioning sensitive subjects that might jeopardize our positions.

The Impact of the Blessing Ways in Red Gap and Pinnacle

All Navajo staff and many local Navajos in both communities attended the two Blessing Ways. Few Anglos did. Only two Anglos in Pinnacle stayed all night to watch key aspects of the ceremony; in Red Gap, only the principal of the school participated in the ceremony.

Notwithstanding, the ceremonies were initially described by participants as moving and efficacious. The Red Gap principal

> felt it had a unifying effect on the staff. For those of us not Navajo, it gave us a feeling of how important ceremonies are to the people and to the students. That raised the level of cultural awareness among the entire staff. . . . We had probably the best school year that I've ever had. There was better teamwork and better relations among staff. The Navajo people felt very comfortable relating their feelings about their culture . . . their feelings as a Navajo.

A high school teacher in Pinnacle said,

> It really changed my feelings about Dr. Sanders. I really thought he was just a politician, and was only interested in education for the publicity it would give him. But when he went through the whole ceremony on behalf of the school district, I knew that he really cared deeply about Navajo people.

Some problems did arise, Red Gap really needed (and had) two ceremonies, one to determine whether or not the school had been cursed and another for renewal and blessing. The actual cost of the rituals was considerably in excess of the Anglo principal's original estimate. Some Anglo parents questioned the appropriateness of having a religious ceremony in the school, even though the principal made it clear to parents and to his Anglo superiors that no school funds were used. In fact, all money had been raised by parents or contributed by the principal.

In Pinnacle, rumors started that Dr. Sanders had not followed all the prescribed observances before and after the ceremony. Several Navajo staff worried that the ceremony had been compromised; as evidence, they asserted that the initial disharmony that led to the ceremony had not significantly improved. Others were distressed that so few Anglos had attended. However, the overall effect was felt to be positive.

The Discourse of Science and Rationality

Two discourses that inform and constrain the educational, academic, and research communities in these two sites contrast with the cultural discourses framing the Blessing Ways in Pinnacle and Narrow Ridge. Both derive from norms that govern rational objectivist Western science; they are framed in the language of specific epistemologies, determine what constitutes knowledge, and constrain the behavior of scientists.

The language of technical rationality describes the bureaucratic structure of schools and other contemporary institutions. It is embodied in the rules, roles, expectations, and obligations that constrain the daily lives of teachers and other district employees (Bidwell 1965; Blau 1955; Weber 1947). The discourse of linear and reductionist analysis informs academic research, even when it is presented in the guise of postmodern critique or critical collaborative and ethnographic research.

Both the technical and analytical discourses are appropriated by educators, both in mainstream school districts and in culturally different communities, to explain or justify what they do and to predict or control future behavior. Administrators use rational "job targets" and "job descriptions" to enforce the compliance of maverick employees; the target or description symbolizes the authority structure and serves to ward off irrational or nonconforming behavior. Incompetence, insubordination, or simple excessive technical difficulty—as measured by technical and objective criteria—explain program failure. However, nonobjective, nonrational explanations, including witchcraft, can have equal currency in the communities where we work. They coexist with the bureaucratic formalism of schools (and the epistemological formalism of our research, for that matter), finding space in what sociologists call the informal structure of everyday life. They represent practical knowledge or practice, and provide explanations for how these organizations really work.

Competing Discourses in Pinnacle and Narrow Ridge

The varying normative discourses that govern behavior and belief in Pinnacle and Narrow Ridge operate from quite different metaphysical frames and they create quite different cultural contexts. Anglos find the normative nature of both rational discourses—the technical rationality of bureaucracy and the analytic linear rationality of academic research—easy to understand. They constitute the givens that explain, predict, or describe how things *ought* to be to Westerners. These explanations are presented as truth because they are couched in the privileged language of science; their legitimacy resides in the power their users have to impose them on the wide range of human experience. Researchers use these explanations to report what they have observed, privileging them over participant rationales as "truer," "better," or "more objective." Even if these explanations lack authenticity or validity to research participants, lack of validity is deemed less problematic than failure to produce real knowledge. A scientist might attribute the "good year," which followed the two ceremonies in Red Gap to improved communication between and among the subgroups in the community, or the continued disorder and turnover in Pinnacle to the perpetuation of isolation and burnout among Anglo staff, rather than to lack of proper ritual observance by participants.

NAVAJO METAPHYSICS

A Navajo ecologist struggling to restore the ravaged spoil piles around the Peabody Coal Company's Black Mesa mine wonders why native plants refuse to return, despite ten years of revegetation efforts. The ecologist is torn between scientific explanations, which cite changes in the soil composition and drainage, and rationales given by traditional Navajos: "The Plant People are displeased. They have moved away, and they won't come back just because we want them to. We have to find out why they are unhappy. Maybe they won't ever return" (Arthur, et al. 1986, 220). Navajo culture addresses issues of causality differently from Western objective science, and it is done in a decidedly nonwestern, unbureaucratic, and nonlinear manner. Knowledge for Navajos does have an empirical base rooted in their experience in the natural environment. However, their empirical base has different antecedents from those of Western science. It is suffused with a history Westerners treat as myth—perhaps because Westerners have replaced their own religious myths and history with scientific traditions. Navajos use empirical evidence such as their knowledge of conditions that plants prefer, which is rooted in religious traditions that Westerners disregard but that Navajo culture cannot.

Both Western science and Navajo traditions can explain the demise of native vegetation; scientists could coexist with the Navajo Plant People by deeming them a metaphor. However, Western hegemonic science privileges its own theories and silences many forms of Navajo belief because they are difficult to reconcile with scientific knowledge. Knowing that a given people adhere to what, in some contexts, appear to be superstitious or unscientific traditional beliefs also justifies silencing those people in many other ways, including dismissing Navajo beliefs about the causal relationships governing their social interaction.

The Silencing of Competing Cultural Discourses

We have already indicated that technical/rational discourses silence Navajo explanations of human and natural causality. In the communities of Narrow Ridge and Pinnacle, the cultural discourse of Western religion is equally powerful as an impediment to Navajo voice. These communities have been targeted for decades by Christian and Church of Jesus Christ of Latter-day Saints (LDS, or Mormon) missionaries, whose goals are the elimination of the indigenous—or "heathen"—religious beliefs that form the core of Navajo cultural identity. The Mormon Church, whose members dominate the Anglo population in Narrow Ridge and who are highly visible among the Anglo population in Pinnacle, claims many teachers and administrators in the two communities. These individuals are a powerful force in silencing traditional Navajo beliefs because the church has used educational institutions as a principle way to reach potential converts. A primary mission of the LDS Church is the conversion of Native Americans and Pacific Islanders, whom Mormons believe are members of the Lost Tribes. Conversion reclaims souls for the church, transforming Native Americans from those whose ancestors' sins caused them to be "cursed with a face of darkness" into "white and delightsome" beings. Members of the LDS Church feel that the loss of cultural identity and self-esteem that the conversion process causes is outweighed by the greater importance of ultimate salvation (Deyhle 1991).

Missionary activity and the widespread practice of "home placement," or temporary adoption of Indian children by Mormon families, has created many converts. Smaller Protestant and Catholic churches also have missions in Pinnacle and Narrow Ridge, and many Navajos are members. Their doctrines also conflict with Navajo identity but are not based so clearly upon a doctrine of racial inferiority as is that of the LDS Church.

Regardless of their sectarian affiliation, however, many Navajo converts compartmentalize their beliefs, refusing to deny their native cultural identity while accepting what they feel to be beneficial from each alien culture—including aspects of religion. However, other Navajos who have been the objects of missionizing or who were educated in boarding schools are left stranded between two cultures, fully accepted by and belonging to neither. They may, for example, feel very Navajo but know little of their own language or cultural traditions. Other people who are ethnically Navajo feel completely alienated from their own culture, although they are treated by Anglos as if they were fully integrated into Navajo culture.

Even the assimilationist policies of state and federal governments, while ostensibly secular, have cast their American Indian educational programs in a language of moral and doctrinal fervor that disguises and legitimates its racist effects. Educational practices—of which the boarding school was the most effective tool—have been designed to lead Native Americans away from their allegedly degraded and superstitious ways and to bring them into the healthier mainstream of American life. The dominance of White religious and governmental policies—especially in schools—has silenced Indian voices and privileged that of mainstream Whites. In schools this has meant denying the legitimacy of Indian patterns of parenting and perspectives on education and goals for their children's future, while giving importance only to those deemed important by Anglo school personnel (Deyhle 1992; Deyhle and LeCompte forthcoming).

Compartmentalization of culture, years of assimilationist policy, and de-racination, as well as an emerging process of Navajo political and cultural self-determination, create competing allegiances that make the cultural discourses and understandings in Narrow Ridge and Pinnacle exceedingly complex, especially for an outsider. Both of us became embroiled in these issues while attempting to initiate teacher education and certification programs in our respective school districts. These experiences proved to be the catalyst for one of the most clear-cut clashes between technical rational and cultural norms. The technical rational norms encouraged the establishment of the programs; cultural norms nearly destroyed them.

Teacher Education Programs at Pinnacle and Red Gap

Barely 8 percent of all certified teachers in the Navajo Nation are Navajo, despite the prevalence in most districts of Indian preference in hiring. This shortage encouraged the school district of Pinnacle to urge local community people to become teachers. Establishment of teacher education programs in Pinnacle was given additional impetus in 1990 when the state education agency imposed higher educational requirements for public school aides and substitute teachers. The new regulations required that all aides have at least an Associate of Arts degree, and that substitute teachers have a college degree. Given the dearth of people with advanced educational credentials in Pinnacle, its school board asked for a waiver of this requirement. However, because the regulations eventually would be enforced, the waiver could only be a temporary expedient.[5]

Bureaucratic norms dictate that jobs be filled by individuals who meet objectively verifiable standards of competence. In educational systems, these standards, which are enforced by states and school districts, are embodied in requirements for teacher certification and accompanied by demands for at least minimal levels of schooling and enrollment in teaching methods courses. These standards often conflict with cultural norms dictating not only that teachers represent the indigenous culture of the community but also that opportunities for good jobs, such as those provided by schools, be available to indigenous persons on a preferential basis. The clear "Navajo hiring preference" established by the school board in Pinnacle reflects these norms.

Certain subgroups in the community—especially the school district governing board and most of the school administrators—approved of the higher standards for aides; they did so by supporting the establishment of teacher education programs for Navajos. This also matched with the self-determination priorities of the Navajo Nation, which wishes to raise the number of certified Navajo teachers to 1,000 by 1995. With the help of the Ford Foundation and in cooperation with local colleges and universities, the Navajo Nation has started a program to provide mentoring and a degree of financial aid to prospective teachers. The program requires participants to become fully bilingual and biliterate in Navajo. The board and the school superintendent had been enthusiastic supporters of LeCompte's attempts to initiate training programs to augment these efforts.

At first, the impetus for teacher education at Red Gap came from McLaughlin. In the fall of 1990, having moved from a school principalship on the Navajo Reservation to a university professorship, he developed a research connection with the school. At that time, Red Gap Elementary School was not unlike many public and Bureau of Indian Affairs schools elsewhere on the Navajo Reservation. The turn-over rate of teachers for the previous five years averaged more than 40 percent; student achievement levels were the lowest in the state; and curriculum planning at best was haphazard. Within a recent three-year span, three different individuals had served as principal. No language arts and literacy curricula existed whatsoever, apart from the mainstream logic embedded in disconnected series of basal texts, even though one-third of the students came to school as native speakers of Navajo and the remainder as speakers of American Indian English. Nearly all instruction took place in standard English, in which few of the students were fluent. McLaughlin sought to develop a teacher education program that not only credentialized Navajo teacher aides and teachers but also developed an appropriate language arts program for the school. It consisted of organizing an on-site Master's degree program in curriculum, which offered courses for both graduate and undergraduate credit.

Pools of potential Navajo teacher education students existed in both districts. As in Red Gap, Navajos were already working in the Pinnacle schools as teacher aides; most had taken at least a few college courses. The Pinnacle school board had been trying to increase its own pool of "home grown" teachers by encouraging Navajo teacher aides to work toward teacher certification. Already experienced in working with children, many aides came from Pinnacle; the school board believed that hiring locals would reduce teacher turnover and produce a more stable teaching staff. The superintendent in Pinnacle thought that, where possible, prospective teachers should enroll in four-year programs away from the community to broaden their perspective on teaching and learning. In the opinion of the district administrators, such programs also were more coherent and of higher quality than those offered in nearby community and four-year colleges.

In 1990, the Pinnacle board began enforcing their policies; they proposed to make continued employment of teacher aides conditional upon their enrollment and satisfactory progress in a teacher certification program. Le-Compte obtained a grant designed to encourage aides to enroll in teacher education programs. This grant paid for recruiting and degree-planning activities for the aides and for a mentor—a former teacher from Pinnacle who was an education doctoral student at an adjoining state university—to provide counseling and support with the myriad problems that minority students face at the university. The grant also provided a family-support stipend to supplement university financial aid packages; this stipend recognized that most of the aides were older women with dependents, whose needs university aid packages normally do not recognize.

Over the course of the year, LeCompte found that many of the aides already had taken a wide range of courses from among those most easily accessible in nearby community colleges. However, despite amassing many hours of university credit, most of the aides were nowhere near completion of a degree. Many had avoided taking prerequisite courses—such as math for teachers—and so were unable to complete the coherent course sequence required for a degree.

Echoes of a conflict between cultural and bureaucratic discourses also surfaced. Enthusiasm among the aides for continuing—or even beginning—teacher education programs did not seem to be matched by the seriousness of school board policies designed to get them certified. LeCompte and school administrators first asked for volunteers among the aides, meeting with the few who came forward in their homes or after school. To help them enroll in the school of their choice, necessary admissions and financial-aid forms were obtained and help was provided in filling them out. Despite many hours of meetings, only three people finished the forms, and none submitted the applications.

Next, the superintendent met with the aides to describe how seriously their jobs would be jeopardized if they did not get certified. After his talk, the mentor spent several hours discussing with the aides problems they felt impeded their participation; only seventeen of the sixty-two aides showed up. At first, administrators felt the aides simply did not want to attend the university involved because it was too far away and too expensive. However, several weeks later, a representative of the Navajo Nation's teacher education program held a meeting in Pinnacle to discuss the tribe's program, which involved local colleges closest to Pinnacle, from which most of the aides already had taken courses. Only seventeen people—the same seventeen—showed up.

The board then directed Daisy Benally, a Navajo woman who administered federal programs for the district, to ensure that the aides began work toward certification. Mrs. Benally and her assistant already had spent several years encouraging the aides to go to school. She felt cornered by the board's directive, since she felt she already had done as much as she could. Reflecting not only her frustration at the difficulty of imposing bureaucratic standards on unwilling individuals but also powerful Navajo cultural norms against interfering in the decisions of other people, Daisy lamented, "I can tell them to come, but if they don't want to, I can't make them."

Each group interpreted the poor reception the programs received in different ways. The aides avoided participation or sabotaged initial efforts to become involved in the programs because of conflict between traditional Navajo obligations to family, community, and the land, and the academic and financial obligations that college entails. Most of the aides were women with families. Some single women without immediate dependents were the sole support of their extended family or were raising nieces and nephews. Some did not want to leave their children, and none could see how they could support them on a university campus. The husbands of some married women did not support their pursuit of a career. Other aides were afraid that if they left even for the summer to take courses, their husbands would stray.

A number of aides did not want to live far from Dinétah, the land between the four sacred mountains of the Navajo. Proximity to the land signifies more than comfort to many Navajo; it denotes the very core of Navajo cultural identity. Others feared that they were too old to go away to school. Unspoken, but very pleasant, was the fear that, once having enrolled, they might fail. Some aides were quite successful as aides, but lacked confidence that they would be comfortable as full-time teachers.

Nonetheless, neither members of the Pinnacle school board, all of whom were Navajo, nor Mrs. Benally were sympathetic. They felt they had made sacrifices, left their husbands and families behind, and gone into debt to obtain their own educations. Why couldn't the aides do likewise? A compromise was suggested for the existing group of aides, such that no new aides would be hired without a prior agreement to continue their education. Training efforts for the existing group would concentrate on those individuals who wanted to be teachers; those who wished only to remain aides would be "grandfathered" into their positions. However, this was rejected by the board, which continued to insist that all aides pursue the AA degree first and then seek teacher certification.

At Red Gap, McLaughlin attempted to solve the immediate problem of distance between the college and community by bringing the college to the community. The grant he obtained provided funds for him to travel from the university to Red Gap. His objective was to teach some initial courses to teachers on-site, desensitizing them to the issues of entry into higher education and getting them accustomed to the demands of academic work. Practicing teachers were to be admitted to a Master's degree program offered primarily at Red Gap, but participants in the program would finish their courses on the main university campus.

In the winter of 1991, McLaughlin taught an on-site introductory class on multicultural education, critical theory, and Navajo-English language curriculum development to twelve Red Gap staff members—seven Navajos, five Anglos. Class participants developed personal histories, reflecting on how their own earlier student experiences suggested better ways to teach Red Gap children. Moves, divorces, the inability to find jobs elsewhere, and altruism punctuated the personal histories of Anglos; by contrast, the Navajos spoke of family responsibilities, family problems, difficulties with English, participation in the Mormon home placement program, and difficulties in K–12 and postsecondary schooling. The class then assessed program development needs for the school. Three-quarters of the teachers targeted the unique language needs of the native language- and Indian English–speaking student body, and decried the lack of an appropriate language arts and literacy program for their students.

Curriculum development began in the summer of 1991 and continued the following school year with a team of seven Navajo teachers from Red Gap and a linguist well versed in the descriptive and pragmatic features of American Indian English. All members of the team probed further into the curriculum needs of Navajo learners at Red Gap School.[6] Three graduate seminars on language and literacy program development were organized for the Red Gap teaching staff plus an additional ten teachers from two other K–6 and two secondary-level schools. All together, twenty-two teachers participated in the effort.

The teachers produced narratives using methods that not only allowed for critical, iterative analysis, but that also could be used as alternative methods for their own students. After discussing story production (Dewey 1938/63; Graves 1988a; Graves 1988b; McLaughlin 1989) and doing a considerable amount of brainstorming, the teachers decided to produce a three-part book that began with an in-class interview on "What Teachers Need to Know About Navajo Students To Teach them Well," included out-of-class interviews on "My Most Powerful Experience in Schools," and concluded with self-generated fictional texts linked thematically to the first two sections of the volume. Class participants then reframed the instructional techniques employed to produce the interview and story texts, using the conceptual language of critical theory and instructional theory, respectively.

As at Pinnacle, conflicts between cultural and rational bureaucrative discourses soon emerged in Red Gap's teacher education program. Initially enthusiastic about creating an on-site Master's program on the Navajo Nation, McLaughlin's university department was sympathetic to the unique situation and needs of Navajo program participants. However, it soon raised concerns over normative academic standards that made it problematic. As in Pinnacle, many of the Navajo participants had received much of their prior training in local educational institutions with low academic standards; many had difficulty with the literacy levels required in McLaughlin's classes. Consequently, he tailored his instruction to the levels of literacy prevalent among the participants. Back at the university, department officials were pressured by deans and the academic vice president to maintain "standards" by not watering down instruction. Course syllabi and standards from McLaughlin's courses in Red Gap were measured and found wanting in comparison to on-campus reading loads, course assignments, and grading criteria. Admission standards to the graduate school, prerequisite to forming the on-site Master's program, also were problematic. Applicants needed 3.0 undergraduate GPAs and high scores on the Miller's analogy test to gain admission to the regular Master's degree program on campus—a goal that had been primary in McLaughlin's efforts at recruiting Red Gap teachers. However, while six of eight Anglo applicants from Red Gap met the 3.0 GPA standard, none of the seventeen Navajo applicants—the target population— came close. Placing high reading and writing demands on participants created consequent difficulties for Navajo teachers, with predictable results. While many Navajos were deeply appreciative of the university's outreach to their school and community, they were frustrated with McLaughlin's readings, which they found undecipherable and meaningless.

Federal funding for the program also failed to materialize, putting the effort in dire financial straits. More problematic was the sudden leave-taking of Red Gap's principal at the end of the school year. As the *only* non-Mormon administrator in the district, he had taken considerable risks by initiating the on-site Master's program. Many, if not most, of the principal's long-time colleagues saw no need for the student- and community-centered curriculum that the program promised. Years of prior complaints about blatant racism and inadequate, inappropriate schooling that groups of Navajo parents elsewhere in the district had voiced had simply gone unheeded (see Deyhle 1992). The principal explained that he had been offered an early retirement package that he could not refuse. Some members of the community claimed that he was pushed out by the superintendent and the school board for, among other reasons, "mishandling" the Blessing Way

Ceremony at Red Gap Elementary School. Others suggested that his support for the ceremony had allowed church—or Navajo religious—and state practices dangerously to mix. This allegation carried some weight in the community, notwithstanding decades of well-documented intermingling between LDS Church and school affairs in the area.

Conclusion

The fledgling teacher training programs at Red Gap and Pinnacle were well-intended and actually did address some of the obstacles that impede the participation of Navajos in higher education. Notwithstanding, they failed to materialize. But why? Which of the competing explanatory discourses of the two communities best frame an explanation for the failure? These questions cannot be answered by resorting to research methods. Rather, they require attention to all specific voices in the community and interpretation of their discourses. Each discourse gives a different account of events, some of which are accepted readily by the school community, while others, though equally valid in specific circles, are rejected. From the technical rational point of view, the teacher training programs failed because potential participants were poorly prepared, underqualified, incompetent, or inadequately motivated to apply, or because they lacked a "future orientation" and did not work hard enough. These victim-blaming explanations permit schools—and universities—to absolve themselves from responsibility for looking deeper into rationales for behavior; were they to do so, they might find underlying premises completely foreign to the world of contemporary bureaucracy and science. Failure to disentangle these premises leads to conflict and, in some cases, unusual alliances. In Red Gap, a technical/rational explanation co-opted a cultural discourse. Some parents said that the principal was fired because his support for the Blessing Way Ceremony inappropriately mixed church and state affairs. However, this explanation ignores the domination of the LDS Church in regional school affairs and its frequent incursions into state- and school-related business. In fact, the LDS Church in Red Gap has been granted legitimate power by dominant groups in the community to interfere in schools, while Navajo religious groups are denied the same privilege.

Conflicts over notions of causality, such as those we described in our accounts of Blessing Way Ceremonies and land-reclamation efforts, may in fact create difficulties for Anglos working in the Navajo Nation. However, while it is tempting to attribute cultural conflict, even in discourse, to cultural differences in metaphysics, such an explanation may simply excuse elitist dominant cultural practices. For Navajos, success or failure of the teacher training programs contained no real cultural mysteries. Potential participants felt that the schools—and Anglicized members of the Navajo community—

still "just don't get it" with regard to the difficulties Navajo teachers and aides faced in going away to college—whether these had a cultural genesis or not.

In the first place, aides did have serious financial needs that district policies failed to acknowledge, even by offering sabbaticals to aides who went to school. In the second place, classes in the local and community college programs where most teachers and aides received their initial training often were no more demanding than high school work. Students amassed poor academic records because they had participated, of necessity, in the lowest (nearest and cheapest) track of the highly stratified higher education system of the United States. These institutions are designed, implicitly or explicitly, to "cool out" those individuals whose aspirations, by virtue of their minority or economic status, are deemed too high (Dougherty 1987; Karabel 1972). If the teachers and aides were poorly prepared and lacked academic self-confidence, it was because they had bought into the myth that all college work was equal and had worked hard for substandard credentials.

The dominant culture also accords little credence or power to a community discourse that rejects economic or professional opportunities, and even success, if it means leaving cultural affiliations, family land, and relatives behind. Anglo culture asserts that the only "rational" reason why aides in Pinnacle did not jump on the higher education bandwagon was that they were lazy, didn't want to succeed, or were unwilling to make sacrifices for their future. Indians who want to stay near their extended family, friends, community, and ancestral land are stigmatized as failures by Anglos. However, this time-honored belief—that the only successful Indians are absent ones—serves the Anglo community well. The Four Corners area of the United States is both ravishingly beautiful real estate and the ancestral home to Anglo communities whose members are as determined as the Native American population to remain near their extended family, friends, community, and ancestral lands.[7] An ideology which holds that a local Indian is a failed Indian encourages the ambitious to leave, thereby eliminating Indian competitors for jobs Anglos want. Since programs that promote Indian empowerment, such as the teacher education programs we described in this chapter, create competition for Anglos who claim the few lucrative jobs in the area, it is in the interest of Anglos—and those who have prospered within the Anglo-dominated political economy—to see them fail. Since programs that accommodate nontraditional students threaten the hegemony of universities and the perpetuation of the status systems they support, such programs, too, are rendered suspect. It also is true that the researchers who set up these programs were unaware of the difficulties that lay ahead of them, participated in the same dominant cultural practices that made the programs problematic, and, in writing this account, left out different versions of their own behavior that might be held by others.

Taken singly, none of these explanations fully explains what happened, and none of them alone provides sufficient guidance for collaborative researchers to use to create better programs. We believe that organizational and community change cannot take place without an understanding of all of the normative discourses that frame behavior in communities such as Red Gap and Pinnacle. Further, it is necessary to place that understanding in the context of the relative power ascribed to each explanatory framework by each constituency in diverse communities. Navajo explanations, even if silenced by the wider Anglo community, still drive Navajo behavior. Ignoring them only dooms our efforts to failure.

Notes

1. All names in this chapter, except for those of the authors, are pseudonyms.

2. Chapter houses are the local governing units for the Navajo Nation; the chapter house president is analogous to the state representative of a legislative district.

3. The "Mormon home placement program" is formally known as the Indian Student Placement Program and has been run since 1954 by the Church of Jesus Christ of Latter-day Saints. It matches American Indian youths with Mormon foster families in order to educate these children in public school settings away from their home reservation communities and to bring them spiritually into the Mormon Church. Most recent figures stipulate that by 1985, more than 22,000 American Indian youths, a significant number of them Navajos, had participated in this program (Deyhle 1991).

4. Some teachers own homes off the reservation that they use during holidays; during the school year they rent housing in teacher compounds constructed by the school district under long-term leases from the Navajo Nation.

5. Pinnacle regularly hired people with high school diplomas as aides, and sometimes was forced to hire people with similarly minimal qualifications as substitute teachers.

6. See Leap & McLaughlin (1991) and Leap (1993) for descriptions of focused discussions of the language-related needs of Red Gap students with the Red Gap teachers.

7. We are indebted for this insight to Donna Deyhle, who details these socioeconomic dynamics in her 1992 article, "Constructing failure and maintaining cultural identity: Navajo and Ute school leavers."

References

Arthur, C., Bingham, S., Bingham, J., Rock Point School et al. (1986). *Between sacred mountains: Navajo stories and lessons from the land.* Tucson, AZ: Sun Tracks and the Univ. of Arizona Press.

Bidwell, C. E. (1965). The school as a formal organization. In J. G. March, ed., *The handbook of organizations*, 927–1022. New York: Rand McNally.

Blau, P. M. (1955). *The dynamics of bureaucracy*. Chicago: Univ. of Chicago Press.

Dean, J. P., and Whyte, W. F. (1969). How do you know if the informant is telling the truth? In G. McCall, and J. L. Simmons, eds., *Issues in participant observation*, 105–115. New York: Random House.

Dewey, J. (1938/63). *Experience and education*. New York: Collier.

Deyhle, D. M. (1991). Empowerment and cultural conflict: Navajo parents and the schooling of their children. *Qualitative Studies in Education* 4 (4) (Winter); 277–97.

Deyhle, D. M. (1992). Constructing failure and maintaining cultural identity: Navajo and Ute school leavers. *Journal of American Indian Education* 4 (January), 24–47.

Deyhle, D. M., and LeCompte, M. D. (Forthcoming). Developing conflict over theories of child development: Navajo cultural goals versus middle school objectives. *Theory Into Practice*. (Summer 1994).

Dougherty, K. (1987). The effects of community colleges: Aid or hindrance to socioeconomic attainment? *Sociology of Education* 60 (April): 86–103.

Geertz, C. (1989). *Works and Lives: The Anthropologist as author*. Stanford, CA: Stanford Univ. Press.

Graves, D. (1988a). *Experiment with fiction*. Portsmouth, NH: Heinemann.

Graves, D. (1988b). *Investigate non-fiction*. Portsmouth, NH: Heinemann.

Karabel, J. (1972). Community colleges and social stratification in the 1980s. *Harvard Educational Review,* 42 (November): 521–62.

Leap, W. (1993). *American Indian English*. Salt Lake City, UT: Univ. of Utah Press.

Leap, W., and McLaughlin, D. (1991). What Navajo students know about written English. Paper presented at the annual meeting of the American Educational Research Association, April, Chicago, IL.

McDade, L. M. (1985). Telling them what they do not want to know. Paper presented at the American Anthropological Association meetings, November.

McLaren, P. (1992). Collisions with otherness: "Travelling" theory, postcolonial criticism, and the politics of ethnographic practice—The mission of the wounded ethnographer. *Qualitative Studies in Education* 5 (1): 77–92.

McLaughlin, D. (1989). The sociolinguistics of Navajo literacy. *Anthropology and Education Quarterly* 20 (3): 275–290.

Said, E. (1978). *Orientalism*. New York: Pantheon.

Schensul, J. J., Schensul, S. L., Gonzales, M., and Caro, E. (1981). Community-based research and approaches to social change: The case of the Hispanic Health Council. *The Generator* 12 (2): 13–26.

Weber, M. (1947). *The theory of social and economic organizations*. A. M. Henderson, and T. Parsons, trans. New York: Oxford Univ. Press.

EMPOWERING THE CULTURALLY DIVERSIFIED SOCIOLOGICAL VOICE (RESPONSE)

John H. Stanfield, II

During the last three decades of the twentieth century, we have been witnessing the advancing attack on traditional modes of domestic and international hegemonic authority traditions and structures. Post–World War II decolonization of the third world has phased into the crumbling of the last European-centered massive empires, as witnessed in the demise of the Soviet Union. The destruction of cold war ideologies as the central means of defining and organizing the global community as well as the disintegration of classical forms of empires have left the world without rigid forms of international hegemonic authority, probably for the first time in over five hundred years.

In the United States, since the Watergate scandal and Viet Nam, there has been a growing skepticism about the so-called natural goodness and unquestionable authority rights of public leaders and professionals. It has become quite appropriate in America to question authority in places once considered sacred, whether in the areas of business, medicine, law, sciences, religion, or the profession of teaching. The post-1970s tendency among many Americans as consumers, clients, and customers to no longer take professional authority for granted, and indeed to be quite skeptical of it, has spilled over to cultural authority issues.

The fact that the world is no longer under the permanent thumb of upper middle-class European-descent males is not a startling revelation in 1993. The Afro-American collective protest activities of the 1950s and 1960s and the other liberation movements such sociopolitical activism inspired in the post-1970s have eroded traditional structures of sociopolitical and economic hegemony and are transforming conventional definitions and functions of dominant culture and institutions. Additionally, for at least the past ten years, the changing ethnic demographics of the United States and of the most central international power holders have made it quite obvious to many public-culture observers that the American nation-state and the global community invented by white males are in a period of rapid decline. In post-1970s America, we see the era of a dying colonialism as it was in the British and French empires some forty years ago.

166

The breakdown and breakup of white male hegemony everywhere we look has been, of course, a very painful process of becoming knowledgeable of what cultural pluralism really means. It is no coincidence or accident, then, that the human sciences and humanities and the American academy have been in the eye of the storm in hotly contested claims regarding orthodoxy and diversity in debates regarding what knowledge is and what knowledge should be. Whether we turn to anthropology, psychology, sociology, medicine, philosophy, literature, theology, history, or elsewhere in cultures of knowledge production, we find mounting dilemmas and controversies over whether there is only one way of knowing; and, if there are two or more ways of knowing, are such interpretations inferior or superior or just different cognitive lenses altogether. It is little wonder, then, that no matter how we cut it, when we turn our attention to the knowledge foundations of education as a profession, the whole messy issues of what we know and, more importantly, how we know in an age in which hegemonic cultural authority is under unprecedented attack become even more confusing.

The confusion comes into play when we consider questions such as those raised by the authors (Foster, and LeCompte and McLaughlin) of the two papers I have had the pleasure of reviewing for this section. Confusion these days in the heat of multicultural debates more often than not hinges on one very simple though disturbing concern—at least to some it is disturbing. It is the issue of insider/outsider ability to study the cultures, institutions, and communities of those under the microscope. It bothers many Whites these days to be told that there is a strong possibility that, due to their outsider status, they are not able to tap adequately into the cultural sites (institutions, communities, networks, and other social organizations) of people of color. Although that concern began to be raised by anthropologists and sociologists of color in the 1970s, it was not until the 1980s and 1990s with the advent of cultural studies and the re-emergence of academic ethnic studies that at least some mainstream scholars began to take the outsider bias issue seriously. But the issue continues to be a sore spot for White researchers interested in doing research in people-of-color cultural sites. The relatively recent advocacy of participatory and empowerment research by an emerging generation of scholars such as LeCompte and McLaughlin is an interesting way to deal with the deepening distrust people of color have when it comes to allowing White researchers to enter into their lives. But, as the authors allude to, participatory and empowerment research becomes rather ineffectual when an oppressed population is rigidly controlled by the political and institutional realities of a "colonial-like" third party such as the Bureau of Indian Affairs.

On the other hand, with the growing number of people-of-color researchers doing work in cultural sites at least ethnically similar to those in which they were reared, there is the rather frustrating paradox of intrusive factors.

The chief intrusive factor is, as Foster so rightfully points out, professional status. Since the professional status of the person-of-color researcher may be enough for the human beings under investigation to view him or her as an outsider and perhaps even as being "really White," the issue of what is knowable becomes a grave problematic.

The professional status issue is critical for understanding the dilemmas and paradoxes experienced by scholars of color and by White scholars. In order to be heard and believed by colleagues in the mainstream, scholars, regardless of their socially defined race or gender, have to abide by discourse rules and knowledge-distribution rules established by the official professional communities. What this means is that despite the personal feelings and alliances of the scholar, the scholar must embrace the jargon and productivity norms of the field if he or she wants to become what some have called "well published." This professional demand becomes especially problematic for ethnically conscious scholars of color and even for White scholars from nonaffluent backgrounds who view the White middle-class discourse and productivity norms to be alien to their reality sensibilities. It also means that more often than not the most conservative dimensions of the ideas of scholars appear in high-profile journals and publication series, while their more "radical" ideas are edited out or published in more obscure ethnic sources (I am thinking here about two historical giants in sociology—E. Franklin Frazier and Charles S. Johnson—and one literary figure with a critical sociological imagination—Richard Wright).

There are several issues that these two most interesting papers focus on, which should be mentioned before moving on to what is perhaps the two most important implicit unifying themes of both documents. The Foster paper offers a fascinating and important case study in how "human subjects" use ascribed and achieved status characteristics to construct and control research processes, particularly when it comes to knowledge access and interpretation issues. This is an important observation since even in the most critical qualitative research methods literature there is a tendency to treat "human subjects" as the passive prisoners of the research process. Instead, as Foster suggests and in some places demonstrates, "human subjects" are all complex human beings with, among other things, consciousness, vested interests, and even hidden agendas.

Although researchers these days wish to be helpful in assisting "human subjects" in their efforts to gain control over their lives, it is easy to forget that, more often than not, the human beings already have control over their lives and negotiate the nature of research processes right under the paternalistic nose of the researcher. We need to learn more about the ways in which subjects participate in research processes as subtle and not-too-subtle negotiators of reality. The ways in which Foster's subjects utilized their age status, racial consciousness, gender, and ethnoregionalism to define the norms of information sharing is an excellent example of how human beings under examination use ascribed and achieved status to structure research processes as interaction relationships.

Feminists have often critiqued the hierarchial character of social research, including the asymmetrical communication styles that mark male-centric logics of inquiry. Whether we consider survey research, ethnography, or experimental design, it is more than apparent that implicit male-centric logics of inquiry insist that researchers talk to rather than with human beings under investigation.

This critique can be extended to racialized ethnic critiques of research traditions.[1] Racialized ethnicity is a political and sociocultural process of categorizing culturally specific populations through linking real or imagined phenotypical attributes to human qualities such as intellectual abilities, moral fiber, and personality. Racialized ethnicity has been a major criterion for building massive domestic and international forms of social inequality in the West for at least the past four hundred years. The hierarchial relations that buttress modes of racialized ethnicity have found their way into the formation of the varieties of knowing that have dominated the West for centuries. During the past one hundred years, the most dominant way of interpreting realities in the West has been the sciences.

The hierarchial relations undergirding the emergence and institutionalization of the human sciences are apparent in the presumptions that have encouraged Westerners to label the nonwesterners they have encountered and studied as primitives, genetically inferior, culturally deficient, underdeveloped, third world, and in other ways inferior. So, it is not too surprising to find that, historically speaking, people of color, even those studied by "their own," more often than not find themselves being talked to rather than talked with when involved in research processes.

Foster gives us a glimpse into examples of Black ethnic discourse styles, which strongly suggest that the usual Eurocentric communication norms and values researchers embrace are not adequate when applied to at least the cultural sites she investigated. For instance, take the example of social status hierarchies as cultural forms in traditional southern Afro-American communities. It is more than apparent that the Afro-Americans Foster interviewed had their own conceptions regarding social hierarchy and how such experiences should be structured with her as an outsider. The notions that people converse rather than be interviewed and that access to information was based upon skin color if not ethnic affinity were important observations for Foster to understand and embrace in order to develop rapport with her informants. Given the social status, ethnic, and ethnoregional diversity of the African-descent population in the United States, more research must be done to flesh out the culturally unique complexities involved in doing first-hand research on Afro-Americans. Mounting empirical evidence, including the Foster paper, indicate that if we want to gain more accurate knowledge about Afro-American experiences, we best pay closer attention to the ways in which Afro-Americans structure conversation as reflections of the ways in which they define and in other ways invent their reality constructions. And perhaps just as well, we need to pay closer attention to the contexts in which such talk takes place—historical moments, political economies, ethnoregional and ecological locations, and community and institutional sites.

The LeCompte and McLaughlin paper brings to mind several matters over and beyond the more obvious concerns of the perils and dilemmas of outsiders looking into the cultures of "Others" and the value of empowerment-oriented research agendas. Perhaps the major important consideration of this paper is the institutional frameworks of the politics of knowing in plural communities dominated by hegemonic ethnic populations. At first glance, the attempt by Navajos to legitimate traditional cultural interpretations and solutions to school problems in contrast to Anglo ways of knowing and problem solving appears to be just another example of knowledge legitimation contests. But the more the paper describes the Anglo institutional control traditions and structures and their "scientific" knowledge foundations, the more it becomes apparent that there really is no contest at all. Even though the most progressive thinking Anglos may have great respect for if not belief in Navajo world views, it is more than obvious who is in control of the schooling structures and processes. From the Bureau of Indian Affairs right down to local reservation levels, even though Navajos are allowed to maintain significant degrees of cultural differences, it is the Anglo administrators who call the shots when it comes to defining appropriate curriculum, teacher training, and the institutional structures of schools. This is what LeCompte and McLaughlin mean, apparently, in their discussions on the ways in which the ethnic hegemony that underlies federal and state approaches to Native American education function to undermine and in other ways discredit the legitimacy of Native American cultural interpretations such as those regarding witchcraft and the Blessing Way Ceremony.

What LeCompte and McLaughlin discuss within the narrow confines of their ethnographic focus certainly is not earth-shattering, at least not in the context of the 1990s. Yet their claims do have very important implications for the general American nation-state. Their observations of the problems Navajos experience in getting their ways of knowing heard and applied and about the communication gaps between Anglos and their Native American subordinates are microcosms of what is going on in the United States today. Specifically, even though there is a great deal of discussion about multiculturalism and growing attempts to implement cultural diversity policies, there is still great resistance to empowering ideas about cultural difference in public culture, mainstream politics, and the business world.

This is because we continue to live in a nation-state in which changing ethnic demographics and political realities have not been matched with efforts to develop a citizenry that really understands what pluralism really means. This is the reason why we still find ourselves entangled in rather absurd debates over the value of cultural diversity and affirmative action. There remains a rather naive assumption in many circles that, at most, multiculturalism means merely indulging in appreciation rituals such as ethnic holidays and wearing ethnic clothing rather than being a mirror of a nation-state which has always been culturally pluralistic.

When we step over the rather simplistic, reified notion of multiculturalism and begin to address structural and political questions about cultural pluralism, it becomes quite threatening to the ethnic status quo. It is one thing to express appreciation for people-of-color cultures and it is another to advocate that Eurocentric power and authority rules be modified to allow Americans of color to be equal if not superior players in the distribution and use of resources. This is why, for instance, whenever Native Americans, Afro-Americans and other people of color begin to demand resources based upon their cultural differences and their human right to build and control their own communities, they have been labeled in negative ways in public culture.

So, my point is, the resistance or, better yet, the indifference or paternalism Anglo power holders displayed toward Native American culture and educational needs discussed by LeCompte and McLaughlin is quite reflective of what is going on in the larger American nation-state. As much as Eurocentric ways of knowing are being undermined by significant ethnic demographic and political economic changes in the United States and on the international level, many powers that be insist on acting as if this were still an unquestionably White world—which it never really has been anyway.

There are two themes running through both papers: first, the political problematics of teaching and schools and cultural diversity, and second, expanding definitions and uses of research in culturally diverse settings. That learning how to teach and teaching are political activities is not a surprising finding. What is important to realize though, as both of these papers point out in unique ways, is that historically speaking teachers as cultural transmitters have been central producers of the sort of knowledge that has created, institutionalized, and transformed historically specific phases of the United States as a racialized, ethnically hegemonic nation-state.

More important, teacher training and teaching are cultural and political practices occurring in schools and other institutional contexts rooted in historically specific, political, economic, and social contexts. In regard to

racialized ethnic inequality, a major function of training teachers and of
the establishment of educational institutions has been on the one hand to
legitimate assimilation and accommodation norms and values and on the
other hand to discredit elements of indigenous non-White cultures that
encourage critical political responses to the racialized ethnic status quo. So,
it is no significant surprise to find that the history of Black education has
been very much the history of tracking Afro-Americans into nonintellectual
tracks and exposing them to obsolete technologies and marginalized voca-
tions. It is also the reason why, although liberal arts have been incorporated
within the curricula of historically Black colleges, the focus has in most
institutions been on Eurocentric arts and sciences with little attention paid to
the validity of Afro-American experiences in need of political empowerment.

Among Native Americans, teacher training and teaching remain under
the political control of Anglos in state and federal bureaucracies and in
home-missionary societies, including and especially those aspects of formal
and informal learning experiences that spring from indigenous cultural elements. As in the case of Afro-Americans and other people of color, Native
Americans who wish to be upwardly mobile in this nation-state learn relatively quickly that the intrusion of Eurocentric ways of knowing and acting
in their lives requires that one at least acts as if one is becoming or actually
is assimilated on the way up the educational ladder. Even in 1990s terms,
there is still a great deal of Eurocentric anxiety displayed toward well-
educated people of color who "act" too ethnic and, more than that, too
independent (even though as Whites continue to rediscover their ethnicity,
it is trendy to boast about one's European immigrant roots; and of course,
being an independent individual has always been a cultural and a political
privilege Euro-Americans have sanctioned and enjoyed).

The issue of contexts in the politics of teacher training and teaching as
theory and practice in a historically plural nation-state is an important point
since ethnographers, oral historians, and other qualitative researchers rarely
peer outside schools' walls in efforts to understand the more macro structures
that influence micro processes of knowledge defining and dissemination.
More than this perhaps, the overstress on schools as primodal learning
settings overlooks or minimizes what some have called nontraditional cultural sites as educational institutions: families, religious orders, street corners, hair-styling shops, and fraternal organizations all supplement and
influence what students learn or do not learn in official schooling institutions.
This point is critical in the issues raised in these papers, since so much of
what people of color are is not picked up in schools or reaffirmed in schooling
processes. As well, teachers coming from culturally diverse backgrounds
who "think" and "act" ethnic can find themselves embroiled in frustration
if not open conflict when confronted with school and government bureaucracies and with community leaders, which at most give lip service to "multicul-

tural appreciation" but which are actually indifferent to social and cultural empowerment issues. This came across quite clearly in LeCompte and McLaughlin's observations regarding the conflicts Navajo program administrators experienced when confronted with Eurocentric teacher training selection criteria which impeded native access. Foster's commentary on the political conflicts between White and Afro-American teachers in a predominantly Black community college in the Northeast is a vivid example of how efforts to educate Afro-Americans in ways that validate and empower unique cultural norms and values is more often than not compromised and derailed (I am thinking of the other example of how, historically speaking, Black-controlled school movements have been impeded in their success by White philanthropists, media, and the federal government withholding funds or labeling such efforts as being racist or militant).

One of the more interesting spins on the post-1970s critique of professional authority is the attack on logical positivism as the dominant definition of scientific inquiries. Whether we turn to chaos and hologram paradigms in the physical and biological sciences or postmodernism and cultural studies paradigms in the human sciences, it has become cutting edge to declare the terminal illness of logical positivism and to promote humane ways of explaining realities. Even in the most conservative circles of sciences, where logical positivism reigns supreme in their very cores, there has been a raising of ethical consciousness which has begun to force scientists as professionals to think twice about the human and environmental implications of their work.

The politicalization of American ethnic diversity in the midst of the rising importance of people of color as major if not dominant domestic and international power players has predictably found its way into rebellions against logical positivistic reasoning in sciences, especially the human sciences. Ethnic arrogance, if not blatant racism and ethnocentrism, have been central to the historical construction, institutionization, and professionalization of human sciences. For years, the universal knowledge and rational reductionism claims of logical positivistic human sciences have been grounded in Eurocentric assumptions applied uncritically and arrogantly to people-of-color experiences. As a consequence, it has been assumed in the logical positivism frame of reference in the human sciences that people of color can be studied the same way Whites are studied, and more importantly that the absence or presence of universal Eurocentric experiences in people-of-color cultural sites (such as "standard English" or "rational thinking") are empirical markers of degrees of "civilization" or "development." It has also been assumed that, through technical manipulations of data, it is possible for even the most racially and culturally biased researcher to be neutral in data interpretations. Last and certainly not least, the logical positivistic traditions that have defined the human sciences promote the view that science is in essence an elitist venture that has to do with the career development of the scientist rather than the empowerment of the human beings under investigation.

A new generation of scholars across color lines are beginning to raise questions about the value of research in a world in which "subjects" drawn from oppressed populations are presently in various phases of political empowerment, if not political and economic liberation. It is within the context of this emerging literature that we are beginning to understand that in a nation-state and world in which the oppressed are more aware of the elitist, if not racist, agendas and outcomes of human scientific research, it is not advantageous for researchers to continue to approach research as a career advancement venture divorced from the lives of those they study. As a friend of mine put it, the natives are getting restless. Those oppressed people who used to allow researchers to enter their institutions and communities freely are now demanding through their advocates, attorneys, and governments and media that researchers be accountable and give something of significance back to them (besides monetary tokens of appreciation or a box of used, dirty clothes). More than that, a growing number of people of color and poor people are beginning to bar researchers from their cultural sites.

So, hopefully because it is the right thing to do but more often than not due to growing access problems, American human scientists are beginning to redefine what research should be and what it should be used for in people-of-color cultural sites. These two papers represent some interesting twists and turns in this emerging discussion. The Foster paper reminds us that research in people-of-color cultural sites should be a two-way learning experience for credentialed insiders as well as outsiders. The research process such as oral-history interviewing or participant observation should be structured in such a way so as not only to empower "subjects" but also to contribute to the human development of the researcher.

The LeCompte and McLaughlin paper reminds us of the virtues of participatory research. It also should be an important reminder of how much work needs to be done to expand the parameters of research designs that attempt to empower residents in examined cultural sites. Usually when we think about participatory research, what comes to mind are researcher attempts to assist the examined human beings in their efforts to improve their quality of life and to have more control over it. This is a good start. But there are other questions that have not been as clearly addressed in the participatory research literature.

For instance, how should "subjects" play an active part in designing and carrying out the research process from start to finish as equal partners of the researcher? In what ways should researchers share career credits with involved "subjects" such as coauthorships, coprincipal investigators on grants, royalties, etc? Should "subjects" ending up in major publications have a say in the evaluation of researchers for tenure and promotion in their universities? These questions radically broaden what is meant by participatory research.

In relation to education, papers such as the two in question suggest new areas of critical inquiry about the politics of racialized ethnic hegemony in schooling processes. There is a steady stream of profound contradictions and paradoxes characteristic of structuring educational institutions in a historically plural nation-state that gives little real political and economic legitimacy to cultural differences, particularly when it comes to people of color. These papers would assist us in rethinking ways in which we conceptualize and study power and authority issues in education through considering the politics of racialized ethnic hegemony as context in the formation of internal schooling processes and structures and their external environments.

Note

1. See "Ethnic Modelling" in Norman Denzin and Yvonna Lincoln, *Research handbook on qualitative research methods* (Newbury Park, CA: Sage, forthcoming).

Section Two

Power and Method in Context

Relationships Within Qualitative Research

ALTERNATIVE METHODOLOGIES
AND THE RESEARCH CONTEXT

Andrew Gitlin and Robyn Russell

During the last decade, traditional research methods have come under constant attack. Whereas research was once seen as a way to rid educational decisions of politics, some feminist scholars are now arguing for openly ideological research (Lather 1986; Weiler 1988). Objectivity, a cherished aim of educational research is now openly challenged both by educational ethnographers and other scholars who champion the need for more interpretive approaches. Who is expected to do research is also in doubt. Where heretofore research has been conducted exclusively by university scholars, academics are now putting forth powerful proposals that suggest the need for parents, teachers, and students to be involved in the research process (Cochran-Smith and Lytle, 1990).

These debates have been invaluable in challenging taken-for-granted assumptions about objectivity, validity, reliability, and who should be involved in the research process. However, by separating out questions about research from the research context, the debate has deemphasized the relation between structures, wider ideological assumptions, and method. In this chapter, we attempt to consider this relation by examining how the research context informs an alternative methodology, Educative Research. The first part of this essay examines some of the ideological assumptions and material conditions that texture the terrain on which research takes place. The second part chronicles our attempts to develop this alternative method, Educative Research, and the final section considers the implications of the research context for this alternative methodology.

Legitimate Knowledge

Historically, the push to have research drive educational decisions was linked in strong ways to the distrust and disdain of experience as a form of legitimate knowledge. For example, the first teacher-training institutions, the normal schools, came under attack in the early part of the twentieth century, primarily because those teaching in these schools relied on their experience, not research methods, to structure their courses. If these institutions were to help professionalize teaching, research needed to replace experience as the basis for determining desirable aims and practices. Any type of research, however, would not do. Initially, it was argued that only scientific research could serve as a corrective for practical experience and haphazard empiricism (Powell 1971).

Over time, as research knowledge became seen as *the* form of legitimate knowledge, the influence of those who based their knowledge on experience was curtailed. While it is true that experiential knowledge has currency within some local contexts, such as schools, at the policy level it carries little weight. This hierarchy between experiential knowledge and research knowledge continues to be reinforced by the fact that large segments of the educational community work in intensified environments where for all practical purposes there is no opportunity to produce research knowledge (Apple 1986).

Work Conditions

Dominant beliefs about what is legitimate knowledge illuminate ideological prejudgments about the relation between research and context; they do not tell us about the influence of work conditions on the nature of research. These material conditions are important because no matter what dominant beliefs may be in vogue, if particular groups do not have the opportunity to produce knowledge that is seen as legitimate, then these groups will inevitably be excluded from participating fully in community decision making (Pateman 1970). The material realities of participants in the community tell us quite a bit about the influence of context on method.

A look at the material realities of the educational community shows that there is a clear division between two groups: those housed within universities and colleges and those working at the level of practice. For those working in higher education, work is structured so that time is available for research. In fact, many professors teach only two courses a term, making it possible for them to spend the vast majority of their time doing research. Furthermore, professors are rewarded for doing research. While all sorts of documents can be found that indicate that teaching and research are of supposed equal importance, research, in the final analysis, seems to be what counts for tenure, promotion and merit salary increases.[1] Finally, while it is true that professors are not immune from local pressures to produce a certain type of research and to publish in particular journals, there are no direct consequences for taking a position that is unique, radical, or esoteric. At least on the surface, universities applaud work that is seen as innovative and different.

In contrast to the general work conditions of professors, teachers have a very intense work situation. Not only are they teaching almost from the minute they step into the school until the final bell rings, but the number of students in a class requires that they make thousands of quick decisions in the course of a school day (Jackson 1968). Furthermore, many teachers correct papers for at least a couple of hours after school. Put simply, teachers hardly have time to grab a cup of coffee, never mind do research.

But even if one could make the case that teachers could engage in research, the question of why they would do so under the current reward structure becomes an important query. Currently, teachers are rewarded primarily for staying on the job. They are neither rewarded for excellence nor demoted because of incompetence. What seems to be most valued by administrators is the ability of a teacher to be nondisruptive. This notion was first made popular by none other than Horace Mann, who stated that teacher professionalism "involved first a deep sense of being called to serve . . . a sense so strong that one would persist in service regardless of the difficulties entailed or the temptations of other activities" (Borrowman 1965, 24). A teacher who is not complained about by parents and who follows administrative mandates without much fuss is exactly such a teacher. On a pragmatic level, there is little or no incentive for teachers to add to their already busy schedules and do research. Finally, even if teachers were rewarded for doing research, it is still the case that teachers are held to local norms much more closely than professors. Given that university research usually does not focus on a professor's own classroom, and that academic freedom still has some meaning (although clearly it is constrained in significant ways), university faculty are able to experiment with ideas and procedures and even miss the mark several times without direct consequences for their students or job. Teachers, on the other hand, are usually most interested in problems and possibilities associated with their classroom. Furthermore, because they are typically thought of as public servants who are to uphold community values, their work is measured in formal and informal ways by community opinions (Bullough, Gitlin, and Goldstein 1984). Those who want to take risks and try new instructional approaches and procedures, therefore, must not only keep in mind what these innovations might do to students but also how the community will react to the research process. As a consequence, the scope of research questions teachers can safely pose is limited by the practical nature of their work and their constructed role as public servants.

Who is Expert?

Related to the above concern about the differentiated work structures found in the community is the question of who is able to be seen as expert. Although all members of any community cannot be considered experts of all sorts, it is important to acknowledge the different types of expertise particular groups may bring to the decision-making process. Parents, for example, may not be experts in matters of curriculum, but most surely have an understanding of the needs of children; yet parents are rarely consulted when it comes to educational matters. Much the same can be said about teachers. Although most understand the limits and possibilities of curriculum implementation, the needs of students, and the problems of working in a crowded classroom, teachers are rarely consulted in terms of overarching educational decisions.

Research, as currently conceptualized, allows a small segment of the educational community to produce a specialized form of knowledge that is typically considered more objective or at the least more insightful than the knowledge produced from experience. Because researchers produce such knowledge, they are considered to be experts—members of the educational community who inform others, such as teachers, how to work within their classrooms. Furthermore, because researchers are viewed as experts by many in the educational community, they can successfully request an unequal share of the community resources.

The Influence of Method

Dominant research practices also help bound the research context. Specifically, it is clear that some community members (teachers, parents, and students) become objects of study who have few opportunities to further their own development, while others (the researchers) are intimately involved in examining their understanding of the world and, more specifically, educational issues. Research, as currently conceptualized, helps create a great divide between those who regularly produce specialized forms of knowledge and those who are supposed to be informed by that knowledge. When research is constructed in this way, it provides a counterweight to a fully participatory form of decision making.

The influence of research on change is an important aspect of understanding the research context. Unfortunately, when research is looked at from the perspective of what difference it makes, the overwhelming conclusion is that while it may make an individual difference for the career of the researcher and may contribute to intellectual debates, it rarely influences classroom practice. Forms of action research and collaborative research that are now gaining some popularity hold some promise in this regard (Kemmis 1984). Most qualitative and quantitative studies, however, rarely find their ways to the classroom door, and, even when they do, the local context usually makes the implementation of the reported insights difficult.

In sum, the following claims can be made about the relation between research and the research context:

1. Legitimate knowledge is narrowly understood as research knowledge. Experiential knowledge tends to be discounted ex-

cept in local situations that have little influence on policy matters.

2. Material work conditions structure a division of labor between practitioners and academics such that those on the lower rungs of the hierarchy are denied opportunities to produce what is seen as legitimate knowledge.

3. Notions of expertise are constructed in narrow ways. This construction denies the knowledge various groups have gained through their lived experiences.

4. Traditional research furthers the division between those who reflect on and scrutinize reality and those who are objects of inquiry.

5. Traditional research does little to foster change and therefore may act primarily to legitimate the status quo.

Educative Research

We turn now to our attempt to develop an alternative methodology, Educative Research. By describing the assumptions and practices of this approach, as well as by providing a case study, a text will be created that will enable us to scrutinize this method in terms of its relation to the research context.

Assumptions

Researcher/"Subject" Relationships

Educative Research attempts to restructure the traditional relationship between researcher and "subject". Instead of a one-way process where researchers extract data from "subjects," Educative Research encourages a dialogical process where participants negotiate meanings at the level of question posing, data collection, and analysis. This dialogical relation allows both participants to become the "changer and the changed" (Williamson, in Lather 1988, 570). It also encourages participants to work together on an equal basis to reach a mutual understanding. Neither participant should stand apart in an aloof or judgmental manner; neither should be silenced during the process (Bernstein 1983). Instead, both participants are united by the quest to examine the topic at hand as well as to reveal contradictions and constraints within the educative process itself. The intent of this dialogue is not to discover absolutes, or "the truth," but to scrutinize normative "truths" that are embedded in a specific historical and cultural context. In this way, taken-for-granted notions can be challenged as educators work to better understand schooling.

VOICE

The central motivation for encouraging a dialogical approach is that it can further the aim of developing voice among those who have been silenced historically. The opportunity to speak, to question, and to explore issues is an important aspect of this process. But the notion of voice can go far beyond the opportunity to speak; it can be about protest. Understood in this way, voice becomes politicized; its aim is to question what is taken for granted and to act on what is seen to be unjust in an attempt to shape and aide future educational directions. Injustice or oppression cannot be defined outside of a historical context. However, members of the educational community are encouraged to scrutinize relations where one group has power over another. Included in this analysis should be the structures that unnecessarily elevate particular groups and stereotype and constrain others. Voice as a form of protest is directed both outward at the social construction of meaning making and the structures that reinforce those meanings, and inward at the way the individual takes part in the production of certain constrained beliefs, roles, and practices.

UNDERSTANDING AND PRACTICE

For this type of protest to make a difference, these insights must be linked to practice. Educative Research attempts to do so by shifting the primary responsibility of doing research from the university faculty member to the practitioner. While the university member still has a role, the focus on the practitioner allows those who are acting at the level of practice to also gain understanding through the inquiry process. There is no need for the understanding to "trickle down," because the institutional separation between those who do conceptual work and those who practice teaching at the very least becomes more fluid.

Enabling practitioners to be involved in the research process goes a long way toward linking understanding and practice. However, there are still potential threats to this linkage. One such threat is the traditional view that research is a product. When research is approached in this manner, even if conducted by a person acting at the level of practice, understanding is still separated from practice within a temporal frame such that understanding occurs and then is applied to practice. Furthermore, this separation of understanding and practice makes it difficult for the research findings to act back on the research question in a continuous, fluid manner.

Educative Research confronts this threat by being primarily a process with turning points that redirect inquiry rather than a product. This allows the research process to alter the questions asked and influence practice as insights are gained.

AUTHENTICITY

Most educational research leaves the author out of the text; the research-er's judgments, biases, and evolving views are not included as part of the report. This omission is not the result of forgetfulness, but rather reflects the assumption that to present data that will be convincing and deemed legitimate, attempts must be made to bracket out the subjective. The illusion created by this bracketing can be very convincing. However, the author is part of the research not only because the questions posed reflect a focus on one set of concerns rather than another, but also because the constructs developed (i.e., the organization of the data) and even the form and style of the communication all are linked to the perspective and orientation that the author brings to the research project. For research to be authentic, the relationship between what is said and the person(s) doing the talking must be made apparent.

VALIDITY AND RELIABILITY

Validity and reliability are the criteria that set the standards on which research is judged. Because Educative Research attempts to alter the meaning of research and its purposes, traditional definitions of reliability and validity must be altered. The validity, or "truthfulness," of the data can no longer be understood as something extracted by an individual armed with a set of research procedures, but rather as a mutual process, pursued by researcher and those studied, that recognizes the value of practical knowledge, theoreti-cal inquiry and systematic examinations. The researcher's knowledge is not assumed to be more legitimate than the "subject's," nor is his/her role one of helping the needy other. Rather, the researcher and subject attempt to come to a mutual understanding based on their own strongly articulated positions.

Questions of validity, however, must go beyond the truthfulness of the data. The influence of the research process on who produces knowledge, who is seen as expert, and the resulting changes at the level of school practice are also part of an expanded and political view of validity. For example, one criteria of validity could be the degree to which the research process enables disenfranchised groups to fully participate in the decision-making process; to examine their beliefs, actions, and the school context; and to make changes based on this understanding. The role of research in establish-ing authoritarian relationships that silence particular groups and limit re-flectivity would threaten validity as we have defined it.

Traditional notions of reliability are also altered when the central aim of the research process is to develop voice. Within traditional methods, reliabil-ity is understood in terms of the ability of independent researchers to come to the same conclusions when the same procedures are used. In contrast, when the aim is the development of voice, it is not expected and is indeed undesirable that independent researcher-subject teams come to the same conclusions. It is also undesirable for the procedures to remain unchanged from context to context. Procedures should be allowed not only to evolve within a specific research study but also to change given the needs and priorities of a particular population. Reliability, therefore, cannot be based on duplicating procedures, but rather must center on attempts to satisfy the underlying principle of voice and its relation to a desired type of school change.

Practices

The two year cooperative Master's program at the University of Utah provided an opportunity to try out and further develop the underlying assumptions of Educative Research. In particular, because the curriculum structure of the program was very flexible, encouraged teacher input, and allowed a university professor to work with a group of teachers for an extended period of time, a long-range process of question posing, data collection, analysis, and action could be attempted.

While most research approaches include practices such as data collection and analysis, our approach differed from others in that these activities, as well as the actions taken, acted back on the questions posed. Put simply, we did not follow a linear approach to research but instead tried to foster a more fluid orientation. Educative Research also differs from other approaches by emphasizing the question-posing process. This process involves the production of "texts" that focused attention on self, context, and the connections between understanding and practice. By examining these "texts" and their relationship, the basis for a research question can emerge.

While the assumptions described produce a snapshot of what is Educative Research, they do not provide an adequate basis on which to assess the relation between context and method. Only an actual account of a participant's journey can illuminate the possibilities and limits of this approach to research. To consider more carefully these possibilities and limits, we turn to Robyn's story—a story shaped by the assumptions and practices of Educative Research.

A Case Study

Typically, researchers are absent from the text. They make themselves invisible not only to bolster claims about their "objective" or unbiased point of view, but also to make clear that their theoretical insights are not contaminated by experiential knowledge. In contrast, Robyn begins with her struggles and considers how these struggles relate to the project at hand and to the initial questions she poses.

The struggle between silence and voice has been lifelong for me. The ramifications of swinging back and forth between the act of speaking out and reticence are markers along a path that defines who I am. Society told me to be seen and not heard, like some naughty child, while an inside whisper begged for a listening ear. It was within this state of fluctuation that I began a journey into further study of the educational system. This story is about my chosen project of developing teacher voice; but more than this, it is about my own travels in this previously uncharted terrain: to speak and to be heard.

When I entered teaching, little did I realize how suited to silence was my occupational choice. My mother promoted it as the "ideal woman's profession." It wasn't until much later that I discovered that teachers have historically held a passive voice in the whirlwind of educational research and theory. This passivity, in my case, was often coupled with strategies to falsify my behavior to please others. As I note in my personal history:

> My "falsifying" or "cheating" took on three main behaviors, recognizable even in my personal relationships. These are described by Jackson (1968) as common to most schools' implicit curriculum . . ." (1) to behave in such a way as to enhance the likelihood of praise and reduce the likelihood of punishment . . . , (2) publicize positive evaluations and conceal negative ones . . . , (3) behave in ways that disguise the failure to comply." (Jackson 1968, 26).

I am still living the imprint of these lessons as I cope with the balancing act of being as others wish me to be and gaining an acceptance of self. Professionally, I face this quandary each time my principal enters my classroom to do a teaching evaluation.

The writing of my school history furthered my understanding of voice and silence by pointing to the way school structures silence teachers. I found the mandated curriculum and required texts used at the school played a role in silencing my educational beliefs and aims. My analysis of a teacher survey, conducted as part of my school history, suggested that other teachers feel constrained as well.

> There is so much already determined by the state core and the district, that many of us limit our involvement to how and in what order the material will be presented. Some don't even do that. This causes one to suspect that teachers have almost completely withdrawn from the professional aspects of curriculum planning and development. But not without hard feelings.

Much of my growing awareness about educational voice and silence was also enhanced when I explored a vast array of literature as part of the Educative Research project. These readings released me from the guilt of what I could not change and gave me permission to change all I could. I gained confidence in my teaching. I began to speak out and not hide behind by "closed classroom door." This signified a major shift in my relation to the system. I had learned to conceal what I was doing to survive in teaching. I recognized how my own hidden curriculum was perpetuating a profession of silent subversion:—a political act that continued the hierarchy and status quo. I realized that I had been a guard in a prison of my own making.

Peer dialogue in the form of Horizontal Evaluation, a process whereby two or more participants attempt to better understand teaching through the examination of interactions, practice, and their relation (Gitlin and Smyth 1989), furthered my desire to understand the issue of voice and silence by providing the first glimpse of what could be done to confront my silence and the silence of teachers generally. I found that when I used this dialogical process, I was increasingly willing to examine and change my old teaching patterns. The benefits of this form of evaluation were numerous, as I noted in one of my Horizontal Evaluation conferences.

> The benefits are spreading as I develop a stronger voice about my values with regard to school issues. Newly found confidence in my teaching and its underlying values enables me to express my views to colleagues, parents, administrators, and the school board. I'm more willing to risk exposing my opinions about our school structures and issues. This benefit has come directly from Horizontal Evaluation as I reflect on my values and express them in the clearest terms to Kathy, my partner.

It was for these reasons that I decided to reach out to my peers, through dialogue, to share in this adventure of the development of teacher voice.

THE INITIAL DEVELOPMENT OF A QUESTION

By creating several texts on self and context and then considering how those texts related to teaching practice, Robyn started to develop a series of questions. As opposed to most researchers, who see their questions coming out of a particular discipline of theoretical orientation, Robyn's issues and queries were linked to self and her everyday practices in the local context of schooling. In particular, Robyn came to believe that, in general, teachers do not have a voice in educational reform. An investigation of school structures as part of the writing of her school history strengthened this belief by pointing to the way job intensification, the schedules of the teaching day, teacher isolation, and the feminization of teaching limit opportunities for teachers to work on reforms and constrain their influence, even when they are asked to contribute in some small way. What follows describes Robyn's initial attempt to develop research questions.

The simple act of talking about these issues began to change my professional life. The empowerment for which I so longed in my profession and my life was within me. This is not to say there were and are no structural barriers, but as I addressed the self-imposed restrictions, the other barriers were more clearly defined and understood.

These changes in my perception of the teacher role caused me to look at how others could also benefit from dialogue. A recurrent question began to appear in my thoughts and writing: How might our school, or even our profession, change if discussion and reflection were made available and encouraged in a wider audience of teachers? As this possibility was discussed with others, I began to look for a way to answer that question.

Toward this end, I decided to: (1) determine teachers' attitudes about professional dialogue, defined as "a discussion among two or more colleagues about issues related to the profession"[2], (2) organize a method for the development of teacher voice through dialogue, and (3) evaluate and analyze the dialogue sessions to better understand their import. Results of the teacher attitude survey were analyzed in combination with the themes and patterns found consistently within the teacher dialogue sessions.

During the week following each of the first four teacher dialogue sessions, and twice during the 1989-90 school year, Kathy, my Horizontal Evaluation partner, and I met to review and compare notes. This comprised a second area of data collection. Horizontal Evaluation was used to compare the intentions for the meeting with the realities of what transpired. Transcripts of my dialogue with Kathy provided an additional text to determine how the process was influencing each dialogue session.

As I transcribe my two-year study, I start with the question of professional dialogue and consider how this concern changed over time. I then discuss my reflections on the meetings, possibilities for change among the participants, and future directions.

REVISITING THE QUESTION

Even though Robyn is well into the Educative Research process at this point and is trying to make a difference by implementing dialogue sessions with other teachers in the school, her gaze is not solely directed at the results and their possible importance, as would be the case of most researchers. Instead, she uses the practices of research to look back toward the assumptions embedded in her initial query. Specifically, she starts to question the relation between dialogue and the teacher's voice. She describes this rethinking process in this way:

When I began this project, I assumed everyone knew what I meant by dialogue. I was warned by several people that this could become an exercise in futility, with teachers merely using the dialogue forum as a gripe session. While I wasn't sure that allowing teachers to gripe was all bad (as a peer pointed out, some might call this "problem posing" if mentioned in reference to, say, someone in business), I did look upon a more formal dialogue about broader educational issues as preferable to the common "presentist" talk of teachers. I have, however, since rediscovered the value inherent in informal conversations among teachers. These informal discussions are a foundation for teachers to break through their isolation and build confidence. It is only where trust and openness are encouraged that a more formal sense of dialogue is likely to take place. Since the more common, informal talk of teachers provides a starting point for more formal dialogue, any combination of the two seemed important for the development of voice. With this developing sense of dialogue in mind, I turned my attention to the question of why, as a group, teachers' voices are not heard.

IN SEARCH OF AN AUDIENCE

It appears that silence and its seeming flip side of talking has a lot to do with the question of audience. At times, silence can be more a lack of acceptable voice, not an absence of voice. Teachers do discuss educational issues, but these issues tend to be skewed toward classroom concerns (what to do about Suzy's behavior, how to deal with yet another district mandate, etc.). Teachers' tendency to focus on these sorts of issues has much to do with the expectation that no one of importance will listen or consider their views. They have grown to anticipate the continuance of school structures and mandates, instigated without their input and often in the face of their objections. The challenge for teachers, as well as for other silenced groups such as Black women, is not to "emerge from silence to speech, but to change the nature and direction of our speech. To make a speech that compels listeners, one that is heard," (hooks 1989). There is much that traditionally silenced people do share and the shift of voice to "one that is heard" is exactly what teachers must do if we hope to have an impact on current educational structures, theories, and aims.

One way to move the conversation from perceived futile griping to one that "compels listeners" might be to incorporate research as a way to cultivate ourselves and validate our views. I found a growing audience as I learned to incorporate research into my expressions. Surprisingly, I discovered a maturing acceptance of my expertise as a practitioner through reading the works of those considered educational experts.

Teachers typically have very little awareness or access to current research. I, too, have been hesitant to read journals that continuously blame the classroom teacher for our educational ills while promoting strategies that are out of touch with the realities of class size, minimal pay, and intensified scheduling. I have also seen how this absence of outside input has limited the expression of my educational views, thus contributing to my frustration and aura of silence. While recognizing the value of practical knowledge, my own as well as others', I have grown to accept and respect the place research can hold in informing practice. If research is to be made more available to classroom teachers, however, the assumptions of the process need to be examined. Research cannot be accepted as "truth" but rather as a focus for discussion and comparison to the practical concerns of teachers.

With these developing assumptions regarding dialogue and the cultivation of an audience shaping her perspectives, Robyn continued meeting with the teachers in what became known as dialogue sessions. What follows differs from typical research accounts, in that Robyn is not only reporting the results of the dialogue sessions but also her journey within them. Included in this journey are her actions as well as her thinking about the sessions themselves. By inserting herself into the text she is able to look critically at her role as participant in the group. The research, therefore, is directed in part at the researcher and can play a role in altering the relationships among the research participants.

REFLECTIONS ON THE DIALOGUE SESSIONS

Twenty-five teachers attended the first session in April of 1989. Teachers were eager to talk to each other, and I felt exhilarated at this successful beginning. Some objected to my request to audiotape the session, even though I assured them I would be the only person who would hear it and that it would be used only for the purposes of my research. Promises of anonymity were rejected, so we went on to the topic of "teacher isolation" solely depending on my marginal note-taking skills. Several teachers continued animated conversation after the meeting had ended, and one teacher enthusiastically commented during recess duty, "Congratulations! You've gotten teachers talking to each other!" I was feeling quite pleased and believed this dialogue session idea was going to work.

As I reflected on the four dialogue sessions instigated in the 1988–89 school year, I realized I had certain naive expectations about how they would transpire based, in part, on this initial success. I thought that, given the chance to discuss educational issues with their peers, many teachers of diverse philosophies would attend often. I expected to establish a core group, at the very least. This was not the case. Attendance had become so erratic by the end of the fourth session that this "core group" was composed of

Kathy, who had to attend for our Horizontal Evaluation conference, and myself. Somehow, these dialogue sessions were not meeting teacher needs. Otherwise, it seemed to me, attendance would be a priority.

A common fear I faced, and with which I continue to deal, concerned my own abilities and qualifications in conducting these sessions. I had never attended a teacher dialogue meeting before I introduced them to my peers. My experience was comprised of faculty meetings. I knew I did not want to duplicate those, but what type of session would be an appropriate model? When few teachers attended or participated, I was certain it was due to my inability to discern their needs and desires. Surely, another teacher with better skills and knowledge could do justice to this cause, yet who was this person?

Other structures and issues besides my feelings of incompetence affected attendance. The lack of trust among teachers, as well as between the teachers and administration, was obvious. The refusal to participate if the first session was audiotaped was one example of lack of trust. The interference of other scheduled meetings also limited attendance. The absence of administrative support, although not altogether unexpected, did surprise me in its intensity. Perhaps inadequate teacher input on the topics for dialogue was an inhibiting factor. Questions about my level of influence in the sessions continued to be raised in my mind. I wrote about my concerns in a reflection on my project:

> Teachers complained of attending meetings where the agenda is determined and manipulated by the administration. How different is it if the agenda is determined and manipulated by me? Probably a minimal difference. The intention of this project is to give teachers a forum to develop their voices, in whatever direction that might be. How can that happen if they cannot have a voice in how the meeting is organized? If I perceive my position as one who is more knowledgeable because I have experienced or read more, am I any different from those in administration? No.

It was within the storm of these previously unforseen obstructions, priorities, and questions that the 1989–90 teacher discussion sessions were approached.

At this time, the notion of dialogue was maturing within my mind. I was hoping that as teachers discussed educational issues among themselves, dialogue could begin with administrators, some level of agreement could be achieved, and we could move forward toward new educational horizons. Unfortunately, this goal was still limited by a number of problems in simply getting the dialogue sessions off the ground, many of which were experienced the year before: inconsistent attendance, time constraints, lack of recognition by the administration, and a lack of ownership.

This last problem was summed up to me by one teacher who said the reason for her inconsistent involvement in the sessions was feeling as though it was "supporting [me] in [my] little deal." How could I make it her "little deal" too? Questions I started asking myself included:

- Why would I, as a teacher, get involved in the group?
- How can I get the teachers past the stage of thinking this is what they do for me and toward doing it for themselves? They picked the schedule and the topics, yet still the meetings were my "little deal."

This question of ownership seemed to further point to the possibility that the professional dialogue sessions were not yet meeting teachers' needs. I decided to take the issue right to the teachers and ask them what they wanted to spend time working on.

During our December meeting, it was decided we would develop a proposal for a computer lab for the school. An earlier request for a lab had been refused. This push for what we wanted in the face of the administration's refusal was an aspect of empowerment previously unseen. The organizational power of the group, in contrast to individual effort, had begun to be realized. Suggestions for researching benefits and detriments found in other schools with labs was pursued, as was exploring costs and potential funding. One of our teachers had studied the philosophical implications of computer technology with regard to gender and class, and was asked to present her findings. With this topic as a focus, and the possibility of change within the reach of teachers, a core group of seven began to formalize.

The developing sense of influence greatly affected the nature of our next dialogue session, which was attended by the district superintendent. (He had previously indicated an interest in our meetings and had finally accepted our invitation.) Our discussion involved the district's recommendation of the use of only one type of kindergarten-through-sixth-grade science program. We discussed possibilities such as funding science equipment and materials instead of classroom sets of textbooks that, for many of us, most likely would sit unused on the shelves. Ideas were explored as we worked around the previously perceived impenetrable structures and mandates of the administration. Many teachers, myself included, were unaware of this potential flexibility on the part of the administration. This was also a significant shift in the teachers' willingness to discuss issues of concern with those in power. The alternatives we explored were taken to the faculty and discussed further. Many intended to follow the alternate path and order equipment, not textbooks. Empowerment through dialogue and our ability to make more substantive choices was beginning to be experienced.

As Robyn concludes the discussion of her journey to develop voice in herself and the teachers in her school, she reflects on what difference if any this process has made. In doing so, she builds on the tradition of action research in that the study is not only conceptual, aimed at understanding, but also directed at making changes. As opposed to some action research projects, however, the change is not simply a form of individual empowerment but rather part of a collective effort to make a difference in the school:

At the beginning of this journey, I asked a question: How might our school, or even our profession, change if discussion and reflection were made available and were encouraged in a wider audience of teachers? Change is an elusive perception, hard to document and prove. Nevertheless, I believe change has occurred for teachers and administrators. While recognizing that changes within me were motivating factors for this project, I too have continued to change.

Teachers discussed some perceived changes during our last dialogue session of the 1989–90 school year. In general, it was enthusiastically agreed that isolation was decreased and trust was growing among members of the group. Often the topics we discussed were continued among a wider audience during lunch, and comments about more sharing between grade levels were made. Barriers of isolation were beginning to break down.

The heightened sense of power a group can hold, as opposed to individual teachers attempting to initiate change, was acknowledged. The speed with which those changes can take place when a group of teachers are supporting them was also explored. This growing sense of empowerment to address and change structures through dialogue and in an environment of trust is in direct contrast to the traditional isolation and acceptance of the hierarchy. As more and more educational issues are addressed, these teachers are redefining and recreating their own sense of professionalism to include the investigation of the aims, as well as means, of education.

While changing the administration was not a goal, it has been an unforeseen side benefit that occurred as teachers began speaking of their views and concerns. Administrators have begun to listen. One change transpired at the beginning of the 1989–90 school year. The principal announced that in our faculty meetings there would be scheduled time for sharing ideas and discussions of professional issues generated by the faculty; only a small portion of time would be taken for business and administrator-generated items. This had not been addressed before, and our principal admitted that this was her response to the interest displayed in our dialogue gatherings.

Our superintendent has spoken highly of our attempts to generate dialogue among the teachers in our school. In a recent letter, he wrote:

> I enjoyed the discussion . . . and was impressed with the importance of the issues you dealt with and the thoughtfulness with which those issues were discussed. I think that you have launched some-thing very important and worthwhile. I would like to see similar groups develop all over the district. I think if teachers had the opportunity to participate in discussions such as [these], they would find their professional work much more stimulating and growth promoting. Moreover, there would be, over time, an increase in the quality and effectiveness of teaching and learning.[3]

It appears our superintendent is redefining traditional notions of profession-alism in favor of the idea that dialogue is conducive to growth. This bodes well for future possibilities for this forum.

The dialogue between the teachers and our superintendent extends the range of this project. As I wrote in a letter to the superintendent after his visit in 1991, "It is important for me and others at my school to see your interest in what we are doing. I'm sure I can no longer speak of 'the admin-istration' as a . . . faceless power structure, as I have been known to do in the past."

Revisiting the Text

With Robyn's journey in mind, we return to the initial questions we posed to understand the relation between alternative methodologies and context. The first query we raised concerned legitimate knowledge. We argued that most forms of research are based on narrow notions of legitimate knowledge that deny the importance of experience as a basis for knowledge production. When Educative Research and specifically Robyn's case study are analyzed, we can see the way this process both challenges traditional notions of legiti-mate knowledge and yet reflects the dominant view.

Robyn's experiences as a teacher, woman, and researcher are integral parts of the research project. Not only does she use her personal history to expose the way questions of gender and patriarchy get infused into teaching, but also examines her role as leader of the dialogue sessions to find some of the contradictions between her aim of developing teacher-initiated dia-logue and her role as leader of the group. In this sense, Educative Research attempts to construct a notion of legitimate knowledge that includes knowledge that is produced through data collection, consideration of other scholarly texts, and experiential knowledge.

It is also the case, however, that as Robyn's study developed there was a tremendous pull to move toward the traditional view of what counts as legitimate knowledge. In the first rewrite of the text, for example, the personal sections were greatly reduced in size while the review of the literature and the data sections seemed to take on more importance. In discussing this trend, Robyn at first felt that this direction was necessary if the paper was to be accepted by others. Only after further consideration did she begin to feel comfortable with a balance between experiential knowledge and research knowledge.

While this result is encouraging, it also shows the limits of Educative Research to alter notions of legitimate knowledge. Legitimate knowledge is normative; it reflects dominant cultural values and the material conditions of various cultural groups that make up a society. Research can challenge the dominant norms, but it cannot change them unless the audience also accepts wider, more diverse notions of legitimate knowledge. What Robyn seemed to understand from the start was that changes in her approach to research (making it more obviously personal and "subjective") without a corresponding change in the audience might do nothing more than cause her text to be discounted. Integrating research knowledge and experiential knowledge does not assure that both forms of knowledge production will be taken seriously. Alternative forms of research will only challenge traditional conceptions of high-status knowledge if the community accepts, or at least takes seriously, this altered view. Educative Research did not direct participants to work with those in positions of power, such as funding agencies, to alter how they would read these alternative texts.

A second question we raised about the relation between alternative methodologies and context concerned the limits imposed by material work conditions on the ability of community members to engage in a particular form of knowledge production. Unfortunately, when Educative Research is viewed from this perspective, it is clear that nothing about the physical work conditions of teachers changed as a result of the process. It is the case that during the project monies were diverted from the normal university funding patterns to support professor-initiated research to enable teachers to conduct research and disseminate results. However, with the project winding down, all the common constraints that keep teachers in the classroom and limit most types of consistent examination of educational issues were still in place. This was very evident in Robyn's struggle to get the teachers to meet for the dialogue sessions. Although the teachers, for the most part, found value in these sessions, attendance was erratic because of the other pressures and priorities that were put upon them by structures such as core curricula and district-mandated testing.

If research is to play a role in altering the "subject"/object dualism that plagues our community, we must radically rethink the research context: the work structures of those teaching in our schools and in the university. Specifically, ways must be found to make it possible for teachers to study their classrooms; importantly, this sort of activity must be seen as having value, not something that is simply added onto teachers' already busy schedule. Alternative methodologies cannot be truly alternative unless structural changes go hand in hand with these developing perspectives.

Another question we posed about the research context was its influence on notions of expertise. When Robyn's case study is used as an example, there are several instances where traditional standards of expertise were challenged. One such instance occurred when Robyn started to view herself differently. Where the world of research had looked imposing and possibly unreachable, Robyn now understood research as doable, yet not necessarily producing a superior form of knowledge. Furthermore, others, mostly teachers, valued Robyn's expertise that was based both on experience and data collection. However, as was true of the query we posed about legitimate knowledge, it is also the case that the larger audience is still likely to see an expert as one who produces knowledge based on data collection and the reading of scholarly texts. Educative Research, therefore, made inroads in furthering a more diverse notion of expertise by suggesting that teachers at the local level have important insights that can be used to reform schooling. But if this modest start is to make a significant difference, strong efforts must be made to challenge the accepted notions of expertise held generally by society. Part of the process of reconstructing these notions involves community work where discussions about expertise can be debated. Parents and others, for example, need to be appointed, where appropriate, to share their understanding with others in the educational community. The message must get out that, while few in the community produce the type of research knowledge that university professors do, other forms of knowledge can be used as a base to foster expertise.

Who gets to tell the educational stories is another concern when scrutinizing the relationship between alternative methodologies and context. As we argued, most community members do not get to speak out and give meaning to educational events. If alternative methodologies are to challenge this divide, community members should have the opportunity to interpret education practice and aims. Robyn's case study indicates that Educative Research had a significant influence in this regard. Robyn not only had an opportunity to tell her story to other teachers and local district staff members but also to present her story at two educational conferences. Robyn's story surely was not viewed by all as important and insightful; however, it challenged the traditional role of woman/teacher as "silent partner." Robyn also examined her own part in the dialogue sessions and even her understanding of what is dialogue. In both instances, she initiated inward protests against her beliefs and actions. The telling of the story, therefore, was important not only because it enabled Robyn to confront historical forces that keep women and teachers silenced but also because it led to personal growth and development.

Unfortunately, these gains are not without side effects. While Robyn told her story, the stories of others in the dialogue sessions were interpreted by Robyn; it was her voice, not theirs, that was coming through. The challenge of storytelling is to enable disenfranchised groups to speak out, without the cost of speaking out being the silencing of others.

Finally, Robyn's case study suggests that the connections between research and practice can be strengthened. Research can foster a type of community change which is based on a questioning of school practices and aims. When it does so, research allows the stories told and the questions raised to be part of an ongoing process of education and change. In particular, several changes occurred because of Robyn's study. Teachers, who had rarely if ever talked consistently on educational issues, not only did so but also influenced decisions made at the school level. Furthermore, the importance of teachers discussing such issues was acknowledged by the fact that faculty meetings were structured to include time for teachers to pose questions and to set the agenda for items to be discussed. Finally, others, including the district superintendent, started to listen. It is too early to make any grand claims about this event, but it is likely that the superintendent will take into consideration the issues raised by the teachers involved in the dialogue sessions.

However encouraging, these results are also limited in several regards. First, all the changes taking place are focused at the school level. As a consequence, wider issues that link schools and teachers together have not to this point been addressed. In addition, because common school structures are for the most part unchanged, it is unclear if these important first steps can provide a foundation for more sweeping changes that influence the nature of the curriculum and the power structure of the institution. If research is to do more than support the status quo, individual school efforts must be linked together such that a spectrum of teachers, parents, and administrators can work together to raise central questions about the education offered in the community and consider the sweeping changes necessary to address these queries.

In sum, alternative methodologies are unlikely to make a difference unless they are accompanied by ideological and material changes. What our reflections on Educative Research suggest is that while methods can enable groups to tell their stories and strengthen the link between research and change, these important results must go hand in hand with changes in work conditions and ideological notions of what is legitimate knowledge. Specifically, structures that create unnecessary hierarchies by arbitrarily elevating specific groups to the status of expert must be challenged. Notions of legitimate knowledge must be reconsidered so that the knowledge produced by large segments of the community is not dismissed. In essence, the challenge for those working on developing alternative methodologies is to work simultaneously at the level of method and within the community. Only then can changes in work structures and widely held beliefs complement the influence of method in furthering educational understanding and more just relations.

Notes

1. At some teaching colleges the course load is as high as three or four courses a term. Research institutions, however, for the most part, limit teaching loads to two courses. Furthermore, while teaching may be seen as contributing in the same way research does to promotion and tenure, at most schools the tenure committee tends to give greater weight to research. Bad teaching can keep an applicant from getting tenure but good teaching cannot by itself enable one to receive tenure.

2. Twenty-one of the thirty-four surveys distributed in Robyn's school were returned, representing about sixty-two percent of the teachers. Their teaching experience ranged from three to twenty-nine years, with grade level assignments from kindergarten through sixth grade, one media specialist, and seven teachers from special programs, (resource, self-contained learning disabled, severely intellectually handicapped, speech, and gifted and talented). Eleven had graduate degrees, while three indicated that getting a graduate degree was a career goal. Two teachers were working on a "Master's equivalency" offered through the district. Sixteen teachers indicated "career ladder" status, a district program devised to determine outstanding teachers for leadership positions.

3. John Bennion, personal communication to author, 1991.

References

Apple, M. (1986). *Teachers and text: A political economy of class and gender relations in education.* New York: Routledge.

Bernstein, R. (1983). *Beyond objectivism and relativism: Science, hermeneutics and praxis.* Philadelphia: Univ. of Pennsylvania Press.

Borrowman, M. (1965). Liberal education and the professional preparation of teachers. In M. Borrowman, ed., *Teacher education in America: A documentary history,* 24. New York: Teachers College Press.

Bullough, R., Gitlin, A., and Goldstein, S. (1984). Ideology, teacher role and resistance. *Teachers College Record* 86 (2): 339–58.

Cochran-Smith, M., and Lytle, S. (1990). Teacher research and research on teaching: The issues that divide." *Educational Researcher* 19 (2): 2–11.

Gitlin, A. (1990). Understanding teaching dialogically. *Teachers College Record* 91 (4): 537–64.

Gitlin, A., and Smyth, J. (1989). *Teacher evaluation: Educative alternatives*. London: Falmer.

hooks, b. (1989). *Talking back: Thinking feminist, thinking black*. Boston: South End.

Jackson, P. (1968). *Life in classrooms*. New York: Holt, Rinehart and Winston.

Kemmis, S. (1984). "Action research and the politics of reflection." In D. Boud, R. Keogh, and D. Walker, (eds.), *Reflections: Turning experience into learning*, 27–54. London: Kogan Page.

Lather, P. (1986). Research as praxis. *Harvard Educational Review* 52 (3): 255–77.

Lather, P. (1988). Feminist perspectives on empowering research methodologies. *Women's Studies International Forum* 2 (6): 569–81.

Pateman, C. (1970). *Participation and democratic theory*. Cambridge, ENG: Cambridge, Univ. Press.

Powell, A. (1971). "Speculations on the early impact of schools of education on educational psychology." *History of Education Quarterly* 11 (3): 407.

Weiler, K. (1988). *Women teaching for change: Gender, class & power*. South Hadley, MA.: Bergin & Garvey.

DISTANCE AND RELATION RECONSIDERED: TENSIONS IN THE ETHNOGRAPHIC TEXT

Don Dippo

This chapter is loosely based on a paper written some ten years ago by Roger Simon and me, entitled "Distance and Relation: The Dilemma of Critical Ethnography" (Dippo and Simon 1982). There have been two or three substantially different versions of that paper produced over the years. We found, however, that the more we worked on it, the worse it got. So several years ago we put the manuscript into an interoffice envelope and filed it away. This current effort at revision has been an opportunity to recover some of what we thought was so interesting and important before we wrote it into something pompous, boring, and irrelevant. Our concern in 1982 was with the possibility of creating ethnographic representations that would challenge readers to reexamine the ways in which they construct their understandings of the world. Rather than follow the more conventional ethnographic practice of making the strange and exotic seem accessible and even familiar, our interest was in using ethnography to make the comfortable and familiar seem strange and disconcerting. We referred to this as the dilemma of distance and relation:

> This dilemma refers to the seeming impossibility of producing ethnographic accounts which will be at one and the same time critical and communicative. Simply put, the question is this: How does one provide the details of concrete social relations in a manner which renders them familiar and sensible yet simultaneously calls their taken-for-granted character into question? (Dippo and Simon 1982, 3)

Our efforts at the time were guided by the example of Bertolt Brecht's "epic theater." Brecht sought always to entertain his audience in ways that were provocative, amazing, and shocking. His technique of alienating the familiar—of making the everyday strange—was intended to turn audiences from passive consumers of theatre into active participants, producers, creators of meaning, and critics of the taken for granted.

Epic Ethnography?

Our own early attempts at Brechtian-inspired ethnography elicited reader responses that ranged from lukewarm to chilly. For example, we became involved in a project designed to foster the "professional development" of staff who teach in the educational programs of institutions like art galleries, history museums, and centers of science and technology. Coordinators/ Directors of these educational programs were primarily, and understandably, interested in program development: How could school visits/tours be improved? The means we proposed for working with them on this project was essentially to get program staff together to talk about what they did and why they did it. Coordinators agreed to set up a series of meetings with the educational staff, and we agreed to provide "accounts" or "portrayals" of actual class visits to the gallery, museum, or science center based on: (a) our own observations of tours/demonstrations and (b) classroom observations and interviews with teachers and students conducted in the school before and after the class visit.

Our approach was based on several assumptions. The first was that improving school tours/demonstrations required understanding them as contextualized rather than isolated events. The second was that "excursions" themselves were bound to have different meanings for different people. We were convinced that talking to students and teachers about their expectations for the trip and reactions to the trip (as well as accompanying them on the trip) would provide the kind of contextualizing information that would enable the education staff to extend their understandings of why some tours/demonstrations seemed to work better than others beyond the usual explanations: "some classes are good and some classes are bad"; "some teachers are good and some teachers are not"; and/or "classes from some neighborhoods are well behaved and appreciative while classes from other neighborhoods are ill-mannered and basically not interested."

One of the "accounts" we produced for the education staff at a large metropolitan art museum focused on a school tour of impressionist paintings. Monologues such as the following, based on interviews with students, became part of the story of the tour.

> Ted: This is my fourth year in Art so this'll be the fourth time I've been to the Gallery with my class. We go every year. I'm not in Urban Studies so this is the only trip I ever go on. I took a class there this past summer on animation. It was good. I'd like to work in film or animation when I finish school. Sometimes when the class was over, the one this summer, I'd go up into the Gallery and look around. So I've seen most of what they've got there. Most of the tours I've been on have been pretty much the same. You

start out looking at some slides and then go look at the paintings. This one was like that but it was the best one I've been on. The tour guide, Philip, was very exciting. He didn't tell you about the paints so much but made you look and figure them out yourself. Like when we were all looking at the Pissarro, which was my favorite of all the ones we saw by the way, I knew that the bridge drew you into the painting but I knew there must be a better answer. And there was. The zigzag was right there in the painting but you had to look hard to figure it out. If he would have told us, we wouldn't care. I thought the slide show was pretty good too, the way they would show you a photograph of something, say a cafe scene, and a painting of a cafe scene right beside it. That was good because you could see how they were the same and how they were different. I thought the slides were explained well. Also, I thought the discussion about modern art was good. I liked modern art before this tour but it made me understand it a lot better. (Dippo and Simon 1979, 24).

Far from being the "authorized" version of "The Meaning of the Tour for Ted," this monologue, based upon several interviews with Ted both before and after the tour, provided at least partial grounds for a reasonable interpretation of what that meaning might be. This monologue, along with others in the account, were expected to contribute to a more complex understanding of the tour as a social and educational event. We thought of the monologues as vehicles for conveying information about the kinds of background experiences and orientations to art that students brought with them to the museum, together with their assessments of the tour itself.

A second component of this particular portrayal was what we called a "story fragment." Together with monologues, these story fragments were intended to provide readers with a sense of the tour as an ongoing event. The characterizations and contexts developed in this way were meant to convey not only the researchers' interpretations of others' meanings but also make evident and available the empirical grounds for the interpretations being rendered. What follows is an example of one such story fragment:

Allison saw Debbie step off the subway car just ahead. Debbie smiled when she noticed Allison on the platform and waited for her to catch up. Both girls, while not close friends, had been together through four years of high school art. Having been to the Museum before and knowing the way, they both headed up the stairs and down Dundas Street talking about mutual friends and their free afternoon.

As the Museum came into view, Debbie said, "I hope it's not

the same tour we had last year. I like the impressionists but didn't we see them before?" She was quite sure she remembered seeing some paintings last year by the artists Miss Robbins had discussed in class yesterday.

Allison just shrugged. She couldn't remember exactly what they had seen last year either. She and Debbie had been on several tours before; in fact every year she had taken Art, the class had gone on a tour. However, all she could remember was that they had seen some slides and then gone in small groups around the Museum. Was it the Canadian Collection, the Old Dutch Masters . . . or . . . ?

"It doesn't matter," Allison offered, "it's really good to get out and see some paintings." (Dippo and Simon 1979, 2–3).

Here again, the point was to contextualize the tour and to show how different students with different experiences brought different expectations to the event.

A third component of this particular account was our inclusion of what we called a "base narrative." This was a fictionalized conversation, based in part on empirical data, among Lynn, the teacher; Anne and Philip of the Museum staff; and Roger Simon and myself, two university-based researchers. In this imaginary conversation, we juxtaposed thematically related interview data from a number of sources with our own commentary on the topic or issue at hand. Our role in the "discussion" was more that of facilitator than analyst. We posed questions, raised issues, and then spliced together the perceptions and observations of our informants. We did not attempt to provide any kind of conceptual or theoretical framework for organizing the discussion at this point, in anticipation of actual conversations between readers and ourselves where we could theorize together around important themes and issues. The base narrative, then, was intended to serve a variety of purposes. First, it was supposed to consciously and continually remind readers that the account being offered for discussion was not to be understood as an authoritative version of "what really happened" on the tour, but rather was to be seen as one of many possible interpretations, the plausibility of which was always open to question and the empirical grounds of which were available for discussion. What's more, the base narrative located us, the researchers, within the story of the tour and provided a way to suggest possible themes for discussion that arose from our own experiences in the classroom and at the museum. Here is a brief segment from the base narrative:

Roger spoke first. "One thing that really struck me were the comments from Debbie and Allison about what they remembered from previous tours."

"Hmm", mused Anne, "It seems that they remembered more of the form than the content."

"Yeah, and we heard similar kinds of comments from other kids," Roger continued. "That's one thing I'll be curious about in the future when we talk to students at some other schools. Will they remember the same kinds of things?"

Lynn chimed in, "I often wonder what they remember. The tour guides can push the kids and they'll perform, but what do they remember two months later? Lately I've been thinking that the thing to do is to relate the content of the tour to their studio work—to help them to achieve a perceptual change that will stay with them long after the tour is over. This way the tour becomes a curriculum resource which is tied to the skill development aims of studio assignments." (Dippo and Simon 1979, 5)

This portrayal was presented to the education staff at the Museum, just as other portrayals were presented to the staffs at other institutions. The discussions were always disappointing. We were often accused of being pseudoscholars and frustrated, third-rate fiction writers. Even when people were being polite or trying to work with the text, discussion rarely developed beyond: "Did Jackie really say that?" or "I just don't remember it happening quite that way." or "Those kinds of kids are just like that. If you worked here long enough, you'd understand." or "It's interesting but so what—I don't see the point." Here is an example from a taped transcription of one such discussion, which dealt with the form versus content issue referred to in the monologues, story fragments, and base narrative.

Roger: One thing that really puzzles us is the repeated comment we received when we asked students what they remembered from the last trip they took to the museum . . . . It's this notion that we saw slides then went in small groups on a tour around the museum . . . and very, very rarely, I don't think we ever spoke to a kid who said, "Well, I remember we looked at that particular painting." or "We looked at (say) Degas or Van Gogh." It's always this . . .

Philip: . . . slides, tour . . .

Roger: . . . slides, tour.

Anne: And sometimes they can't even remember the theme . . . if it's sculpture, or the Canadian collection . . . .

Pat: They can't remember what they're doing in their own classes either (*laughter*). Or at least that's what they tell us!

Philip:	What are you doing at school? "Nothing."
Pat:	NOTHING!! (*laughter*)
Anne:	The teacher will tell you at the end . . .
Philip:	The poor teacher with a red face will tell you that they are doing this, this, and this . . .
Pat:	Or, they say they're doing something quite different from what the teacher says they're doing.
Philip:	Yeah.
Anne:	I think that's teenage philosophy anyway.

Leaving aside, for the moment, questions of narrative form (which we then spent a lot of time considering), what was the problem here? Years ago Schutz and Luckmann observed that, in daily life, people are primarily concerned with the mastery of typical, recurrent situations. None of us, they concluded, are interested to the same extent in all objects and events that take place within our taken-for-granted world.

Plan-determined and situationally related interests (in the biographical molding of the acquisition of knowledge) organizes the world in strata of greater and lesser relevance . . . . I know that there are more precise explanations for the events which are familiar to me and even that there are certain people who can transmit this knowledge to me . . . . Although I know that, I am really not interested in acquiring further knowledge about it. I am sufficiently familiar "for my own purposes." The interest involved here is in the broadest sense a pragmatic one that determines the acquisition and the interruption of knowledge. I would, perhaps, in principle be "interested" to know more about these things, but under the principle of "first things first," I have "no time," since I must "first acquire knowledge more relevant for me." I want to keep a "place" open for more important or more urgent experience. (Schutz and Luckmann, 1973 138–39).

The museum staff may have "perhaps, in principle been interested to know more" about the meanings and understandings represented in our account. In practice, however, as the discussion illustrates, they found little in our portrayal that was relevant or important to them. What we found fascinating, puzzling, and complex, they found ordinary, routine, and self-evident. The provision of multiple perspectives on an event—"The Tour" as seen through the eyes of teachers, students, and tour guides—while interesting, was not necessarily compelling when it came to reexamining taken for granted. The director of educational programs at the museum summed up her response to the experience this way:

The thing is, when we discussed it originally, I thought it was going to be a three-part experience—before the tour, the tour, and after the tour. But the whole concentration seems to have come on the tour and, you know, the other things that have been brought in. But the main focus has been on what has happened here in the museum itself, and—as I guess I tried to explain before,— and— I'm not being critical 'cause I think you've done a super job,— but I think that all of us here are pretty experienced and I think that, — I'm speaking for the staff,— and I'll speak for myself too,— but I feel that everybody who tours here is extremely competent, to put it just mildly. So I feel, then, that, ah, what we really wanna see is the results because that's what's going to make us change. I think we feel that we can give a good experience here for the kids. But if, we are really . . . if we saw results that were totally different, and had no closeness to what we thought we had taught here, then we would want to change. (Simon 1980, 25)

In hindsight, what is striking here is the clear discrepancy between our interest in providing empirically based accounts that might provide the occasion for reflection and critique of practice, and the museum staff's interest in program evaluation. Where we tried to provide the kind of circumstantial information that would enable the tour to be seen in context (what the director refers to as "the other things that have been brought in"), the staff was interested in evidence of "results." As the director said: "if we saw results that were totally different [from] . . . what we thought we had taught . . . we would want to change." We had assumed that once the museum staff became aware of the diverse expectations of multiple perspectives on and conflicting responses to the tour that they would be interested in discussing the implications for practice and reconsidering at least some of the assumptions they held about what they did and why they did it. What we discovered, however, was that merely multiple was insufficient. Short of a kind of shocking document that reported, for example, that students were confused about or didn't understand the differences between a salon and an impressionist orientation to painting, or that they mistook pointillism for a breakfast cereal, the confidence of the museum staff in their own competence remained unshaken. For them, the tour was self-contained. It began when the students walked into the museum and ended when they walked out the door. They knew that they toured well and wanted to know that they did it effectively; that they had taught "what we thought we had taught here." Clearly, our account was not powerful enough to provoke the kind of radical crisis in understanding required to challenge those who felt "extremely competent" in terms of their knowledge of and practices in the everyday world of museum touring.

Our own curiosity about (and maybe even preoccupation with) the pedagogical possibilities of having people reflect upon and discuss our depictions of their practices might have focused our attention too much on technique

(alienation effect, narrative structure, etc.) and not enough on more fundamental questions: What do we have to say, as outsiders, to the museum
staff? and Why are we doing this, anyway? How are we invested in this
project? One of the most significant things missing from our account of
the Impressionist Tour was a conceptual framework—a set of organizing
concepts and principles, which could have helped link the local, the situated,
and the circumstantial data we had collected through interviews and observations to the immediate concerns of those with whom we were working and
to a larger set of socio-historical, political, and economic issues. While the
danger of oversimplification and distortion is always present, this linking
up and making connections need not be done in a theoretically reductive
way (real life as an illustration or instanciation of reified concepts). Rather,
the framing and connecting can be done in a way which supports more
complex and contextualized understandings. In "The Tour," for example,
we might have dealt directly with the issue of why and how the ubiquitous
"good class/bad class" explanation of successful/unsuccessful tours made
so much sense to museum staff. We might have introduced more theoretically
sophisticated and/or powerful problematizing concepts into the discussion.
The notion of "cultural capital" might have been particularly effective, but
even introducing the ideas of "legitimate school knowledge" or "dominant/
subordinate culture" might have been useful. I would say now that we
were too timid in our assertion of theory/politics, too worried about being
impositional. We were interested in representing multiplicity (maybe even
polyvocality, although we didn't know it at the time), but at the expense
of being clear about the political project which must inform research if it
is to be critical: the project of resisting cultural hegemony and creating
possibilities for social transformation (Brodkey 1987, 67).

It seems, then, that our own efforts were much better at achieving "distance" than at establishing "relation." We were not interested in creating
polemics or propaganda, but were convinced that accounts with an overt
political/pedagogical agenda would be dismissed out of hand as uninteresting
and irrelevant. Our reluctance to infuse sociohistorical, political, or economic themes for fear of being heavy-handed and distancing our audiences
too much, in the end, was misplaced. Polyvocality and the representation
of multiple points of view without a clearly articulated sense of project is
an ineffective as a single-minded commitment to a project without the ability
or inclination to accommodate polyvocality. So we return to the question
of distance and relation.

> Ethnographic studies are often communicated through interpretive
> accounts of the social relations in a setting which attempt to portray
> meanings from members' points of view. In order to render in
> discourse a sensible version of what those perspectives might be,

the author must rely on commonly held sense-making practices which will enable readers to interpret and make meaning of the text. To be critical, however, requires more than communicating that which is commonly held. It requires providing the occasion for a reflexive consideration of the grounds and limitations of what is known to be common sense and practical knowledge in a manner that situates such knowledge and its production in historically delimited and culturally specific social practices. However, to challenge familiar assumptions and values through a discourse which, to be understood, is compelled to reproduce in its very content and organization the assumptions and values of the discourse itself, seems like an impossibility. Thus, as Catherine Belsey points out, "To challenge common sense is to challenge the discourse of common sense" (Belsey 1980, 46). Yet, if we let such reasoning serve to fully legitimate the production of new, unfamiliar and therefore initially difficult discourse, we run the risk that our accounts will never be read (let alone understood) by anyone outside of a closed circle of like-minded colleagues. This then is the primary dilemma of critical ethnography—the dilemma of distance and relation. This dilemma refers to the seeming impossibility of producing accounts that will be at one and the same time critical and communicative. (Dippo and Simon 1982, 2–3)

An Update

Discouraged and frustrated at not being able to *do* better what seemed to us such a good idea and what we were encouraging others to do (Simon and Dippo 1986), we shelved the project and took to writing more conventional texts. At the time it seemed easier to think about disruptive texts than to produce them, to imagine them easier than to find them.

In recent years, however, our interest has been renewed partly due to the attention being paid to the writings of Walter Benjamin—critic, essayist, and contemporary of Bertolt Brecht—and partly due to the appearance of better, more serviceable, contemporary examples of "disruptive representations," or what Benjamin would have termed "dialectical images" (Buck-Morss 1981; Simon 1992). These are texts, broadly speaking, which create the kinds of "textual tensions" and "startling juxtapositions" that disrupt unproblematic readings and call attention not only to productive and interpretive processes, but also to the discourses upon which such processes depend. Examples would include:

- advertising, especially television ads and public service anti-advertisments that juxtapose consumer pleasures with social/environmental costs (antidrinking-and-driving ads, which juxtapose scenes of traffic accidents with the sounds of a party; antifur ads, which depict blood dripping from the fur of a coat being modeled)

- painting, photography, and performance art, especially the use of captions in painting and photography (see Linda Hutcheon's *Splitting Images* [1991])
- postmodern poetry and literature (e.g., Salman Rushdie's *Satanic Verses*)
- postmodern music/performance art (e.g., anything by Laurie Anderson)

More important, however, has been the recent appearance of excellent examples of dialectical imagery and tantalizing textuality (Dippo 1992b) in educational ethnography (see, for example, Britzman 1991; Brodkey 1987; Lather 1991). Before commenting on these texts and talking about what I think can be learned from them, I want to briefly describe how issues of textual construction and ethnographic representation fit into the context of my own work in teacher education, and to establish why I think it is important to develop a more self-consciously critical ethnographic practice that makes explicit the links between research interest, research method, and research product.

My interest in disruptive texts is not mere curiosity nor a simple attraction to texts that exhibit a degree of intellectual playfulness (though there is certainly a place for curiosity, playfulness, and textual pleasure). Rather, the disruptive, the interrogative, the "writable" text addresses real concerns I confront everyday in my teaching. I use educational ethnographies in a preservice, educational foundations course I teach. Elsewhere I have commented on the difficulty students have in taking up these texts critically (Dippo 1992a). Beyond judging whether or not a text is "good" or "bad," students seem unaccustomed and ill-prepared to ask more critical questions: Whose voice(s) am I hearing in this text? Whose knowledge is represented? Why should I pay attention? What difference does it make? It may be that I haven't prepared them well enough to take up these texts in a critical way, but I think that it's also that the texts themselves don't inquire. They show, and they tell, but they don't ask. This is not surprising. Good ethnographies, after all, tell good stories. Published ethnographies are generally well written and have a literary quality which makes them better reading than most other social science texts. They represent tales of other lives, other cultures, other worlds. Tightly told, they are seductive, persuasive, confident. Is it any wonder, then, that readers (and I include myself) are readily drawn into these texts; willing to believe, as Deborah Britzman says, "that subjects say what they mean and mean what they say" (Britzman 1990, 2) and that their stories somehow tell themselves. They/we are all too willing to forget that such naturalism is a textual construction. Which brings me to the second site of my interest in textuality—thesis supervision.

It is now commonplace to speak of ethnography as both method and product, which is to say it refers to both techniques for investigating and narrating culture, which culminate in an "ethnographic text." The more I supervise, however, the more I begin to wonder about how much the *product*, or an *image of the product*, influences or determines the application of method. What I find particularly troublesome is how the mainstream, modernist, ethnographic text—finely crafted, eminently readable, unambiguous—encourages students to reduce the complexity of what they've found out through interviews/observations/analysis in order to produce a plausible, conceptually coherent version of an actual world peopled with noncontradictory subjects.

Two Examples

I recently sat on the committee of a student who was a speech pathologist. She was interested in oral language development in "whole language classrooms." As someone whose understanding of speech pathology had changed rather dramatically over years of practice, she was professionally invested in integrated (as opposed to withdrawal) approaches to speech and language therapy. Her reading of the "whole language" literature supported her own belief in the superiority of integrated approaches. Her study did not set out to prove such superiority (although it was based on the assumption), but instead to document and describe the effectiveness of integrated, whole language approaches to oral language development. In the end, what she wanted to do was make the case for redefining the relationship between the speech pathologist and the classroom teacher based on a better understanding of oral language development in "whole language classrooms."

In the beginning of her thesis, there is a lengthy discussion of developments in linguistics and implications for speech and language pathology. The section concludes with a metatheoretical discussion of paradigms and the shift from "mechanistic" to "holistic" understandings of language. What she's looking for as she begins her empirical work is an instance of this paradigm shift, an actual manifestation in classroom practice that can be understood and explained in paradigmatic terms. What she finds is complexity and contradiction. This is good news, right? For her it is not: It is a major problem.

The "whole language teacher" upon whom the study is focused uses direct instruction methods, talks about "positive reinforcement," "shaping behavior," and "building self-esteem." As well, she admits to "having a thing" about inventive spelling. The problem for this graduate student is that her "holistic" teacher says some pretty "mechanistic" things. From the student's point of view, this teacher is still quite effective in facilitating oral language in her classroom. So her case for integration is not really in jeopardy. What is coming undone, however, is the seamlessness, and consistency, and coherence of her original image of the thesis.

She can no longer equate holism with integration and effective therapy, and mechanism with withdrawal and ineffective therapy. What's most unfortunate, however, is that she cannot appreciate (or even enjoy) such complexity, not because she cannot/does not understand it, but because she's unsure about how to represent it. Mostly she fears the implications of this complexity and contradiction for her thesis. Theses she has read have been neat and tidy: no loose ends, no rough spots, no contradictions.

My second example tells a different story. I am on the committee of another graduate student, also a speech pathologist, who works in a school for the deaf. There is an historical "tension" within the deaf community and among communities of deaf people, parents of deaf children, and teachers of deaf people. Some within these communities argue for oral approaches to education for deaf people. These approaches emphasize lipreading, speaking, mainstreaming, and integration based on the assumption of long-term benefits. Others advocate for bilingual and bicultural approaches that are based on an understanding of deafness as difference (as opposed to defect) and that emphasize signing as a first language. These divisions are often profound. And when the hearing public learns about these issues, it is often from hearing people speaking on behalf of the deaf. This student knows the debate well. She works in an oral school but is doing graduate studies in a program committed to bilingual and bicultural approaches to deaf education. There is a sense in which, to use her own words, she "sees both sides" of the issue. What she plans is to interview deaf adolescents and adults and to talk with them about issues of language and identity. She is hoping to be able to "make more complex" what is usually described and discussed in either/or terms.

This student is less far along in her program than the student in the first example. And so she has had the benefit of reading more disruptive texts like Patti Lather's *Getting Smart* and Deborah Britzman's *Practice Makes Practice*. This student is confident in her ability to, and enthusiastic about the prospect of, writing a thesis and creating a text that represents complexity and contradiction with clarity and does it in a way that is respectful of her subjects without precluding her own critique and commentary or admission of ambivalence.

Where does encouragement and support for this kind of venture come from? (Not from me anymore, recommending Brecht!) It comes from researchers like Deborah Britzman:

I recently completed an ethnographic study of secondary student teachers, *Practice Makes Practice: A Critical Study of Learning to Teach*. My goal was to write a "Rashomon" of student teaching, an ethnographic opera where voices argued, disrupted, and pleaded with one another; where the high drama of misunderstandings, deceit, and conflicting desires made present and absent through language complicated what is typically taken as the familiar story of learning to teach. I tried to speak against the discourses that bind the disagreements, the embarrassments, the unsaid, and the odd moments of uncertainty in contexts overburdened with certain imperatives. (3–4)

Here then are my contradictory desires: to textualize identities at their most vulnerable moments, to speak about and for individuals by juxtaposing their words with my own, to dramatize the ordinary days that make time seem like no time at all, and to persuade readers of the credibility of my interpretive efforts yet warn them that all I could constitute were partial truths and my own guilty readings of other people's dramas (6).

I do not know, at this point, whether Britzman's text will fare better in the "catalytic validity" (Lather 1991, 68) department than did the now-nearly-forgotten "Impressionist Tour." I have not yet had the opportunity to use *Practice Makes Practice* in my own preservice teaching. What I suspect, however, is that the "partial truths" and "guilty readings" of others' lives narrated would strike a resonant chord in my students. They would surely be compelled to ask: "Could this be my story?" (Britzman 1990, 5). At the same time, I suspect they would find Britzman's analyses disturbing, unsettling, and disruptive, especially those that challenge discourses of experience and subvert the authority of common cultural myths related to teachers and teaching. Their encounter with provocative contradiction and ambiguity would be not so much a feature of what I used to think of as the "dilemma of critical ethnography," as an example of the kinds of textual tensions that enable ethnography to be critical. Beyond providing contextualizing information and/or multiple perspectives, as we attempted to do in the "Impressionist Tour," Britzman's study of learning to teach is imbued with both theory and politics. Yet, the ways in which she is able to interweave the unremarkable with the unexpected prevents the text from becoming either an all-too-familiar story or an incredible tale from beyond the fringe. But there is another, probably more significant, balance achieved here as well. The text is playful and disruptive enough that, rather than compromise, encode, or conceal its agenda of theoretical and political concerns, it can be overt, direct, and up front without being heavy-handed or impositional.

And the text is theoretically sophisticated and politically powerful enough that, while playful and at times puzzling, it is difficult to dismiss as mere methodological curiosity or cult-intellectual entertainment.

Britzman's text is but one example of what for me is an encouraging development in educational ethnography. Not that it should become a template for critical ethnographic representation, but rather it stands as an example of what can be done when producers of ethnographic texts take up the challenge of creating works that teach readers and writers how to read and write differently.

References

Anderson, L. (1991). Empty places: A performance. New York: Harper Perennial.

Belsey, C. (1980). *Critical Practice.* New York: Methuen.

Britzman, D. (1990). Could this be your story? Guilty readings and other ethnographic dramas. Paper presented at the Bergamo Conference, October, Dayton, OH.

Britzman, D. (1991). *Practice makes practice: A critical study of learning to teach.* Albany, NY: State Univ. of New York Press.

Brodkey, L. (1987). *Academic writing as social practice.* Philadelphia: Temple Univ. Press.

Buck-Morss, S. (1981). Walter Benjamin—Revolutionary writer (I). *New Left Review* 128: 50–75.

Dippo, D. (1992a). Ethnographic, near-ethnographic, and not-so-ethnographic accounts of school life: Searching for the teachable text. *The Review of Education* 14 (2): 95–105.

Dippo, D. (1992b). Tantalizing textuality. *The Review of Education* 15 (1): 29–40.

Dippo, D., and Simon, R. (1979). An impressionist tour. Unpublished manuscript. The Ontario Institute for Studies in Education.

Dippo, D., and Simon, R. (1982). Distance and relation: The dilemma of critical ethnography. Paper presented at the Ethnography in Education Research Forum, March, Philadelphia, PA.

Hutcheon, L. (1991). *Splitting images.* Toronto, CAN: Oxford Univ. Press.

Lather, P. (1991). *Getting smart: Feminist research and pedagogy within the postmodern.* New York: Routledge.

Rushdie, S. (1988). *The satanic verses.* London: Viking.

Schutz, A., and Luckmann, T. (1973). *The structures of the life-world.* Evanston, IL: Northwestern Univ. Press.

Simon, R. (1980). Program portrayal and reflexive inquiry. Paper presented at the annual meetings of the American Educational Research Association, April, Boston, MA.

Simon, R. (1992). *Teaching against the grain: Texts for a pedagogy of possibility.* Westport, CT: Greenwood.

Simon, R., and Dippo, D. (1986). On critical ethnographic work. *Anthropology and Education Quarterly* 17 (4): 195–202.

EXPANDING OUR NOTIONS OF "CRITICAL QUALITATIVE METHODOLOGY": BRINGING RACE, CLASS, AND GENDER INTO THE DISCUSSION (RESPONSE)

Louise Lamphere

As a White female feminist anthropologist, I come to these essays on "Critical Qualitative Concerns" not only from my own experiences as a participant-observer among Navajo families in the 1960s and in a New England apparel factory in the 1970s, but also through the debates that have rocked anthropology for the last decade concerning how we conduct research and how we write ethnography.

As the quintessential colonial discipline, anthropologists have over the last ten years done much to undermine and critique their own discipline's construction of the "primitive," the colonial "Other," the "object" of research. This questioning and repositioning has been greatly aided by postmodern theory, by studies of colonialism (Stoler 1989; Cooper and Stoler 1989; Comaroff and Comaroff 1991; Stocking 1991), by an interrogation of the history of our own discipline (Stocking 1987), and by the history of the writing of ethnography (Clifford and Marcus 1986; Marcus and Fischer 1986; Clifford 1988). In some ways we have been long on critique and short on solutions, though several authors have written treatments that bring themselves into the texts (Tedlock 1992; Tedlock 1993), have constructed life histories that are really stories about both the anthropologist and the subject (Behar 1993), and have experimented with new forms of more dialogic ethnographic writing (Rabinow 1977; Dwyer 1982; the Hajj, Lavie, and Rouse 1993). Anthropologists have generally worked toward more collaborative forms of research (Bahr et al. 1974), often elevating their "informants" to the role of "consultants" and coauthors in an attempt to make them subjects rather than objects of research.

I have also been influenced by my role as editor of *Frontiers: A Journal of Women Studies*, a multicultural journal that seeks to be interdisciplinary as well as to publish work that analyzes and depicts the lives of women of differing class, race/ethic, and sexual identities. Struggles we have had in the process of publishing the journal have led me to see how many blind spots White-middle-class academics often have, as well as the difficulties (but important necessity) of bridging differences among women and between women and men. Recent feminist theory has also grappled with many of the epistemological and methodological issues that have been addressed in anthropology, but with the added focus of gender and race.

It is refreshing to find that these methodological transformations are also taking place in other disciplines, particularly within educational research that impacts on the lives of our children as well as on the structure of one set of major institutions—schools, universities, and museums here in the United States and Canada.

The contributions to this section engage rethinking both sides of qualitative research: the research process, including the interaction between researcher and subject, and the writing up of research as ethnography. Andrew Gitlin and Robyn Russell focus on the researcher/subject relationship through an account of Russell's case study. Russell attempts to rearrange the researcher/subject dichotomy and the whole research process, making it more "participative" and less driven by a problem the researcher defines and instead something that is mutually arrived at by both researchers and teachers. Don Dippo recounts the difficulties he and Roger Simon had in conducting their research on high school tours at a metropolitan art museum (presumably in Canada). In doing so, he focuses primarily on the difficulty of writing ethnographic accounts that jar the readers, be they the museum staff he and Simon observed or those his doctoral students studied in whole language classrooms and in a school for the deaf. These subjects and other "lay persons" in our own society take many relationships for granted and have difficulty understanding the structure, underlying patterns, and cultural assumptions of the interaction described by researchers since these ethnographic accounts are about their own "culture."

In sum, these two chapters pay attention to both the research process and ethnographic writing and how both these might be transformed into a new kind of educational research. There is an attempt to break apart the traditional scientific paradigm (adopted by social scientists and educational researchers in the post–World War II period) that enshrined in the objective researcher, the object of study, and knowledge as articulated by experts.

In an era in education when there is so much stress on testing and statistical measurement, and in a political environment in the United States in which there is pressure to institute national standardized testing and objective measurements of how well schools are doing, this is all to the good. This sort of critique makes it clear that solving our educational problems will not be an easy matter and that there is an important place for qualitative research.

What I found missing in both these papers, however, was sufficient attention to gender, class, race, ethnicity, and sexual orientation. I realize that these themes are the focus of other papers in other sections, but we must be careful not to ghettoize each of these attributes, putting the feminist papers in one section, those that deal with ethnicity in another, and those on sexual orientation in a third, leaving the papers on "ethnographic method" to a section where authors may feel they do not have to deal with those issues, just "how to do research."

Let me say that this is not just a plea for political correctness, nor a simple-minded argument for putting "politics" into research (although I do subscribe to the notion that there is a political aspect to all research in terms of its choice of subject matter, methodology, and theoretical approach). I think that to ignore or brush aside the need to examine race, ethnicity, gender, or sexual orientation by claiming that doing so is mere political rhetoric is to dismiss many of the theoretical advances of the last decade. After all, individuals are not marked by just one of these variables at a time. Not to interrogate the shifting boundaries of these identities and the ways they are implicated in social interaction and in the structure of our educational institutions is to move us back to the old set of assumptions that everyone is really a heterosexual White middle- or upper-class male.

What I liked so much about the Gitlin and Russell paper was both the summary of the model of educative research that the authors propose and the fine account by Robyn Russell of her attempt to institute teacher dialogues. The first year of her sessions was a failure; by the end of the year only she and one other teacher were attending. But the next year, after she had redefined her methods, a core group evolved out of teachers' own interests in putting together a computer lab. The superintendent attended one of their meetings and was supportive; teacher communication and trust evolved, and even the principal saw the need to have more open dialogue during faculty meetings.

The authors acknowledge the importance of Russell's position as a woman to the conceptualization of the research and its trajectory. However, I wanted to know more about this; how did her role as a female teacher bring her to the analysis of hierarchy and silence she enunciates? She mentions her mother's influence on her choice of profession but does not fully explore the way in which silencing and the passive acceptance of hierarchy feeds into women's gender roles. Were all the teachers in her study female? Did they seem to have the same sense of being silenced, pushed apart, and isolated? Were all the female teachers from the same class background, and if not, did those from rural or working-class families have more difficulty in terms of transforming their level of participation? Were there any male teachers? Did they come to dominate discussions, take leadership roles, not participate?

I never understood whether this was a grade school, mid school or high school—a crucial issue if one is to understand the school structure, the position of males or females in authority roles, the ratio of male to female teachers, and the way in which hierarchy operated. Was the school class homogeneous? Were the students and teachers all White? Even if all the participants in the study were White, and even if they all came from the same class background, we need to explore what this homogeneity meant for the possibility of dialogue, confronting power, and taking action. Where did patriarchy lie? In the structure, in the role of the superintendent, in the way female teachers kowtowed to male authority or female authority as well? How did the female principal fit into the system that dominated and silenced? What about sexual orientation? Did marriage as a badge of heterosexuality make a difference? And since I assume this school is in Utah, what about Mormonism? Did it play into gender and patriarchy as enacted in the school?

Raising such questions might lead Gitlin and Russell to the literature of male and female styles of leadership, communication, and relationship to power. My suspicion is that women are much more silenced by power than men, but women also have very different ways of coping with powerlessness. Going the next step and asking how whiteness and middle-class status impact on female relations to empowerment is more difficult, but it is an important next step. White privilege and women's middle-class status might give them an ability to break through feelings of powerlessness and to act in a more concerted way. But I often think that African-American women (who sometimes have strong female role models) are able to resist patriarchy and domination more quickly than White women. One might be able to draw effectively on Patricia Hill-Collins's many examples of Black women's community work to theorize about the difference that whiteness makes in this instance.

What does come through vividly is that power as well as empowerment played a crucial role both in the first year (which netted little in Russell's terms) and in the second year where more was accomplished. If the authors could have explored the issues of race, class, gender, and sexual orientation in more detail, we would have had a much more subtle analysis of how power operates differentially through actors in different social positions and through a structure that shapes and rewards only certain of those actors.

Likewise, I felt that Don Dippo could have probed the issues of gender, race, and class in his study of museum tours, even in hindsight. It took several readings for me to make the "educated guess" that the students taking these tours must be White, middle-class students (probably from public high schools, but this was never clear). I kept wondering if there were any immigrant, nonWhite, or working-class students. Did or could they relate to impressionist painters in the same way that the articulate middle-class teenagers were able to? Did their own histories or experiences give them a different approach to the "meaning" of these paintings?

There is some sense in which art museums epitomize "high culture." In what way do these tours represent an inculcation of particular elite cultural values (or even national ones, through the Canadian Collection)? Through institutions like museums, these aesthetic standards become crossnational and transhistorical. After all, it takes a leap of experience to get middle-class Canadians teenagers to see something in nineteenth-century French male painters.

Certainly females and males might take away different messages from these paintings. There is now a good deal of feminist theorizing about the history of painting and the use of women as "objects of the gaze" within paintings. This perspective could provide questions to pose to teenage tour participants and a way to critique what is taught by the tour guides.

Dippo and Simon were clearly disappointed in their efforts to encourage museum staff to understand the nuanced reactions of teenagers to a tour of impressionist paintings. They concluded that they had lacked a conceptual framework. In response, Dippo turns to ways in which Deborah Britzman's book *Practice Makes Practice* and Patti Lather's study *Getting Smart* produce disruptive texts, those that push the reader to see the conventional in an unconventional way. Dippo suggests that, in the case of the art museum, "startling juxtapositions" like advertising that juxtaposes consumer pleasures and social costs (such as advertisements for beer versus scenes of DWI accidents) could be effective in jarring the museum staff to see through the accepted cultural codes that guide their own praxis.

My own sense is that by bringing class, race, and gender to the fore, similar "startling juxtapositions" could emerge. Thus, overturning the implicit assumptions concerning the male versus female viewer or the male versus female subject in relation to impressionist painting could dislodge the "given" quality both of the staff's narrative and the assumed student responses. Women are often the subjects (or objects) of impressionist paintings, and I would imagine that young female viewers take on the "gaze" of the painter, putting themselves in the position of the nude model, for example, rather than assuming the male position of the painter. Likewise and equally important, the notion of race (a presence often by its absence, or sometimes metaphorically dealt with through images of darkness) could be addressed in a way that disrupts our notions that realist or even impressionist painting depicts "reality." Finally, following up on the notion of "dominant/subordinate culture" or "legitimate school knowledge" would have been a wedge into issues of class. For example, museums exclude some forms of artistic expression (graffiti, for example) and include and celebrate others. What does the content of a particular museum's collections, plus the etiquette of entering and viewing, have to say about the creation of class divisions, the teaching of class differences, and the hardening of class boundaries?

Disruptive narratives can be written using the differences already present in our own and Canadian society and could be a very useful tool for the kind of research Dippo advocates.

Bringing gender, race, and class more clearly into the discussion poses the questions about how these variables shape the research process. What about the male who researches female populations, the straight investigator who looks at gay and lesbian teachers, the White female researcher studying Black and Chicano/Latino students? How can White women write about Black women without cultural stereotypes informing their analysis?

At this point in time, there is widespread skepticism, at least among feminists, that women in one social position (White, middle class, heterosexual) can research, represent, or write about women in other social positions (Black, working class, Latina/Chicana, lesbian). This sense has emerged from the critique by women of color of the White women's movement and also from the analysis by feminists of various standpoint epistemologies (the notion that one constructs knowledge from a particular social location, or standpoint, shaped by race, class, and gender) (see Hartsock 1983; Harding 1986; Hill-Collins 1990).

Given this critique, the actual implementation of research (even if there is a sensitivity to the different class and race positions of the researcher and subject) is still fraught with difficulties and mis-steps, partly because the power of those in research positions (as "representatives" of or as implicated in particular forms of knowledge and particular kinds of institutions) has not been diffused. But also, the possibility of "recognition" has not been actualized in much research. Feminists have asserted the importance of "situated knowledges" (Haraway 1991) and have reminded us that individuals are not just a set of individual attributes that are added on to each other (Spelman 1988). For example, a Black lesbian is not just a woman plus an African American plus a homosexual, but someone whose identity, experience, and knowledge are simultaneously shaped by all of these attributes as they are played out in social structures where power is often (but not always) in the hands of White, heterosexual males. The challenge of conducting qualitative research is not only to recognize the socially constructed nature of diverse identities and knowledges (on the part of both the researcher and his/her subjects), but also to work toward ways of bridging them.

In general, these two essays are promising beginnings, ways in which qualitative research can be less hierarchical, more geared to the needs of its subjects, and less dependent on the creation of "experts." Yet the approaches these papers take need to be pushed further to take account of difference both as it enters the relationship between the researcher and subject and among the subjects themselves. I am not naive enough to think that the process of creating a critical ethnography is or will be easy, either within anthropology or education. However, if we are to succeed we must include our own positionality as researchers in our conceptions of research and address the impact of race, class, gender, and sexual orientations on the institutions we analyze and the subjects of our research. These essays clearly show the importance of examining power in relation to method, but only through examining the institutionalization of power as it utilizes race, class, gender, and sexual orientation and the way our subjects are both shaped by these attributes and struggle against their defining and limiting qualities can we show how power really operates and how individuals can become empowered.

References

Bahr, D., Gregorio, J., Lopez, D. and Alvarez, A. (1974). *Piman shamanism and staying sickness*. Tucson: Univ. of Arizona Press.

Behar, R. (1993). *Translated woman: Crossing the border with Esperanza's story*. Boston: Beacon.

Clifford, J. (1988). *The predicament of culture*. Cambridge: Harvard Univ. Press.

Clifford, J. and Marcus, G. (1986). *Writing culture: The poetics and politics of ethnography*. Berkeley: Univ. of California Press.

Comaroff, J. and Comaroff, J. (1991). *Of revelation and revolution: Christianity, colonialism, and consciousness in South Africa*. Chicago: Univ. of Chicago Press.

Cooper, F. and Stoler, A. (1989). Introduction: Tensions of Empire: Colonial control and visions of rule (special section). *American Ethnologist* 16 (4): 609–621.

Dwyer, K. (1982). *Moroccan dialogues: Anthropology in question*. Baltimore, MD: The Johns Hopkins Univ. Press.

the Hajj, Lavie, S., and Rouse, F. (1992). Notes on the Fantastic Journey of the Hajj, his anthropologist, and her American passport. *American Ethnologist* 20 1(2): 363–84.

Haraway, D. (1991). *Simians, cyborgs, and women*. New York: Routledge.

Harding, S. (1986). *The science question in feminism*. Ithaca, NY: Cornell Univ. Press.

Hartsock, N. (1983). *Money, sex and power*. Boston: Northeastern Univ. Press.

Hill-Collins, P. (1990). *Black feminist thought: Knowledge, consciousness, and the politics of empowerment*. New York: Harper-Collins.

Marcus, G. and Fischer, M. (1986). *Anthropology as cultural Critique*. Chicago: Univ. of Chicago Press.

Rabinow, P. (1977). *Reflections on fieldwork in Morocco*. Berkeley: Univ. of California Press.

Spelman, E. (1988). *Inessential woman: Problems of exclusion in feminist thought*. Boston: Beacon.

Stocking, G. (1987). *Victorian anthropology*. New York: Free Press.

Stocking, G. (1991). *Colonial situations: Essays on the contextualization of ethographic knowledge*. Madison: Univ. of Wisconsin Press.

Stoler, A. (1989). Carnal knowledge and imperial power: Gender, race, and morality in colonial Asia. In M. Leonardo, ed., *Gender at the crossroads of knowledge: Feminist anthropology in the postmodern era*, 51–101. Berkeley: Univ. of California Press.

Tedlock, B. (1992). *The beautiful and the dangerous: Encounters with the Zuni Indians*. New York: Viking.

Tedlock, D. (1993). *Breath on the mirror: Mythic voices and visions of the living Maya*. San Francisco: Harper.

Section Three

Power and
Method Revisited

EXTENDING POWER AND SPECIFYING METHOD WITHIN THE DISCOURSE OF ACTIVIST RESEARCH

James G. Ladwig and Jennifer M. Gore

When this volume was planned, we were asked to write a brief concluding chapter that would provide an overall response to the positions, conversations, and dialogues interwoven within and among the preceding chapters. However inviting initially, such a charter posed (at least) three major difficulties as we formulated our response. First, we saw a problem with speaking about a single volume in which chapters represented clearly divergent projects without drawing tenuous and probably unfair generalizations. Second, there was a potential problem in the two of us trying to speak in a single voice. Third, there was also the problem of writing a review as part of a book. In keeping with what might be called a "deconstructive inclination," we asked, "How is it that these issues become problems?"

It seems to us that each of these difficulties can be connected to, and is made recognizable by, a general concern about "voice" articulated by many contributors to this volume. Many of the authors in this book would argue, we would guess, that speaking in a single voice from multiple positions blurs differences and recreates the Grand Narrative of the Master's Voice. Similarly, drawing summary conclusions from these individual (or multiple) narratives, by abstraction, could be seen as eliminating the voice(s) of the Other(s). Furthermore, our position as both internal and external to the volume requires that we choose our words more carefully than if our charter enabled us to explicitly adopt only one of these positions. The dilemma of not wanting to accept the paralysis that could come from what we might call this "regime of voices," nor wanting to indulge in the tempting presentation of multiple voices within and between us, seemed to place this chapter in a rather precarious position.

Despite these difficulties, in carrying out our charter we have attempted to collectively write an argument in which we take as our major responsibility raising broad questions that might be of concern to each of the positions/stances brought together in the volume. To do this, we draw on two insights. First, having immersed ourselves in the literature typically cited in poststructural analysis, we accept one of the rhetorical challenges posed by Foucault when he asked, "What matter who is speaking?" To the extent that this challenge shifts the analytical focus away from the works of any particular individual within the book and toward the discursive threads that can be seen to connect them, we acknowledge but attempt to go beyond the individual arguments. The second insight we have relied on in constructing this chapter is that no matter what we write, readers of this volume will make up their own minds about all of the issues raised herein. What this common-sense disclaimer signals is that we firmly believe the political effects of any text cannot be determined simply by its encoding (however skilled, sympathetic, or even wise). We raise this issue here simply to encourage readers to take each chapter in this volume (ours included) both very seriously and as a very open text.

Caveats aside, our approach is designed to allow recognition of both difference and commonality in what we think is a loose amalgam or, dare we say, a "movement" of scholars pushing toward a greater prevalence of oppositional education research. It is worth considering that this volume appears at a very interesting and (potentially) politically significant time. Together, the chapters represent an historical point at which it is legitimate, indeed profitable, to question the orthodoxy supporting extant societal relations of power. We briefly examine the context in which this volume has been produced, outlining the historical contingencies that help to explain its appearance, and importance, at this time.

Difference Seen

According to Gitlin's introduction, past qualitative researchers have paved the way for the current reconceptualization of research. In particular, Gitlin points to the work of Willis (1977). This general claim (about past qualitative researchers) certainly helps to position the current volume historically. The more specific loyalty shown to Willis may, to a writer of "critical ethnography," carry some validity (although, after reading Lather, we hesitate to specify what kind of validity). Granting such centrality to the "critical" tradition in an overall framing of this volume is not surprising given the self-proclaimed primacy of the critical tradition in opening up radical discourses within the educational research community. Such framing, however, minimizes other significant histories that have made the project of the volume viable and plausible today. Each chapter builds on a long history within its own field and with its own social group constituents, and is located at a unique historical moment within that context. In this light, we wish to highlight difference among the chapters.

Each section of the volume can be understood in relation to particular social movements or specific marginalized segments of the U.S. populace. At a time when women have entered the academy in unprecedented numbers, it is not surprising that the feminist perspectives in this volume focus on traditional research methodologies that have (for example) often explicitly excluded women and look to rewrite the categories that legitimate those research methodologies. The mere presence of a section on gay and lesbian perspectives, not to mention the disruption of public spaces—particularly those havens of homophobic discourse covered in the guise of "traditional family values"—by Queers is possible in the context of growing gay and lesbian and Queer movements. That some Queers are in a position (as academics) to publicly write about these activist interventions highlights political advances made within these movements. It is not surprising to find, therefore, a chapter that conveys some urgency in the project of gay men recollecting personal histories, collectively building hope, at a time when a large portion are living with HIV/AIDS. Similarly, three decades after the 1960s' civil rights movement, it is not surprising to find a Black woman educational researcher working to rearticulate, maintain, and expand scholarship about Blacks working within historically racist institutions. Moreover, three hundred and seventy years after the White settlement of North America, it is not surprising to find surviving Navajos trying to get something of value from paternalistic institutions that seemingly have been designed to colonize nonbureaucratic cultures. After the fall of the Berlin Wall, the Soviet Union, and the so-called New Sociology of Education, we are also not surprised to find what used to be an agenda associated with economic class struggle to have purged its explicit Marxism and to have generalized in the "Critical."

Clearly, and this is one of the strengths of this volume, the different stories told here build on unique and important histories, histories that overtly seek to lay bare societal-level power relations. The importance of the presentation of diverse voices within the texts cannot be overstated. In a field of research (and indeed practice) in which the perspectives of feminists, gays, lesbians, and people of color have long been marginalized, the accomplishment of this volume in not only providing space for such voices but also bringing them together in ways that do not gloss over the differences, is timely.

Educational research has been a particularly conservative field. This volume celebrates a shift in that terrain wherein it is possible for academics from a range of specific political perspectives to tell their own stories, retain their jobs, and potentially expand their audiences. The stories told in this volume advance a broad activist agenda within educational research in a way that no other single volume has. If this agenda is to advance even further, however, we believe that explicit discussions of the key terms in the title of the volume—"power" and "method"—will be necessary. In the remainder of this chapter we focus on what the volume contributes to understandings of power and of method. How do the perspectives presented here portray power? How do they address method? As a first step in that process we consider what these divergent histories seem to bring to the process of producing educational research. This step next leads us to explore what we see as two paradoxes of the volume and some possibilities for activist educational research that moves beyond these paradoxes.

In the feminist chapters, informed by poststructural or postmodern theorizing, it is declared that we are working in a postpositivist era where we must attend to questions of insider/outsider and/or self/other. Here, these feminist educational researchers identify as their task working in the fractures of difference. Fine's advocacy of such an activist stance is explicit, while Lather's is enacted in her redefining of validity.

The chapters on gay and lesbian perspectives provide an extended argument against so-called positivist philosophy.[1] With Leck and Tierney enabling "authentic voices" to be spoken, there are firsthand reports of political intervention and the negotiated construction of a life history. Here, too, the relation of researcher to researched is of concern, as is the development of multiple voices.

In the chapters addressing race, the relationship of researcher/researched or insider/outsider is again explicitly addressed in Foster's account as a Black woman working as an ethnographer in Black communities, creating histories. Foster and LeCompte and McLaughlin point out an argument familiar to us about the relationship between power and the knowledge produced by research: that to understand relations of power that dominate a particular social group's experience, the knowledge of those on the nondominant side will be more accurate or hold "stronger objectivity" than knowledge created from the dominant perspective. This argument was made explicit by Foster and demonstrated particularly well in the chapter on Native American culture. Arguing for the development of research working with communities and against so-called positivist tenets on the separation of the researcher and researched, support for the knowledge of the nondominant is applied in the advocacy of constructing research within the framework of "critical ethnography."

"Educative research" and "disruptive texts" are the banners raised within the chapters labeled Critical. Working both sides of the modernist/postmodernist distinction, Gitlin and Russell and Dippo also question the gap between the researcher and the researched by making explicit different working conditions of academics and teachers, questioning who is expert, letting a "subject" develop her own research in a critical collaborative endeavor. In a search for less closed frames, we are also guided by Dippo, in the end, to consider yet another disruptive text, Britzman's *Practice Makes Practice*.

Interestingly, our analysis of the chapters for the relationship between specific methodologies or methods and the divergent histories outlined above leads to the observation that what has been done in the name of educational research within isolated segments of difference really is not all that different. There is a common foe, positivism. There are oft-repeated tensions, for example, researcher/researched or insider/outsider. There is support for the knowledge of the oppressed. There are peer reviews, collaborative relations, disruptive texts, new forms of validity, and authentic (if multiple) voices. And there are both explicit and implicit calls to activism.

Difference Made Similar

Recognizing these similarities begs the questions, "What is the relationship between research and specific social groups?" and "Is there a methodology unique to each of these social groups?" There is certainly a substantial literature on feminist methodology (and substantive criticisms of this literature from within feminism). To our knowledge, the same observation holds for these other groups, to varying degrees. From what is presented in these chapters, however, there seems to be little that is unique in terms of research methods and methodologies particular to the social groups represented by a feminist, gay, lesbian, antiracist, or critical research agenda.

In this regard, we think the volume does not go far enough. To claim a reconceptualization of research with a focus on power as the major task of the volume and to pay careful attention to each specific social formation without also paying careful attention to specific methods and methodologies is to limit the potential of the volume and the advancement of political activism within educational research.

What we see as this neglect of methods would make sense if the point was, for example, to prop up wider support around a failing Marxist/critical foundation. After all, the activist concerns of the authors in this volume could be rearticulated within a traditional "critical" triad. Habermas's call for holding a utopian point of reference to ground social critique, accounting for a theory's own history (theoretical reflexivity), and speaking to specific agents (e.g., Habermas 1990) of change are all common features of the sections in this volume. Naming the entire enterprise "critical" probably would seem attractive to some but, we assume, this is not the point.

Such a move might make sense if the agenda of the volume were simply to band together currently battling factions of the nonmainstream. After all, the obvious heated debates within feminism; the historically well-known criticisms of U.S. White "progressives" from the perspectives of African-Americans, Native Americans, or other nondominant groups living in the U.S.; and the longstanding standoff between feminism and Marxism are evidence of battles among nonmainstream groups. While some commentators would see the vision of a Rainbow Coalition as offering a response to these conditions, many of the authors of these chapters explicitly seek to maintain multiplicity; thus, we assume, coalition building is not the point of not articulating divergent methodologies.

Two Paradoxes

Of course, this move, this ignoring of specific methodologies, could have happened with a whole host of unquestioned assumptions about what is meant when using the terms "method" and "methodology." It could have happened because the contributors were not asked explicitly to address method. It could have happened even if they were asked to address method, but if they chose to do so by telling stories of their research rather than by systematically analyzing the procedures of their research. No matter what the intent of the individual authors, we think this neglect of specific methods is indicative of at least two paradoxes enacted within this volume. The most obvious paradox we call the *paradox of nondifference*. That is, as we have outlined above, while these chapters have clearly been designed to illuminate important differences between social groups, the volume as a whole presents a remarkably singular view of research methodology (one of its ostensible major foci). The second paradox evident in this volume (and acknowledged by some of the authors) is well known as the internal tension of advocating political activism within the confines of an academic endeavour. We call this latter tension the *paradox of academic activism*. We consider these paradoxes in turn.

The paradox of nondifference found in this volume, we think, results from a peculiar and unfortunate logical slippage. That is, if we take the major relationship at issue in the volume to be the possible connection between specific social groups and the research methodologies appropriate for creating knowledge about any one group, we have a relatively simple two-sided relationship to consider. On the one hand, there are specific social groups to be considered, each with its own history and social conditions. On the other hand, there is the question of research methodology. Examining the relationship between these two dimensions and drawing insights about them seems both reasonable and very important. In fact, we acknowledge that many reasons may exist for thinking each social group would be associated with unique methodological implications. In this volume, we ask, "Where did this difference go?"

To explain the lack of difference, we would point out two analytical moves. First, when seeking to understand the power/ method relationship, the authors of this volume seemed to assume some form of "mainstream" methodology against which they each argued. This assumption is evident in the repeated opposition to so-called positivism, for example. In terms of research methodologies, the similarities among the chapters in the volume are related to their shared oppositional stance. Unfortunately, by arguing *against* an assumed enemy, most authors did not concern themselves with helping readers understand what was being argued *for*, on anything other than the most general activist level. Second, there also seems to be an assumption that as soon as research (method) is moved into the context of some specific nondominant social group (power), then issues of power and method have been addressed. This second assumption facilitates the general oppositional stance taken with respect to methodology, and also helps explain why the authors did not seem to stop and ask, "What is different about studying with this oppressed group as opposed to studying with that oppressed group?"

Within the context of U.S. educational research, these authors work within (or, perhaps more accurately, against) particular principles of legitimation when constructing research. As has been widely documented, adopting a qualitative methodology in North America has carried oppositional implications (constructed in opposition to various forms of quantitative methods or, more specifically, quasiexperimental design). In that context, for those authors seeking to oppose dominant educational research practices on explicitly political grounds, the adoption of qualitative methods follows from a particular sense of research practice. The historical association between U.S. radical educational research and qualitative methods is testimony to the practical sense of what it means to construct radical educational research in the United States.

There are, however, a number of interesting ironies in this association. For example, considering the radical opposition to large scale, macrolevel structures of domination, employing research methods specifically designed to examine "microlevel" phenomena leaves much of the radical research agenda untended or undocumented. What this means is that the macrosocial inequalities addressed in a radical agenda become background assumptions. Here, the concern is simply one of matching an appropriate method with the context to be examined. Further, and more importantly for our argument, the adoption of qualitative methods in association with an explicit political opposition creates a tension between a "larger" general political agenda of the research and the qualitative methodological tenets of foregrounding the specificities of local sites. If such research does not examine the specific nature of its methodology in detail, beyond a seemingly generic adoption of qualitative concerns, then the "products" of these agendas remain open to serious attack. In this regard, however, the attack would not come from a wider "quantitative" audience but from other qualitative researchers who do not share the political sympathies of a radical agenda. What we have identified here is not simply some hypothetical possibility: current debates among British defenders of qualitative methods demonstrate that the adoption of qualitative stances, in and of themselves, provide no sure defense for those researchers seeking to support an explicitly political agenda (see Hammersley 1993; Hammersley and Woods 1993).

The second paradox has been discussed by many authors in a variety of ways. We have no intention of belaboring it here; but we do think that part of the activist academic paradox helps explain the surprising singularity we found. Put simply, as some of the critics in this volume point out, academics work in an industry that requires them to stand on "new" ground, distinguishing themselves from their colleagues.[2] When activism served this function, simple opposition was enough. Given the social space demonstrated by the presentation of this volume, however, we think there is now an opportunity to push even further. In a manner similar to our concern with the paradox of nondifference, one danger associated with the paradox of academic activism is a failure to think clearly about the relationship between the audience for the research and the contest that is supposedly opened up for change. We think it is helpful to ask, "How is writing a volume to be read by other academics going to contribute to the overall political concerns of the authors?" This question is not meant rhetorically to defeat such a project, but is a sincere call to clarify the goals of reporting such research.

The Problem of Power and Method

Both paradoxes also can be understood as connected with the particular approach to the problem of power and method that dominates this volume. We identified at least three approaches to questions of power and method throughout this volume: (1) power and method as a *problem of the utility of particular methods* and methodologies for producing "good" research; (2) power and method as a *problem of the relations between researcher/ researched*, privileged/subordinate, insider/outsider, self/other; and (3) power and method as a *problem of the production of academic discourse*. The preceding chapters, it seems to us, primarily take the second of these approaches in relation to questions of power and method; namely the approach most closely connected with traditional concerns of critical and feminist intellectuals (i.e., power and method as a problem of the relations between privileged and oppressed, marginalized and centered, insider and outsider groups). In taking this approach, questions of positioning, voice, difference, empowerment, and oppression through research are central.

The dominance of this approach to power and method is not surprising, given the activist agenda that characterizes the volume. Such an approach follows from the notion of power implied in the explicit concerns for historically marginalized and oppressed social groups. That is, while there are no explicit discussions of the concept of power in these chapters, the very organization of the volume and the foci of the specific chapters point to a structural notion of power wherein relations between dominant and subordinate social groups are to be addressed and redressed. From such a perspective, the focus on relations between researcher and researched, privileged and subordinate, and so on, in discussions of power and method, is both logically consistent and reasonable.

However, the paradoxes we have identified also follow from this approach to power and method. If academics are to be successful in their advocacy to other educational researchers of activist research, the field within which they work will demand that persuasive arguments be presented that incite and demonstrate methodological alternatives. The mere existence of debate within the three feminist chapters in this volume indicates that activist researchers might not be all that persuasive to each other, let alone persuasive to holders of more conventional stances.

Our own sympathies for each of the political agendas addressed in the volume meant that we found the stories told in each chapter interesting (in some cases, also astonishing and compelling)—but interesting as *stories* of activism and the development of overt political awareness rather than as arguments about the conduct of research. More expansive discussions of problems of power and method in the conduct of research, such as specific issues of methodology, may be necessary in strengthening the discursive power of any activist research agenda advanced from within the academy and aimed at persuading other academics.

Likewise, the paradox of nondifference can be addressed by giving greater attention to power and method as a problem of particular methods and methodologies. While many chapters provided principles of methodology, such as starting from the standpoint of the nondominant, there was little direct discussion of the relations between research methodology and methods. As a result, the book provides minimal guidance to researchers seeking assistance with, for instance, questions of truth, authorship, reality, objectivity, validity, and generalizability.

While such concerns may have been evaluated by contributors to this volume as the wrong questions to ask in the current climate, questions of how to conduct research and questions about the impact of particular methods on researchers, participants, and their fields remain salient concerns for the enactment of the very research advocated. The focus in this book on "larger" questions of relationships to research subjects and so on could be read as a signification that research techniques require no further debate, that they can be treated as already given. While there may be only limited numbers of particular methods or techniques available to researchers, there is still room for considerable exploration of how those methods are to be technically enacted.

Similarly, approaching power and method as a problem of academic production can provide direction through the paradoxes we have identified. Detailed attention to the effects of one's own arguments and explicit discussion of those effects may be necessary in advancing the academic activist research agenda articulated here. Without such elaboration, readers of this volume may well wonder what dynamics have produced the particular structure of the book. Naming, ordering, and classification are practices of power, the effects of which are only too deeply inscribed on those social groups represented in this volume. Gitlin's clear attempt at inclusiveness, evident in the structures of the book and diversity of contributors, however, does not quell questions of power in the "method" of the book.

For instance, if we focus on the overall structure of the book, the attempt to address nondominant social groups through the assemblage of contributors from various fields of educational research, and respondents from different academic locations (not in education), is not without its own tensions and enactments of power. Naming and separating gender, sexuality, and culture as primary foci (despite the naming of gender, class, and race in the introduction) of a book entitled *Power and Method* constitutes an explicit attempt to bring attention to historically marginalized social groups in the field of educational research. Moreover, in the endeavor of centering particular social groups, which groups are left out? Which other social formations have caused groups to suffer marginal status, and which deserve an ear/voice at this point in history? How is one to make such decisions and who gets to make them? How is the poststructural insight of multiple subjectivities to be incorporated within such a structure.

Challenges for the Discourse of Activist Research

Given the nature of academic work, we can expect (indeed, hope) that activist research agendas will remain an important part of the academy. But if such work is to reach beyond the already converted and move closer toward the social transformation sought, then strategic deployment of all three approaches to power and method may be necessary. In a volume that gives primacy to questions of social privilege and power, greater attention to questions of *academic* privilege and power, competition, and contestation seem extremely salient. In concerns about positioning relative to one's research participants, there is much less concern articulated about one's position relative to one's peers or one's audience. The extent to which the production of research and commentaries on research are themselves connected to struggles over power in various fields of intellectual and political endeavor is only addressed by a couple of authors. In short, the contributors to this volume share (with us) a complicity in the very issues addressed. As power and method are discussed, they are enacted.

We do not mean to suggest that there was no recognition of the social context in which academics work within in the volume. Clearly there was some. However, we do think the connection between the academic context and the relative generality of methodologies and methods presented was not addressed. That is, it seems that difference was apparent when discussing matters directly connected to the social groups grounding each chapter; but when discussing, choosing, and criticizing methodology, it was as if being an activist academic was the overriding analytical determinant. If this observation carries any veracity, it suggests that the "methodologies" created in this volume make sense primarily within an academic context. That is, declaring oneself an activist researcher in the context of an overwhelmingly conservative institution does not require of academics that they do much more than signify their difference in this way. Facilitating the impact of those research agendas in bringing about the kind of social transformation espoused will probably require more attention to a wide range of issues and concerns that are contained within the terms power and method.

Is this a challenge? Yes. It is a challenge built on the recognition that those activist academics now working in the North American academy have an opportunity to use their positions in a manner that is more politically productive and defensible than ever before (in our lifetimes, at least). As demonstrated by this volume, we would argue that historical conditions are such that there is now room in the U.S. educational academy to do much more than worry about arguing against technocratic educational research (which, we would point out, has not provided the glorious educational answers it might claim to have in its grasp—even after about a century of dominance). The time is ripe, we think, to address, with much more specificity, alternative methodologies for activist educational research in relation to nondominant social groups. The stories of research told in *Power and Method* highlight central issues of activist research from a range of specific political perspectives. As a volume, these stories combine to provide a stimulating entree for the uninitiated and much food for thought for those already doing related kinds of work. If a wider community of educational researchers is to help legitimate and encourage these newer forms of research, however, the challenge remains to build on the strengths of this volume by extending understandings of power and specifying methodologies in ways that make them even more persuasive and useful to new communities of scholars and activists.

Notes

1. We use the qualifier "so-called" to indicate a commonly recognized point, that characterizations of opposing positions are not necessarily accurate representations. In this case, what gets labelled as "positivist" in a critical agenda often holds little resemblance to most of the historically recognized forms of positivism.

2. This argument about the relationship between academic work and the methodological stances of educational researchers has been explored in much more detail in Ladwig's *A Theory of Methodology for the Sociology of School Knowledge*, Ph.D. dissertation, Univ. of Wisconsin - Madison, 1992.

References

Habermas, J. (1990). Moral consciousness and communicative action. Trans. C. Lenhardt and S. Weber Nicholsen. Cambridge, MA: MIT Press.

Hammersley, M. (1993). *What's wrong with ethnography?* London: Routledge.

Hammersley, M., and Woods, P. (1993). *Gender and ethnicity in schools.* London: Routledge.

Willis, P. (1977). *Learning to labour.* Westmead, UK: Saxon House.

INDEX

CONTRIBUTORS

Don Dippo is Associate Professor and Director of the Graduate Program in the Faculty of Education at York University, Toronto, Canada. His research and writing have focused on the social and political organization of knowledge, critical ethnographic practice, and the sociology of work and occupations. He is coauthor of *Learning Work: A Critical Pedagogy of Work Education.*

Michelle Fine is a social psychologist interested in the ways in which race, class, and gender operate inside high schools, and inside the relationship of schools to community, facilitating and obstructing educational justice for adolescents. Her work has focussed on high school dropouts, race and sex segregation in public schools, and the construction of "community" within and beyond public schools. Active in both educational advocacy and courtroom testimony on school discrimination, she is the author of numerous publications which include *Disabled Women: Psychology From the Margins* (with A. Asch) and is editor of *School Dropouts: Patterns and Policies.*

Michèle Foster is Associate Professor of Education and African-American and African Studies at the University of California at Davis. Her writings have appeared in a variety of scholarly journals and as chapters in numerous books, and she is editor of the book, *Readings on Equal Education, Volume II: Qualitative Investigations into Schools and Schooling.*

Andrew Gitlin is Professor of Educational Studies at the University of Utah. His research interests include alternative methods, evaluation, and teacher education. His recent work includes a coauthored book with John Smyth entitled *Teacher Evaluation: Educative Alternatives*, a coauthored book with several teachers entitled *Teachers' Voices for School Change: An Introduction to Educative Research*, and (forthcoming) a coauthored book with Robert Bullough entitled *Becoming a Student of Teaching: Methodologies for Exploring Self and Context.*

Jennifer Gore is Senior Lecturer in Education at the University of Newcastle, New South Wales, Australia. She is author of *The Struggle for Pedagogies: Critical and Feminist Discourses as Regimes of Truth* and is coeditor (with Carmen Luke) of *Feminisms and Critical Pedagogy*. Her current research is an empirical investigation of the functioning of power in a range of pedagogical sites.

James Ladwig is a Lecturer in the Department of Education at the University of Newcastle, New South Wales, Australia, where he teaches sociology of education, curriculum theory, and educational policy. His work has appeared in journals such as *Educational Theory, Review of Education, Theory and Research in Social Education*, and the *American Journal of Educational Research*.

Louise Lamphere is a Professor of Anthropology at the University of New Mexico, with interests in race, class, and gender. She has edited two recent collections on new immigrants in the United States: *Structuring Diversity: Ethnographic Perspectives on the New Immigration* and *Newcomers in the Workplace: Immigrants and the Restructuring of the U.S. Economy*. She has also coauthored *Sunbelt Working Mothers: Reconciling Family and Factory* with Patricia Zavella, Felipe Gonzales, and Peter Evans (1993).

Patti Lather is Associate Professor, Educational Policy and Leadership, at Ohio State University, where she teaches qualitative research and feminist pedagogy. Her work includes *Getting Smart: Feminist Research and Pedagogy with/in the Postmodern* (Routledge) and *Within/Against Feminist Research in Education* (Deakin University Monograph Series). She has an essay in *Ideology Critique and Beyond*, edited by Herbert Simons and Michael Billig (Sage) and her current work is on researching the lives of women with HIV/AIDS. Her favorite academic achievement thus far is a Fulbright Scholarship to New Zealand in 1989. Her hobby aspiration is to learn to play the accordion.

Glorianne M. Leck is a Professor of Educational Philosophy at Youngstown State University. Her work continues to process through activist/applied philosopher perspectives and career working in and through the civil rights, antiwar, alternative life styles, feminist, lesbian and gay, multicultural, diversity and queer movements in and related to the politics of human rights and free public education.

Margaret D. LeCompte is Associate Professor of Sociology of Education at the University of Colorado-Boulder. Author of over one hundred articles, technical reports, and scholarly papers, her books include *Ethnography and Qualitative Design in Educational Research* (with Judith Preissle Goetz), *The Handbook of Qualitative Research in Education* (with Wendy Millroy and Judith Preissle) *The Way Schools Work: A Sociological Analysis of Education* (with Kathleen Bennett), and *Giving Up In School: Teacher Burnout and Student Dropout in America*.

Daniel McLaughlin is a former classroom teacher, school principal, and university professor. At present, he works with program and curriculum development at Kayenta Public School District on the Navajo Reservation.

His main areas of interest include curriculum, critical literacy, and American Indian education. He is the author of *When Literacy Empowers: Navajo Language in Print* (Univ. of New Mexico Press), coeditor with William G. Tierney of *Naming Silenced Lives: Personal Narratives and Processes of Educational Change* (Routledge), and editor of the *Journal of Navajo Education*.

Daphne Patai is Professor of Women's Studies and of Spanish and Portuguese at the University of Massachusetts at Amherst. Her teaching and research interests focus on Brazilian literature and culture, utopian fiction, oral history, and feminism. She is the author of *Brazilian Women Speak: Contemporary Life Stories, The Orwell Mystique: A Study in Male Ideology,* and *Myth and Ideology in Contemporary Brazilian Fiction.* She has coedited (with Angela Ingram) *Rediscovering Forgotten Radicals: British Women Writers, 1889–1939,* and (with Sherna Berger Gluck) *Women's Words: The Feminist Practice of Oral History,* among other books. Her latest project is *The Women Who Walked Away: Feminism in the Academy* (Basic Books), coauthored with Noretta Koertge.

Roger Platizky is an Associate Professor of English at Austin College. He has published a book of literary criticism, *A Blueprint of His Dissent: Madness and Method in Tennyson's Poetry.* As a Victorianist, he has also published articles in *victorian poetry, Literature and Psychology,* and the *Victorian Newsletter.* His poems on feminist, psychological, and gay themes have also appeared in *Changing Men,* the *Evergreen Chronicles,* and *Empathy.*

Robyn Russell is an elementary school teacher in Salt Lake City, Utah. Her research interests include teacher extraction and feminism. Her recent publications include a coauthored text, *Teachers' Voices for School Change: An Introduction to Education Research.*

John Stanfield, II was the Frances and Edwin Cummings Professor of American Studies and Sociology, Scholar in Residence for the Commonwealth Center for the Study of American Culture at the College of William and Mary from 1988 to 1993. He is currently Professor of African-American and African Studies and Professor of Sociology at the University of California at Davis. His research interests and publications include studies in the sociology of knowledge, especially pertaining to race in science issues.

William G. Tierney is an Associate Professor of Education and a Senior Research Associate in the Center for the Study of Higher Education at Pennsylvania State University. Tierney has written numerous essays on organizational culture and change, equity and multiculturalism, and critical theory and qualitative methodology. He has published six books: *The Web of Leadership, Collegiate Culture and Leadership Strategies* (with Ellen Chaffee), *Curricular Landscapes, Democratic Vistas: Transformative Leadership in Higher Education, Culture and Ideology in Higher Education, Official Encouragement, Institutional Discouragement: Minorities in Academe, Naming Silenced Lives: Personal Narratives and the Process of Educational Change* (with Daniel McLaughlin), and *Building Communities of Difference: Higher Education in the 21st Century.*